MW00657797

Spirituality

THE UNIVERSAL PATH TO GOD

By Keyth Dickson

Comment from one of the most spiritual men I know:

All perfect living Masters teach the same thing, namely, the truth that our real home can be found only within ourselves. The Masters have come from all cultures, all nationalities and all periods in history in response to the seekers who exist worldwide. Keyth Dickson's work does great service to seekers all over the world by bringing together brief life sketches of several Masters both from the East and the West. I am sure this book will remove several doubts and skepticisms from the minds of seekers who think Masters have only come once for special people.

Ishwar Puri

SPIRITUALITY

Published by:

C. KAVENAUGH BOOKS

e-mail: dondickson@ centurytel.net

Editor & Prepress Planner
Richard E. Wrate

Designed by: Darby's Type & Design, Inc.
Anaheim, CA

Printed by:
Meridian Graphics
David D'alessandro
davidd@mglitho.com

1st. edition 2012

ISBN: 978-0-9825700-3-6

Dedication

To all who are seeking spiritual truth and
To those who are sowing the seeds of love
and peace in a complex world.

And to those who ponder these words of Maulana Rumi:

"All day I think about it and then at night I say it.
Where did I come from and what am I supposed to be doing?
I have no idea. My soul is from elsewhere, I'm sure of that,
And I intend to end up there. . .
Who looks out through my eyes? What is the soul?
I cannot stop asking. . .
I didn't come here of my own accord, and I can't leave that way. Whoever brought me here will have to take me home." **(Barks 1997:2)**

It has been my pleasure and honor to prepare for publication: "SPIRITUALITY, THE UNIVERSAL PATH TO GOD." I received such love from reading the words of Meister Eckhart, St. John of the Cross and others that my job as editor was nearly forgotten. With guidance from my Master, Kirpal Singh, I completed the task assigned.

These words from Keyth Dickson sum up my labor of love.

Love makes the heart young, and like a flame it burns away years, fears and tears. Those alive with love join hand in hand, heart in heart and soul in soul, and their flame produces a brilliance that makes hatred, sorrow, and darkness vanish into nothingness. They recognize the One in many. Being forced to break the habits and affections of a lifetime is traumatic but endurable; severing the intensity of love's perfect moment is impossibly tragic, because that moment touches eternity. Only a master of love really comprehends this truth.

Biographical Statement

Keyth Dickson has worked as a teacher and as an archaeologist, and has spent several years in radio and television. He is the author of two books and many articles on archaeology and natural history. He is also a published poet. Keyth has studied spiritual topics and practiced spiritual disciplines for over 50 years under the guidance of Saint Kirpal Singh.

Keyth was born in September of 1934 in Arkansas, where he resides at this time, although he has lived in California, Oklahoma and briefly in several other states.

Table of Contents

Acknowledgments

Many individuals have contributed toward the publication of this volume. Satguru Kirpal Singh put the concept in my mind and motivated me to complete it. Various individuals have read portions of the manuscript and extended valuable constructive suggestions. Ms. Lynn Crotser pointed out a few places where the text needed some clarification and Aleksandra Hadjioannou, and Jim and Theresa Crawford of Vancouver, B. C., Canada made helpful remarks over the telephone. Steve Curtis of Shrewsbury, Massachusetts provided some data on the life of Mother Millie Prendergraft.

Several individuals have read the total manuscript or most of it and made useful suggestions. Ishwar Puri graciously read the entire manuscript and recommended two important changes. Also Royal Craig of California and Dr. David Copeland of Montreal, Quebec, Canada commented upon portions of the manuscript that they had read. Mr. Richard Wrate, the publisher, has made various recommendations and has gone to considerable effort to find suitable illustrations of the many Master Teachers considered in this book. I wish to thank artist Roberto Casale for his excellent depiction of the fourteen Masters and also to thank artist Laura Fontinot for preparing the illustration of Kabir. One disciple with tremendous inner ingress has informed me that it is a very good depiction of what Kabir really looks like.

Comment **gratefully received from:**

Royal Craig, a spiritual writer and poet.

There has been only one truth throughout the ages - one loving God, changeless, eternal. From the beginning, the Divine message of our return to the father has been offered through the agency of His appointed Masters of Truth who have conveyed the message tirelessly; but man for the most part has ignored or perverted it to something more suitable to his limited understanding. Keyth Dickson has succinctly told the story of those Messengers who tell us again and again that the Truth lies within. All we have to do is go within and begin the journey back to our True Home.

Comment **gratefully received from:**

Dr. David Copeland, M.D.

Beyond the particularities of individual human experiences and viewpoints as well as social, religious and environmental influences , there is an underlying similarity of conscious potential searching for higher truth.

Spirituality as the core of identity beyond words and human experiences is an absorbing study of a subjective science. Those seeking a careful and comprehensive overview of spirituality as it has been taught throughout the ages will find Keyth Dickson's work most rewarding.

***The central thesis of the book is** ......*

the fact that religion deals with outer rituals, while spirituality emphasizes contacting the Divine through the Word. Of course, as previously stated, religion has its function, and that is to prepare the way for the higher teachings by inculcating ethical precepts and endorsing pure living. It is not an end in itself.

In this work an attempt will be made to indicate how a genuine seeker may be able to recognize those teachers with authentic spiritual status.

To the assertion that one loses his or her individuality upon returning to God, the reply is simple: one discovers his or her true nature. And it is much greater and more wonderful than any egotistical concept of ones self.

Spirituality differs from philosophies, religions or creeds in that it gives you a method of testing the assertions of its teachers. One is not asked to embrace blind faith in some religious doctrine and wait until death to see if you are right. A genuine spiritual teacher helps the devotee experience the higher truths he or she teaches during this lifetime if the devotee develops a pure heart and discrimination. A pure heart opens the door to higher illumination, and discrimination helps one separate higher reality from transient phenomena.

Many people ask why God forced us to come into the turbulent realms of change, suffering and death. The answer has been given by many spiritual teachers: God did not force us to enter these realms; we chose to explore the lower regions. However the souls were told when they left the Home of Peace by focusing attention upon lower worlds that if one cried out to God for deliverance from realms of suffering and death, God would himself come in the form of a saint to help that soul to return home. We always have this option since there are saints in the world in every age.

Each person is entitled to judge for him or herself what is the most appealing and beneficial religious or spiritual practice he or she can perform and endorse. In fact, each individual is obligated to seek the level of inner truth that resonates most beautifully within his or her mind and soul. Then each person must allow every other entity to choose as he or she has chosen and respect that choice.

Love makes the heart young, and like a flame it burns away years, fears and tears. Those alive with love join hand in hand, heart in heart and soul in soul, and their flame produces a brilliance that makes hatred, sorrow, and darkness vanish into nothingness. They recognize the One in many. Being forced to break the habits and affections of a lifetime is traumatic but endurable; severing the intensity of love's perfect moment is impossibly tragic, because that moment touches eternity. Only a master of love really comprehends this truth.

The spiritual Master never charges for teachings, advice, initiations or guidance of any kind. It is certainly legitimate for one to recoup the cost of publications being distributed, but no great amount of profit will be made on these. If a small gain is made from book sales, this profit is never used to personally benefit the instructor. Those who charge for initiations, psychic help, personal guidance or anything else are not true teachers of the highest order.

The need for love is more basic than the need for food, clothing and shelter. The desire to love and be loved is built into our consciousness. Individualization allows love to be expressed toward others and this seems to be a primary reason for the original separation of souls from the Divine Source of all. Love constitutes the only genuine happiness. A person may have a superfluous amount of worldly goods and great wealth and still be unhappy and isolated, even in a crowd of people who do not love each other.

The divine spark at the core of each soul is truly above evil, but human beings are ruled mostly by the mind and this is the origin of all negativity.

Only a truly sincere and pure seeker can see behind the mask worn by a charismatic teacher.

St. John of the Cross states that if people knew how many blessings they are losing because they do not raise their desires above trifles, they would be amazed. He, like all other divinely inspired teachers, advises us to ask God for God and nothing else.

Foreward

Today many people are not satisfied with orthodox services at churches, temples, mosques and synagogues because these religious procedures do not satisfy an inner need to experience a deeper spiritual insight or divine fulfillment in their lives. Certainly, the stately and majestic structures and lovely interior furnishings inspire awe, and the solemn services, devotional music, and traditional rites and rituals may stimulate faith in ultimate salvation. But none of these superficial facilities and ceremonies instills true inner peace today or promotes a divine awareness beyond an emotional involvement. Thousands, therefore, who sincerely seek a more meaningful revelation of truth, leave the orthodox religious establishments to search for higher enlightenment. Unfortunately, many of these seekers end up following teachers or "gurus" of questionable spiritual integrity and attainment or individuals who are the victims of delusion themselves. Certain clever men or women are capable of putting on convincing acts and may seem quite sincere to those seeking something better. As Jesus put it: *"When the blind lead the blind, they end up in the ditch together."* This ditch is that of uncertainty and illusion. Of course, a few teachers actually may have limited spiritual attainments and not be aware of higher levels of consciousness. Very few individuals, and from all major religious traditions, seem to have achieved exalted levels of awareness, and these exponents all seem to have expressed comparable teachings. A few teachers today expound the same truths.

When they face the obvious corruption, blind faith, religious intolerance and numerous uncertainties involved in most orthodox religious movements, many sincere souls embrace science because it employs methods that can be tested. One can prove certain things, especially mundane ones, beyond a reasonable doubt. Is that not better than accepting the opinions of an authority figure who gives you no way to check the validity of his or her assertions? The promise of a reward after death is not a reliable assurance of correctness now or in the future because you have no way to check for truthfulness before taking the leap from mortality.

Of course modern science has distinct limitations. After a physicist, via quantum physics, has broken down matter to such rudimentary particles as protons, neutrons, electrons, bozons, quarks or leptons, and defined such fundamental forces as gravitation, electromagnetism, the strong nuclear force and the weak nuclear force, he or she still faces the unanswered question of ultimate or initial causation. Science beautifully explains how life forms have changed once evolution was in progress, but it does not explain how complex life forms and mind evolved from inert substances or sprang spontaneously from nothing. In fact, this seems to be approaching the issue from the wrong direction. It appears more rational to suggest that life developed from a higher vibratory state than to assume that it evolved blindly from some random manipulation of unconscious elemental particles. Why? Because matter can be shown to be congealed or crystallized energy. A relevant question is *"what is the ultimate source of energy?"* This question must be answered before one can reject the concept of a superphysical origin for life on earth.

Most scientists today accept the concept of a *"Big Bang"* or infusion of energy into this universe at its inception about 13.7 billion years ago, but was this creative explosion a cause or an effect? Did this big bang originate at one spatial point or did it simultaneously take place at many or at all locations? Have there been multiple "*Bang*" episodes throughout history of the universe, and has inflation been uniform in all areas? Also, is the universe maintained by the influx and outflow of energy through white and black holes? In other words, does energy cycle from one realm of existence to another? These are questions scientists have not been able to answer in a totally convincing manner.

Spiritual exponents from many religious traditions have claimed that there are levels of existence beyond or more subtle than what is apparent in the corporeal universe that we inhabit. These sages have asserted that space and time permeate these other dimensions of life in different ways than they influence this world. For example, change alters mental and highly spiritual realms far more slowly than it does more mundane environments. The heavens, as some of these regions are called, seem to be eternal and full of joy and light, but time does influence them. Sages from the several religious traditions have even named these dimensions using terms such as Astral, Causal or Celestial, Par-Brahm, etc. But they cannot demonstrate the validity of these concepts by any objective means. Conversely, scientists cannot disprove the reality of spiritual realms or mystical experiences either. So we face opinions. A perceptive student may notice that science and spirituality are slowly adapting similar visions of reality. For example, modern string theory postulates the existence of at least 11 dimensions existing simultaneously in every time-space continuum. Although the scientific concept of a dimension differs from that entertained by spiritual proponents (scientists assert that this universe has four dimensions, for example), both schools of thought seem to agree that existence is not limited to one physical expression. Things in the objective world can be misunderstood and interpreted variously, and, as we shall indicate later, the reliability of subjective phenomena can be open to question because of the creativity of the mind in subjective realms. In other words, you may see what you want to see. To those who assert that their subjective experiences seem more real than do objective ones, we can reply that judgments of reality vary from observer to observer. Certainly dreams can seem extremely vivid and real while people are having them. Even in this physical world, the various observers of a specific object or event may register many different perspectives. The well-known poem about the blind men and the elephant, while not a literary masterpiece, conveys an important lesson about "*seeing*."

The vastness of the expanding universe with its millions of galaxies, each consisting of several hundred billion suns and probably planets as well as nebulas and vast regions of dark matter does not suggest that any causative power could be a small anthropomorphic being as some religions with roots in antiquity imply. Many ancient peoples could not conceive of a greater power than a mighty king or the noble heroes of mythology. Their concepts of God were more those of tribal creator or, at best, the fabricator of a limited heaven, a well-defined hell or place of punishment, a flat or round earth, one sun, one moon and a few thousand stars. They had no conception of a Creative Source responsible for a vast physical universe and many subjective realms of unimaginable cosmic scope and grandeur. And yet those prophets, seers and mystics from all religious traditions, to be mentioned later, assert that such states exist. And the careful student of religious scriptures quickly notices that the teachings of these sages from many diverse cultures present essentially the same message. Another interesting thing is the fact that these several exponents of spiritual doctrine had no physical contact with each other in many instances, having lived in various parts of the world at different times. Few of these teachers had access to extensive libraries of religious literature either. In this work, the subtle thread of spirituality found in the teachings of many proponents of subjective truth will be contrasted with the beliefs, rites and rituals that have, through time, obscured that inner essence of spirituality revealed by the founders of most religions. The role of religion is to serve as an important first step in the development of higher consciousness, but religion is not synonymous with spirituality or superconscious awakening. Many teachers promote religious doctrines with promises of heavenly or celestial rewards, but only a few enlightened individuals deliver spiritual instructions that may awaken sincere seekers for truth during the present life. In Chapter 4 of this work an attempt will be made to indicate how a genuine seeker may be able to recognize those teachers with authentic spiritual status.

There have been hundreds of enlightened spiritual teachers during the last two thousand years, for example, and each of them cannot be considered here or the project would get out of hand. Several criteria were used to choose from the many great sages or teachers that have visited this world. First of all, did they actually write down the teachings they delivered, or do we have to depend upon the memories of disciples or upon the interpretations of later students? In this work, the actual words of each selected teacher are quoted as accurately as possible and the opinions of disciples are avoided. Memories and sincere opinions are often fraught with mistakes. One must also consider the insights and skill levels of each translator of spiritual writers and the presence of bias. In other words, is the interpreter trying to promote a particular point of view or is this writer simply trying to present with accuracy a great teacher's words. And of course, the availability of authoritative translations is very much a factor, for one has to use available texts.

Sources of information used in this work are documented in the text using the same form of documentation employed in most modern scientific writing. The name of the author, date of publication and page cited are inserted in abbreviated form in the text. For example, (Eusebius 1995:108) refers one to the References Cited section at the end of the book where the name of the work by Eusebius, date of publication and data on the publisher are recorded. It is most disconcerting to read a short quote in a book and have no way to check the context of that quote. Some authors of dubious honesty will excerpt a short passage from a text in an effort to back up their contentions. But if one reads what was said before and after this short quotation, he or she will arrive at a completely different conclusion. So many Christian denominations extract a few statements here and there from the Bible to sustain personal beliefs. And completely contradictory opinions can be "supported" by selectively choosing other biblical references. The same factor applies to selections taken from scriptures of other faiths. Admittedly the insertion of reference sources in the text makes reading a work less fluidic because these references seem to intrude in the line of thought. But it is important to document each source so others may consider the same materials that you selected and, perhaps, draw a similar or a different conclusion. The use of footnotes can be distracting to a reader also. As a writer of scientific works, I prefer to insert references in the text.

All readers have not been exposed to similar categories of literature, so some terms in this book may be unfamiliar to you. If you do not understand a certain word or name, please consult the glossary of terms at the end of this publication. Most readers who are familiar with a specific spiritual or literary tradition do not like it when definitions for every term used are inserted in the text. The glossary is included to explain terms.

Illustrations are included for many master teachers, but only William Blake, George William Russell, Soami Ji and Baba Sawan Singh are accurately depicted beyond a reasonable doubt. The illustration of Kabir is based upon a very early painting of this saint, but it still may not represent his actual appearance. Most of the other depictions are artist's conceptions.

There will be substantial repetition of ideas in those chapters that consider the teachings of the greatest spiritual exponents from the west and from the east. This repetition is essential because all genuine teachers of the highest order taught the same things in their own words. It seems important to show the unity of concept and purpose in the spiritual doctrines of these genuine master souls. Also, this repetition can be of value in emphasizing the most important precepts because most of us need to go over a lesson more than once.

Keyth Dickson

Chapter 1

THE QUESTION OF GOD

Since the dawn of history, human beings have tried to explain or symbolize their finite conceptions of an ultimate power. While these individuals have stated little that may actually apply to a Supreme Being, they have said much that reveals their own evolutionary state. In our modern rational age, most people still cling to some belief in a higher power or divine origin of life and try to harmonize this belief with that which is perceived by scientific study.

Modern scientists disagree on the probability of some Supreme Power or God. Many authorities assert that they can explain the universe and the presence of life on earth without recourse to some divine source or creative event (**Thuan 1995:248**). The concept of multiple parallel universes containing every possible combination of physical conditions and laws has been postulated. But, as astrophysicist Thuan suggests, this hypothesis is not convincing because such universes are inaccessible to observation. After a very intelligent appraisal of many scientific hypotheses, Thuan (1995:249) said, *"For myself, I am prepared to bet on the existence of a Supreme Being"*. Admittedly, quantum physics does tell us much about the nature of matter, and evolution helps explain how life forms have changed throughout time after they developed, but no objective scientific process to date has adequately described any ultimate source of energy and consciousness or a cause that is its own excuse for being. Most religions believe in some primal condition or being, or some creative authority, referred to by such diverse names as Allah, Jehovah, Ram, Radha Swami, Anami, or God. We will now consider the various opinions regarding an Ultimate Power.

Probably the most ancient concept of God is that of the "*Big Man*" or anthropomorphic being who created the apparent world. This is explained by the fact that the human ego generally considers itself to be the ultimate creative expression. So, God must be a greater or more powerful human-like entity with such human and emotional traits as anger, jealousy and strong desires. The "*wrath of God*" is often mentioned in ancient scriptures, while such expressions as the "*love of God*" are more commonly found in recent revelations. Many modern intuitive thinkers have entertained the opinion that although human beings in an unrealized ultimate sense may have a spiritual connection with an ultimate state, the Supreme Being may not have any of the characteristics of the typical embodied soul because mind and emotions may not reflect ultimate qualities. In other words, although each person may inwardly possess a divine potential, the almighty is certainly above all human limitations and weaknesses.

According to Christian scriptures, God appeared to Moses as a flame in a burning bush that was not consumed (**Exodus 3:2-20**). Notice that in verse 20 the hand of God is mentioned. In the first three chapters of Revelation we find a clear depiction of a man-like being. John, while in the spirit on the Isle of Patmos, saw an entity that referred to himself as "*the first and the last.*" John described this being as one like unto the Son of Man with white hair, flaming eyes, and brass-like feet and hands, one of which held seven stars. He was dressed in a robe and his voice was like the sound of many waters. The text leads one to assume that this is the risen Jesus or one like him. Then, in Chapter 4, John tells us that *"a door was opened in heaven"* and he was invited to *"come up hither"* in order to be shown future events from a higher perspective. Twenty-four elders sat around a throne from which proceeded lightning and thunder. Upon this throne sat one referred to as God. Clearly He had human characteristics since His right hand was mentioned.

According to Joseph Smith, he had a vision in which God and Jesus Christ appeared before him in the spring of 1820. Both God and Jesus were described as having bodies of flesh and bones (see explanatory introduction to **Doctrine and Covenants and D & C 130:22**). The Holy Ghost was called *"a personage of spirit."*

Some statements in the Bible seem to be contradictory. For example, in **John 1:18** it states that *"no man has seen God at any time."* The Son has declared Him, but no one has seen Him. In **Matthew 5:8**, it says, *"Blessed are the pure in heart for they shall see God."* How do we harmonize these several statements? One interpretation could be that no one can see God until the Son reveals Him. Since human beings are residing in bodies in a physical dimension, someone in a physical body must be used to contact them with messages from God. In contrast to this concept is the possibility that what Moses, John, Joseph Smith and others have seen are manifestations of God but not an Absolute State that cannot be seen. This concept will be considered more fully later.

A second concept of God is that this power is the transcendent reality or force behind the universe and nature. The latter are God's objective manifestations. Such a pantheistic view denies that the divine has a distinct personality but expresses itself through laws of nature. Such visible phenomena as the sun and other celestial bodies have often been venerated as symbolic expressions of the divine power responsible for their manifestation.

A third conception of God is that He is a great mental power or repository of intelligence that can manifest in some form or stay unseen. Via intelligence, he designs natural laws, organizes universes and solar systems and is responsible for human and other evolutionary lines. The universe and human destiny are goal oriented with the great intelligence providing either route or routes and destination. While this being is responsible for objective phenomena, he is generally aloof from them. By this view of divinity, God may be considered to be the Universal Mind and individual human minds but fragments of this super intelligence. The object of religious practice in this system is to reunite with the Universal Mind by merging the individual mind into the great repository of thought. This is done after considerable purification and augmentation of the individual mind by spiritual practices and devotion.

A fourth conception of God agrees that a Universal Mind state exists. However it considers this Universal Mind to represent the negative pole of a creative sphere. The Positive Pole or Power is purely spiritual and exists beyond both mind and matter as we conceive of them. Thus God consists of an Absolute Spiritual Quality that has always existed and both positive and negative polaities that sprang from this Absolute State. This viewpoint suggests that the role of mind, the highest quality of the negative state, is to enable the spirit to contact mental and lower dimensions and to engage the attention or spirit in these regions to keep them there. The Universal

Mind pretends to be the positive power, going so far as to introduce Satan at a lower level to serve as a lesser tempting agent. Only those who overcome the mind and the egotistical characteristics it introduces can return to the positive pole of creation (**Revelation 21:7**). Proponents of this view of existence can be traced back into history at least 800 years, although these teachings are obviously much older than this. Such teachers have appeared in all religious communities, including Christian, Judaic, Islamic, Hindu, and Sikh traditions, expounding a golden thread of spirituality that transcends the creeds and rituals of these widely accepted faiths. We will now consider this view of God in greater detail since it seems to be more inclusive and appealing to sincere seekers for truth than do faiths that insist they have an exclusive claim to spiritual inspiration.

The nature of Ultimate Reality can never be explained via language because this state of being exists beyond all material realms and even mental planes. However, several assertions may be made about it. These may be supported by quotations from the greatest spiritual teachers who have appeared on earth throughout the ages. According to such spiritual luminaries as Meister Eckhart, John of the Cross, Sarmad, Kabir, Bulleh Shah, Shamas-I-Tabriz, Khwaja Hafiz, Guru Nanak, Tulsi Sahib, Soami Ji, and others, the Absolute State of God is a condition of oneness that is its own excuse for being. Before we consider this ultimate unity, one might point out that Eckhart and John of the Cross appeared in the Christian tradition; Sarmad was a Jewish Saint; Kabir, Bulleh Shah, Shamas-I-Tabriz and Khwaja Hafiz were in the Islamic tradition; Nanak and Tulsi Sahib were in the Sikh lineage (although Tulsi Sahib appeared after the ten Sikh gurus); and Soami Ji allegedly was the founder of the Radha Soami faith. It is interesting to note that all of these great spiritual teachers taught precisely the same concepts about God, although they expressed them in the contexts of the religious traditions in which they appeared. From a Saint's perspective, God is too great to fit inside of one religion.

A review of many Saint's teachings and personal intuition suggest that the Absolute State of God is of a Unity of four basic qualities. First, there is ultimate consciousness or awareness (attention). Second, this State contains the supreme source of power or energy. Third, this state is imbued with unfettered creativity via the Word or Naam. And finally, this State is the repository of Perfect Love. In fact, love may be considered the cohesive affinity that promotes the oneness of God. This Ultimate State of God can be experienced or merged into, but it cannot be seen. This may be the meaning of the **John 1:18**: *"No man has seen God at any time"*. In order for something to be seen, one must stand apart from it and observe it. In other words, there must be an observer and the observed. If all is One, however, this cannot happen. To the assertion that one loses his or her individuality in such a state, the reply is simple: one discovers his or her true nature. And it is much greater and more wonderful than any egotistical concept of one's self.

Modern scholars are beset with the smallness of orthodox concepts of God especially when they consider the awesome vastness of the physical universe. But those sages or saints that claim some personal knowledge of God assert that the whole physical universe is but a dismal pinhead when one compares it to the Ultimate State of Being. As our awareness expands, our concepts of God expand, because God expands our awareness. Members of a primitive tribe consider God to be a great chief who rules the sun, thunder and wind. Such a god has a hot temper, strict laws and mostly human qualities. To citizens of a civilized nation, God seems like a great father figure, a combination of Washington, Lincoln, Churchill and Gandhi, full of compassion and justice. He has controlled emotions and refined attributes. When a soul evolves to a state where it recognizes the immensity of the universe and considers the probability of higher dimensions of existence, God becomes more than a great chief, a national founder or a superman. God becomes indescribable. Higher teachers refer to this absolute spiritual state of God as the Positive Power.

Time and space emerged from the Eternal Essence as all lower and changeable dimensions came into being. All emerged from this Source, and all can return to it. As the Sufi exponent **Hazrat Inayat Kahn (1988:117)** stated: *"Our beloved is that which is our source and our goal."* The lower creation was manifested with time not in time because the Eternal State is beyond both time and space. These qualities existed before the Causal, Astral and physical dimensions came into being. Thus the big bang did not introduce time and space into an expanding universe, as some quantum physicists believe. Cause and effect govern the Causal and Astral planes in different orders of time and space.

When God expressed creativity, this power did so through what might be considered a process of fragmentation. The results of this creative impulse will now be considered from the highest dimensions of being to the lower realms of life. From perfect Oneness the four basic attributes of Consciousness, Energy or Power, Creativity or Manifestation (as Sound and Light), and Love manifested as distinct qualities. In spiritual dimensions immediately below the Absolute God, these powers or qualities work in harmony with each other in a positive way. In lower realms, these qualities are subdivided or diluted. Individual souls are fragments of the Divine or drops from the ocean of God with the same qualities as God, however they are weakened by descent into realms of cause and effect where the harmony of these qualities is divided in a personal sense.

After the creative life current has descended to the mental regions, often called the Celestial Dimensions or Causal Realms, it divides into several evolutionary or developmental lines: human, devic (angelic or nature spirits) and subhuman (animal, bird, fish, reptile, insect, microbe, etc.). In the animal kingdom such carnivores as lions, tigers and wolves draw on the power quality and consume other animals while docile vegetarians, are most closely affiliated with peaceful and loving primal qualities. In humans, and to some degree animals, consciousness has been blended with the intelligence and reason of the Universal Mind or Brahm, and the personal consciousness becomes the ego or "I". Attention is now outgoing into the seven Causal subplanes, or further down into lower realms of creation. Power or energy, coupled with creative force or manifestation, instills such concepts as order and justice, intuition and creativity. In this way individuals become little creators of conditions under the direction of ego and thus assume responsibility for their thoughts and actions. This is the initial origin of cause and effect (or Karma to use an oriental term). The initial "sin" committed by fallen souls took place in the Celestial Abode when ego asserted itself. And yet this assertion was necessary if entities were to learn by experience. Sin may be defined as any thought or activity that separates the attention or spirit from an awareness of one's spiritual or true nature.

Higher teachers often refer to the Causal Plane or abode of Brahm, or OM, as the Negative Power. Existence may be compared to a magnet that has both positive and negative poles. Both of these poles are essential if a magnet is to function properly, and both poles are needed if entities are to gain experience in material dimensions. To consider the Positive Power good and the Negative Power bad is to paint a misleading picture of the situation. The power going outward from God sustains the Negative Power and lower realms, while the current that travels back to God is an action of the Positive Essence. The Negative Power is not an entity as most of us think of such, but this power can manifest in any form it chooses. In the purely spiritual regions, all powers are united as one, while in the Causal Plane and below, these powers are divided and attention can be focused outwardly or inwardly as individual egos introduce factors of cause and effect. These agencies direct the destiny of each entity until this soul rises up and reunites the divided forces into the initial state of Oneness. Only entities in the human evolutionary line can return to the Source or God.

The results of each thought and action on the part of each individual are stored in the Causal Plane, and this mountain of karma has to be eliminated before souls can escape the lower worlds. Gender first arises in this realm so procreation can be achieved in lower dimensions. The Zohar, a 13th Century book in the cabalistic tradition, considered God to be half male and half female, and a belief in the *"divine mother"* is found in many faiths. Although the concept of a union between the male and female aspects of God in the Celestial Realm is believed by some faiths, gender is a result of division of higher qualities. For example, power and energy manifest as male attributes, and love and intuition express themselves most fully in female forms. Because divine qualities are further fragmented in the Causal Plane, love is diluted into exalted compassion and forgiveness. The concept of *"soul mates"* arises from recognition that these powers must be reunited as souls move back to the primal origin. However, each soul has the potential to express either male or female attributes depending on the emphasis attention, or the soul, places upon each of the four basic attributes. Karma also influences the gender of individuals. But gender does not exist above the Causal Plane. Life in the Causal dimension seems to be permanent, but it is not entirely stable because dissolution takes place after extremely long periods of time. Souls may *"die"* to the Causal Plane and descend to lower dimensions, or they may rise above the Causal Realm into higher spiritual states. But to do this they need the guidance of a higher teacher.

This leads us to the origin of evil, a concept that has bewildered some of the most acute thinkers and theologians throughout the ages. Simply put, evil originated when power, ruled by egotism, became separated from the higher consciousness and love. In the oneness of the Supreme Being, all spiritual qualities work together in perfect harmony. But in the Causal plane the ruling force considers himself to be separated from the Positive Power, and he establishes conditions and laws that keep his dominion intact. He even represents himself as the ultimate being or God and does everything possible to prevent souls from learning about the Positive Power. The Negative Power is also known as Universal Mind. Perhaps the term *"ultimate ego"* might be a better description; however, there are reasons for this division of authorities into positive and negative forces. As has already been stated, this separation was necessary for contrasting attitudes and freedom of choice to develop in lower worlds. William Blake understood this and stated,

"Without contraries there is no progression." From the Causal Plane to the physical world, both gods and men have their own free wills and are karmically responsible for every action. They can choose which divine qualities or negative qualities they wish to emphasize, and they are rewarded according to their thoughts and actions. Certainly the Unity of God is present at the core of each entity, but when egos begin to operate through mind, entities tend to forget their divine origin and emphasize one of the four basic qualities. When these divine qualities are kept together and influence the entity equally, love and compassion temper power, and leaders are compassionate and just. Without a fusion of these qualities, egos that focus upon power begin using compulsion to obtain their desires. In the Celestial realm we find Satan campaigning for his agenda, using force to elicit obedience to authority, and Michael fighting for the dominance of free will in the mental and lower planes. **Revelation 12:7** mentions this war in the Celestial or Causal dimension, but it does not explain the cause of this conflict. The implication in **Revelation 12:9** is that Satan was deceiving other souls, but actually he wished to dominate others and be looked upon as a leader. Down in the physical world this concentration upon power alone has produced such dictators and tyrants as Nero, Aurangzeb, Hitler and Stalin, ultimate examples of authority devoid of love for others.

On the other hand, those who focus upon creativity become artistic geniuses, and souls who develop the higher love express amazing compassion. Such great artists in visual media as Michelangelo, Vincent Van Gogh, or Edgar Degas and great composers of music like Mozart, Beethoven and Tchaikovsky all emphasized the creative part of their inner natures. In recent years, Mother Teresa and Albert Schweitzer are examples of people whose love stimulated great humanitarian accomplishments.

The Celestial manifestation of God is no more the absolute Being of God than the physical body is the complete essence of a human being. The Celestial Power is an office filled by a highly evolved but still developing entity or Causal manifestation with higher connections. Among Christian denominations, the Latter Day Saints Church expounds the doctrine that God is expanding and developing (into what they do not say). Brigham Young in one of his talks asserted that *"as man is, God once was, and as God is, man may become."* While these precepts may not be acceptable to most Christian denominations, they are certainly worth considering thoughtfully. The Sikh and other eastern traditions also expound this concept of a creative power (called Brahm) that is subject to change and even dissolution (**Puri 1940:45**). Interestingly, the eastern Saint Kabir and the book of Revelation both give similar descriptions of this Celestial Power. Kabir said that around Brahm in the Celestial Plane *"clouds thunder and drums roar. Red colored is the light of this sun"* (**Puri 1940:44**). **Revelation 4, verses 1-5**, states that a door was opened in heaven (apparently the Astral realm of eastern faiths or *"spirit world"* of western traditions) and John ascended to a higher state where he saw a being with a reddish countenance sitting on a throne from which proceeded lightning and thunder. This accentuates the fact that similar concepts are found in most religious traditions. Many exalted prophets, seers and great world teachers, as well as inspired or advanced artists, musicians and writers were sent into the world from this radiant realm. Many pure and more perfected souls enter this state when they leave the physical body at death.

From the Celestial Realm (Universal Mind or Brahm-Lok of some eastern faiths), the soul descends into the Emotional Realm or Astral Plane of many religions. Here creativity is channeled through a power variously called Jyoti, Jehovah, Allah, etc. It should be emphasized that this is an Astral manifestation sustained by the Supreme Power. Various individuals sometimes apply these terms to the Supreme Power also. This is not recognition of a polytheistic system of many gods acting independently but rather an acknowledgement that the Supreme God or Power sponsors various levels of authority. Or one may say that one divine power manifests variously in the several dimensions or heavens just as one actor can assume many different roles on the stage. The higher one rises into perfection, the more exalted will be these manifestations since they reflect the levels of consciousness present in the several dimensions. As Christ said, *"Blessed are the pure in heart, for they shall see God"* (**Matthew 5-8**). Many lesser prophets were sent to the earth from the Astral dimension, a plane that has seven levels or subdivisions. The upper ones are considered paradises or heavens while the lower divisions constitute what have often been called hells. God did not create any of these places of punishment. These dismal and dreadful states exist because wickedness, hatred and selfish egotism have created them or a need for them. If all people were loving and perfect, hell could not exist. When people die on earth, their souls gravitate to the realm or dimension that corresponds most closely with their purity and integrity. A wicked soul could not maintain consciousness in a highly spiritual or divine state. While there certainly is a judge that evaluates souls after death, in a genuine sense a person's life acts as a judge also. At the bar of judgment, one cannot hide any imperfections because they appear as part of his or her nature. Denizens of the Astral plane live longer than do people in the physical dimension, but Astral death does occur, and souls may go up into the Causal or downward to one of the planets in the physical dimension.

In the Astral Realm love generally is reduced to intense emotional attachment to a limited number of close relatives or associates. The denizens of this realm have all of the qualities of people on earth. For example, they manifest such emotions and mental states as anger, lust, strong attachment and greed. All of these ultimately can be traced back to the development of ego and a desire for domination, and they reflect a state of insecurity on the part of residents of this realm. Perhaps these occupants inwardly sense that this state of being is not permanent. As Jesus stated in **Luke 21:33**, *"Heaven and earth shall pass away."* This agrees with the Sikh assertion that the lower heavens are destroyed in what they call Pralaya (**Puri 1940:45**).

In the physical world each individual seems to be an isolated entity, separated from others throughout life. Because he or she feels alone, each person interprets everything in relation to oneself, a strange identity that is seldom understood. Usually this isolation is so icy and intense that communication merely bounces across an impersonal void that adds hollowness to the words and presents ideas as lifeless specters to the minds of others. He or she tries to pacify the inner nature with constant and varied activities and by accumulating an abundance of material things, but the latter never bring genuine happiness. In fact, almost no one is really happy in this world. Poor people are unhappy because their poverty does not allow them to obtain adequate necessities, such as good food, sufficient clothing and decent shelter. They may be unemployed or poorly paid for their services. The wealthy are not happy because they are afraid someone will steal their money or goods. They are never satisfied with what they have. If a million dollars is obtained, they strive for five million; and when they get that, they labor to obtain 50 million because they equate wealth with security. Yet they languish in distress because they sense inwardly that none of this can go with them. Both the poor and the rich suffer from a plethora of diseases, the result of improper thinking, unhealthy activities and poor diet. Certain individuals are in despair because they cannot find a husband or a wife, and others are miserable because they find no happiness in marriage.

The ego or self is an artificial construction that enables the soul to gain experience in a world of relativity. Isolation forces it to examine itself, something it cannot do in Eternity where no basis for comparison exists. Pathetic indeed is the person frozen in self through fear, doubt or inexperience. In the course of living, each entity meets many other individuals who are also in the world to gain experience. People have the greatest affection for those with whom they feel most comfortable or are most attracted to for a variety of reasons. Physical appearance and vitality, warmth of personality, mental acuteness, self control and range of experience all attract one entity to another. Friendships often result from such attractions if the sentiments are mutual. But friendship rarely induces more than emotional and physical involvement. Karmic debts accumulate as factors of cause and effect produce them, and these obligations must be balanced sometime during the course of living in lower worlds.

The spiritual and physical cosmology explained here is mentioned in many scriptures, even those expounded in ancient times. For example, in the **Katha Upanishad 10-11** it states that beyond objects and senses one finds the mind and intellect. Beyond the mind is the Great Atman. Beyond the Atman is the Unmanifest, and beyond the Unmanifest is the Purush. Beyond this state, the supreme goal, is nothing (**Nikhilananda 1949:152**). Although the astral stage is omitted in the above passage, other stages are obviously those mentioned by modern spiritual teachers. As we have already explained, many religious texts refer to the astral and causal planes quite clearly. These statements reinforce the obvious fact that higher spiritual teachers have been coming into this physical world for many thousands of years.

What many religious texts and philosophical treatises do not explain is how souls are kept in the lower dimensions via laws of cause and effect and how the Negative Power or Universal Mind and subordinate agents manipulate the arenas of life. In the Causal, Astral and physical dimensions, conflicts occur constantly between individuals, religious groups, nations and even conclaves of angelic hosts in the heavens. (Remember how it states in **Revelation 12:7** that Michael and his angels fought the Dragon and his angels). From one perspective, these battles seem to rage between the forces of good and those of evil, but this is a highly superficial view that does not reflect the real stimuli behind these Cosmic, Astral and physical struggles.

The primary cause behind this series of irrational and heartless dramas is the fragmentation of once-united qualities into isolated units of power, creativity and love infused by consciousness. That focus of power at the top of the Causal Plane, looked upon as God by most people, has written via his will uncounted cosmic dramas to be enacted in Causal, Astral and physical dimensions. The actors who participate in these Celestial or lower dramas seem unaware that egotism and emotion are the driving forces behind their actions. Love rarely enters into the picture, and when it does to some degree, emotion dominates it and makes it impure and selfish.

The average participant in these games of hell fails to see the broader picture of a cosmic puppet master pulling strings by mental suggestion. Since this power is a mental phenomenon and each living person has a mind, it is easy for him to influence the mental nature of people. Certainly individual souls have free will, but the ego is an amalgamation of spirit, mind and emotions. Most spirits or souls have been associated with mind so long that they consider it a part of their natures, and they heed the suggestions of mind.

Incarnated souls are unaware that uncounted dramas are being enacted on a multitude of temporal stages and that the god of ego and emotion views these epic struggles much like a theater visitor views an enactment upon a stage or a television viewer watches a performance on a personal TV set. Of course, a TV has many channels available and a viewer can switch from one to another. But this cosmic power can see innumerable dramas simultaneously on the screen of his awareness. In a sense he is constantly entertained or mentally diverted by dramas in the realms of emotional strife and those featuring bloody physical conflict. However, it sometimes becomes a real challenge to keep these blind forces from almost annihilating themselves via hatred and greed, and so avatars and prophetic entities are sent into lower worlds to correct extreme excesses. It is not in the interest of the Negative Power to allow things to get too far out of hand. Another challenge for this power is to prevent souls from escaping from his prison of desires, so he uses these activities to keep the participating souls in realms of his control. This is done because each act or cause has an effect and these effects comprise binding karmic bonds. Forgetfulness regarding our pasts and the manacles of religion are also used to prevent escapes.

These games of conflict are instigated between warriors with irrational causes to promote or defend. Often these are religious in nature and not spiritual, where each participant sees his or her position as ethically, morally and theologically correct and worth dying for. This is a strange contradiction of values, since most religions claim to endorse love and peace. These satanic "holy wars" are driven by selfish motives, especially the promise of a heavenly reward for dying as a martyr in a holy cause. But the truth is that each taking of a life, unless in self-defense, and each instance of torture, rape, destruction of property and unjust domination of others only strengthens the karmic chains and adds to the awesome burden that one must carry. All of these transgressions must be paid for in the realms of hell. While there are hells in other dimensions, this world is certainly a hell, and we are all trapped in a sticky cosmic web spun by the spider of deceit. In a sense this spider devours us by appropriating our energies and by keeping us helpless in its domains.

In these dramas of time, no one really wins because each conflict sows the seeds for future struggles as karmic laws keep pitting the same souls against each other. Consciously they may forget past experiences, but on subconscious levels they respond to the same old stimuli and maintain desires to take revenge for past wrongs. The Negative Power justifies these endless wars by claiming that people learn important lessons from the barbaric and inhumane actions that they perform in these struggles. Savage clashes of one religion against another, one nation against a second nation and one family against another family allegedly instill desires for peace sooner or later. Thus, they are slowly elevated to more perfect plateaus of being. The Negative Power knows that no one truly dies or is permanently annihilated in these conflicts. Remember the story of Krishna and Arjuna in the Bhagavad-Gita. Arjuna, facing the evil sons of Dhritarashtra on the battlefield, lamented that he did not wish to kill any of them because he was a compassionate man. Krishna told him to forget such scruples because both he and his opponents had always existed and always would. The unborn and undying Atman or Godhead in each entity is deathless although bodies die. Therefore he was to fight without desires for victory, pleasure or pain, because a controlled mind does not see itself as the doer and is not held responsible. Since few people can work or fight without desire or some emotional involvement, this attitude is more of a rationalization than a freedom from bondage. And someone at some time has to pay for each action undertaken in realms of cause and effect.

When power dethrones love or is separated from it and establishes cold mental rigidity or emotion-laden pride, the results are catastrophes, countless tribulations and a constant reshuffling of theological cards under the direction of a causal or astral stage manager. The Dramatist of Time or the Negative Power authors or allows the scripts people follow, and that includes wars in heaven and gruesome chaos on earth.

In another sense the Negative Power tries to persuade us to enjoy the challenge of living by our wits in an arena where the strong prevail and the weak are slain. While a higher intuition tells us that all wars are crimes against humanity and that our real challenge is to escape from the dungeon of time, we listen to the power that employs our minds to keep us in bondage and subservient to its strategies.

Many people ask why God forced us to come into the turbulent realms of change, suffering and death. The answer has been given by many spiritual teachers: God did not force us to enter these realms; we chose to explore the lower regions. However the souls were told when they left the Home of Peace that if one cried out to God for deliverance from realms of suffering and death, God would himself come in the form of a saint to help that soul to return home. We always have this option since there are saints in the world in every age.

If people had no plight or pain and never faced death, they would be satisfied with a lesser state of existence. Also, they would have no basis to fully appreciate the love and permanence of the True Home. When we return to God with the fruits of experience, we discover upon our return that a basic part of us never left that Divine Realm. A spiritual portion of our higher nature was always anchored in divinity. This is one reason why we can return to the realm of God after gaining lifetimes of experience and overcoming all imperfect tendencies.

These lower dimensions or realms of action promote or test the evolution of each entity. The personal actions and desires of a specific soul can move it further downward into gross material realms or upward into dimensions of light and beauty. Each one of us is really the architect of a personal destiny in physical, Astral and Causal realms. As the late Saint Faqir Chand (**N.D.:7**) said, *"You create your own world with your mind and thought, and (you) remain ensnared in it."* Our interactions with others test us thoroughly until we realize the relative values of bad and good conduct. In other words, we learn various lessons by reaping what we have sown. The ultimate objective of life is for each entity to realize the relative values of material and mental things, all of which are impermanent, and seek for the highest and self-existing state of Truth. In other words, we are to awaken from the cosmic dream of life in temporal dimensions and merge into the eternally awake and all-encompassing existence of God from which we originally departed. Those who really seek ultimate reality or God are destined to succeed, but this search must become a dominant or driving passion. When this takes place, one or more saintly teachers are sent to assist the true seeker and guide him or her through the myriad trials or tests and pitfalls that exist in all temporal dimensions. It is essentially impossible for a soul to return to the Ultimate Source without guidance.

Chapter 2

WAYS DESIGNED TO MEET GOD

The original intent of most major religions was to reunite an errant humanity with the Creator or Original Source of life. Because materialism, superstition and emotionalism dominated human ethnic groups when most religions were first expounded, the higher teachings were expressed in terms of symbols that might be partly understood by many people and encourage them to seek the higher truth. The inner truth or spiritual thread was introduced to the chosen few who were capable of understanding and practicing it. As an example, Jesus taught the multitudes via parables or stories containing an inner significance. His disciples, however, were given insight into the spiritual meaning of these parables. When the original spiritual luminary or luminaries responsible for each religion left the world, the followers, having incomplete understanding of the spiritual part of his or their teachings, emphasized the outer rituals, symbols and scriptures venerated today by these particular faiths. Thus the outer shell of religion remains while the inner divine spirituality has vanished into obscurity.

All of the major religions except Hinduism, and many of the lesser-known ones, were founded by a prophet, seer or saint who acted as an agent of the divine level that he or she had reached via prayer and devotion. Judaism was expounded by a series of prophets, particularly Abraham and Moses. In the first chapter of Genesis, the word translated as *"God"* was *Elohim*. This is the plural form of the word *Eloah* (Allah in Arabic). The *"El"* part of this word refers to God while *"him"* is a plural suffix. A proper translation would be *"the gods"* or *"the powers"*, but this denies the monotheism that Judaism and Islam postulate. Some have supposed that this refers to the trinity of persons in the Godhead or denotes the sum of powers displayed by God (**Smith and Peloubet 1884:220**). The other word used for God or the Lord was *Yahweh* or *Jehovah*. Early in the Judaic tradition this name was too sacred to be uttered and such words as *Shema* or *Adonai* were employed in its place (**Smith and Peloubet 1884:220**). An interesting fact, possibly related to the veneration of names, concerns *Abram,* as he was originally known (**Genesis 17:5**). God changed his name to *Abraham,* often interpreted as *"father of nations."* Perhaps it is coincidental that the name of God among the Hindu and other eastern faiths is *Brahm,* and Abram could be interpreted as one endowed with an awe of Brahm. Being a name for deity, it may also have been considered unsuitable as a name for a human being, even a prophet.

Christianity was inspired by Jesus the Christ and delivered to the world through immediate or successor disciples since Jesus did not state his concepts in writing. Most of the accepted gospels were written from personal memory or from tradition by various disciples between A.D. 60 and 90. Within 50 years of his crucifixion, three broad divisions of Christianity had arisen. The Ebionites were Jewish Christians who kept Jewish laws and customs but who believed that Jesus was the Messiah who continued and fulfilled the Law of Moses. These Christians did not believe in the virgin birth or in the divinity of Jesus as part of the Godhead. They claimed to follow James, the brother of Jesus, and had their own gospels.

They believed that one had to become a Jew before he or she could become a Christian.

In his several letters of encouragement and doctrine to the various churches that he established, Paul expressed most of the Christianity that we recognize today (**Maccoby 1986**). He articulated or explained how Jesus' life and crucifixion fitted into a cosmic plan of salvation, basing his views on a personal understanding of the visions and spiritual transports he experienced (**2 Cor. 12:2** is a modest statement regarding one of these transports). Paul believed he was chosen to bring Christ's message to the Gentiles, and he asserted that converts did not have to join the Jewish faith and keep Jewish laws, such as circumcision. All they had to do was have faith in the atonement of Jesus that was made possible by his death and resurrection. Paul's version of Christianity came to dominate throughout most of the Christian world and ultimately evolved into Catholic, Eastern Orthodox and Protestant divisions. Most of these branches accepted the Apostle Peter as the first head of the church after the crucifixion of Jesus.

Early Christian writers, such as Eusebius, paint a different picture of early Christianity than is usually believed by most orthodox Christians. Eusebius makes it clear that James the Just succeeded Jesus as the main authority or bishop at Jerusalem, not Peter as most believe. In his *History of the Church*, translated by **G.A. Williamson** (**1965:302**), Eusebius clearly states that James, the brother of Jesus, received authority from Jesus and his apostles. The modern writer, **Eisenman, author of *James the Brother of Jesus* (1998)** supplements the records of Eusebius with the results of recent scholarship and also concludes that James, the brother of Jesus, led the early church in Jerusalem.

A third early division of Christianity consisted of Gnostic exponents. These people believed that the world came into existence due to a conflict in heaven. Many souls were cast down into a world filled with ignorance, hatred, sorrow and error. Souls are trapped in this evil material world and are kept there by an imperfect negative being (Satan). Since souls are sparks from the ultimate divinity, God sends spiritual beings (or Aeons) into the world to impart the truth and assist souls to escape from these mundane realms. According to the Gnostics, Jesus was a divine Aeon who revealed the truth about the divine nature of each soul and who taught the way of liberation. He saved souls not by dying for their sins but by delivering truth and by providing guidance back to God.

There were many subdivisions in each of these three general categories of early Christians, and new views of Jesus Christ and Christianity continue to appear. No one has defined the historical Jesus, although many have tried with various degrees of success. And no one can present a convincing summation of his teachings because, as **Bloom** (**2005:8**) has said: *"...Jesus Christ is totally smothered beneath the massive superstructure of historical theology..."* Each portrayal of Jesus represents a reflection of personal faith in the context of individual religious background or skepticism. Every generation in each nation where Christians are found conceives and teaches a different Jesus Christ. That is why each Gnostic view differed from the Catholic opinions and why the Catholic Jesus Christ varied from the Lutheran perspective and why, in America, Pentecostal Holiness, Baptist and Mormon concepts of Jesus Christ are very dissimilar. Each Christian tradition erects a theological stable in which their concept of Jesus Christ can be born. Then they nurture and worship this view of Jesus until he is crucified by a newer tradition and buried in another tomb of theological obscurity.

Islam is based upon a series of revelations given to the Prophet Mohammed (or Muhammad) between A.D. 610 and 632. Muslim tradition regards Mohammed as the last and greatest of the prophets sent with Allah's final message for all mankind. Old Testament prophets, such as Noah, Abraham and Moses are accepted as divinely inspired, and Jesus, the son of Mary, is also accepted as a prophet in the Koran (**Surah XIX: 30-34**). In fact both Jesus and Mary are extolled in Surah XIX of the Koran. Mohammed stated that Mary would be the most blessed of all women in paradise. Islamic tradition stipulates that both Judaism and Christianity were branches of the one true religion. They were valid until the Prophet Mohammed arrived with the final message. Moses and Jesus spoke only to Israel, while Mohammed delivered a message for the whole world.

Two main divisions of Islam, the Shiites and the Sunnis (or Sunnites), developed over a dispute about the succession to Mohammed. After the assassination of Ali, the fourth Caliph, in AD 661, those who claimed that Ali had the right to succeed Mohammed directly became Shiites. In their opinion, the other Caliphs had been usurpers and only descendants of Ali and Fatima (Mohammed's daughter and wife of Ali) were entitled to rule the Muslim community. Shiites believe that those descendants of Ali whom they call Imams are sinless religious and political authorities sanctioned by Allah. The last Imam disappeared in AD 880 and Shiites await his return to establish justice on earth. Modern Shiite leaders reflect the authority of the 12th Imam (or the 7th if one is an Ismailis adherent). Shiites believe that beneath the literal meanings expressed in the Koran are secret levels of meaning known only to the Imam and those to whom he reveals them. Shiites are in the majority in Iran, but in the minority elsewhere.

The Shiite doctrine of legitimism was rejected by the Sunna who developed a complete theological system during the 10th Century. They rejected the views of the Kharijites and Mutazilites as well as those of the Shiites. The Sunna placed a strong emphasis upon the power and will of Allah that contrasted with the Mutazilite belief in the absolute freedom of the human will. Four schools of law, the Shafi'i, Hanafi, Malaki and Hanbali, developed in the Sunnite tradition. Sunnite Muslims comprise the vast majority of Muslims in the world today.

The mystical Sufis also are considered to be within the Muslim tradition. A few of the well-known Sufi exponents include Shams of Tabriz and his disciple Maulana Rumi, Rabia of Bosra, Hafiz and the recent Sufi exponent Hazrat Inayat Kahn (1882–1927). These Sufi purveyors of spirituality taught that God could be approached via meditation under the guidance of a spiritual adept. Such views were not accepted by the other divisions of Islam.

The enlightened Siddhartha, also known as Gautama Buddha, inspired Buddhism. After renouncing family wealth and power, he investigated Hinduism and wandered as a mendicant until he obtained Satori or enlightenment under a Bo tree. His first sermon, given at the Deer Park near Benares is often compared to the Sermon on the Mount of Jesus because the concepts stated in each of these talks are very similar. Buddha taught that all suffering is the result of ignorance and attachment to impermanent things via desire. The Eightfold Path of right views, right intention, right actions, right speech, right livelihood, right effort, right-mindedness, and right contemplation allows the practitioner to overcome the causes of suffering. Karma, or actions followed by their ethical consequences, determines all facets of one's life. This is the same concept as the *"as you sow, so shall you reap"* doctrine of Christianity or the law of cause and effect recognized by science. Enlightenment was clearly described as a state beyond the physical and emotional dominions, a place of nothing (no thing). In fact, truth existed beyond thought and was a condition where the mind was totally stilled. Almost 2,500 years ago Buddhists proposed the concept that the material worlds sprang from this nothing. Some scientists today assert this premise. Conflicting interpretations of the teachings of Buddha resulted in the formation of 18 schools of Buddhist doctrine before 383 BC. Many sects of Buddhism have developed from the Mahayana, Theravada and Tantric schools of thought in various Asian countries. Important examples are the Zen and Pure Land Buddhist traditions. All of the divisions of Buddhist thought will not be considered in this discussion.

The long history of Hinduism extends back to at least 1500 B.C. The four Vedas, the Rig-Veda, Yajur-Veda, Sama-Veda and the Atharva-Veda, represent the oldest scriptures in Hinduism, while the Upanishads were composed about 600 B.C. Many seers and holy men were responsible for compiling these lengthy scriptures. In the earliest writings, the deities venerated seem more like personified natural forces, such as the sun, fire, earth and rain. By the time the Upanishads were composed, mystical meditations on the meanings of life and the universe were being extolled. It seems apparent that the various sages who contributed to Vedic literature represented several levels of spiritual attainment. Many of the earliest writings reveal sacred formulas, chants and charms designed to assist the devotee in daily living.

A detailed description of these major religions or a summary of the many lesser-known faiths cannot be given here. As the Introduction implies, the objectives in this work are to contrast religious doctrines with spirituality and to show that spirituality once infused all major religious systems to some degree. The outer shell of the major faiths will now be discussed. Such things as religious structures, venerated rites and sanctioned rituals will be considered briefly and comments will be made regarding the real significance of such factors.

Most religions have placed great emphasis upon the architecture of synagogues, churches, mosques and temples. Certainly these magnificent structures inspire awe in the hearts of those that worship or perform rituals there. Vast amounts of money have been spent on such lofty edifices, often using the argument that God deserves the very best. **Paul Johnson in *The Quest for God* (1996: 76)** states a prevailing opinion among devout religionists when he says: *"There can be little doubt that among the most privileged of human beings are those who have the honor to erect a great church to God. They must be considered the most fortunate of artists, and dearest to their maker."* However, spending lavish sums on religious structures does not take into consideration the fact that the real work extolled by most religions is service to humanity. Jesus never advised people to erect great structures in his honor. He taught from a boat or under a tree. He considered the church to be the body of believers and said: *"Inasmuch as you have done it unto one of the least of these, my brethren, you have done it unto me."* (**Matthew 25: 40**). Buddha never encouraged the erection of magnificent temples. In fact the enlightened one taught that attachment to material things leads to misery, and temples are certainly material structures. Much of the money spent on great and impressive churches and temples could more effectively be used to benefit the poorer segments of humanity.

Almost all religions place great emphasis upon certain rites and rituals. Repetition of set prayers, chanting scriptural verses, ringing of bells, beating of drums or gongs, singing of hymns or bhajans, lighting of candles, partaking of sacramental foods and drinks (or communion), partaking of parshad or blessed foods etc. once had deeper shades of significance than they do today. Candles once symbolized that higher divine light present in each person and manifested in higher levels of consciousness. Bells and drums reminded one of celestial sounds that elevate the spirit, etc. The sound of a large bell is said to resound at the top of the Astral plane, while thunder and drums are heard in the upper Causal regions. Sounds of lute, flute and bagpipe permeate still higher planes (**Puri 1940:41-61**). Of course these higher sounds are far more beautiful and enchanting than sounds produced by earthly instruments, but these are the closest similarities one can suggest. Today worshippers have forgotten the real or spiritual significance behind the various rites and rituals and simply perform them because they have been taught to do so. They assume that engaging in these rites and rituals will confer salvation upon them, but, as we will indicate later, only the practice of that spirituality symbolized by these rites and rituals will lead to genuine peace and freedom. Churches or religious organizations are like wooden legs. With them one may stand upright, but he or she cannot run as fast as they could on God-given natural ones.

The subject of fundamentalism will be considered at this time. Many religious traditions have dogmatic groups that claim an exclusive grasp of ultimate truth. Only membership in their sect or denomination can save you. All other groups or faiths are in error and followers of these faiths will either end up being eliminated by death or suffer forever in some hell or place of punishment. This is a satisfying ego trip to those with feelings of superiority, and it has served as a motivation for countless wars and extensive religious hatred. Christian groups that claim correct understanding of scriptures and an exclusive authority to represent Christ, and who persecute those with other opinions, forget the injunctions of Jesus to *"love your enemies and bless those that curse you... and pray for those that spitefully use you"* (**Matthew 5:44**). He further said, *"resist not evil: but whosoever shall smite thee on the right cheek, turn to him the other also"* (**Matthew 5:39**). If enemies are to be treated with such love and respect, how should one treat a member of another denomination or faith who is following his or her personal conscience? Common sense should provide the answer. The Sermon on the Mount of Matthew chapters 5, 6 and 7 should be the creed of a real Christian. Obviously, many so-called Christians have never practiced what is stressed there. If they did there would be no conflict between Catholics and Protestants (as in Northern Ireland, for example), and those with differences of opinion that cannot be reconciled by reason or prayer would let God decide who is theologically correct (if any of the disputants are on sound doctrinal ground). The Ultimate God has love and concern for all of his children, and could not support any religious scheme that condemns most of them to hell or annihilation for honest differences of opinion. Even an imperfect human parent would not arbitrarily select among his or her several children, blessing some and cursing others whom he or she had placed where they could not hear the *"message of salvation."* If, as John asserted, *"He that loves not knows* *not God, for God is Love"* (**I John 4: 8**), then how can any so-called Christian hate or persecute another? Peter reinforces this doctrine when he states, "see that you love one another with a pure heart" (**I Peter 1: 22**). Certainly some hate groups quote scriptures to support their agendas and ego trips, but they carefully avoid those many passages that expose their distorted minds.

Today one hears much about the Moslem concept of the jihad or holy war. The original meaning of jihad is the battle with one's self against personal negative tendencies of mind. In other words, one must fight a battle to overcome all negative inclinations in his or her nature. This is the only true holy war. The same concepts of a personal holy war are found in Christian scriptures too. As it says in **Revelation 21: 7**, *"He that overcometh shall inherit all things; and I will be his God, and he shall be my son."* **Surah II: 263** of the Koran states "a kind word with forgiveness is better than almsgiving followed by injury or violence." This does not suggest that vengeance is desirable or sanctioned by Allah. Those Moslem groups that oppose each other on theological or traditional grounds, such as the Shi'ite and Sunni Moslems, do not consider such Koranic injunctions as *"...begin not hostilities. Lo! Allah loveth not aggressors"* (**Surah II: 190**). Or *"show kindness unto parents, and unto near kindred, and orphans, and the needy, and unto the neighbor who is of kin unto you and the neighbor who is not of kin, and the fellow traveler and the wayfarer..."* (**Surah IV: 36**). While one has a right to defend his or her life and property, God has never encouraged the righteous to go out and kill others of different religious views. In fact, He has inspired such injunctions as *"thou shall not kill"* (**Deuteronomy 5: 17**) and *"love thy neighbor as thyself"* (**Luke 10: 27**). One cannot practice love and vengeance at the same time. Anyone who thinks sincerely and deeply cannot condone any fundamentalist doctrine that promotes hatred for other faiths; such irrational and egotistical precepts lead one far from the real essence of spirituality. To concoct a *"holy war"* is like trying to label the insane hell of strife a sacred act.

Members of the several divisions within each major faith should not make the egotistical assumption that they alone are perfect judges of truth, but let God decide who, if anyone, is right. Members of each faith should allow a higher judge to assess theological or spiritual correctness. It is easy to become convinced that the religious tradition one was born in is the correct one due to the bias of familiarity. If one has heard certain precepts taught since childhood, they seem both plausible and logical. However, deeper thinkers and true seekers consider several important factors. First of all, what were the historical contexts and social conditions prevalent in the area where each religion was introduced and at the time it was started? What did each religion do to improve social conditions and to institute higher spiritual precepts among believers? And finally, how exalted and pure are the teachings of each faith in comparison with the teaching of other religions?

Whenever one carefully studies the basic doctrines of each major religion and most minor ones, he or she is impressed with how much these teachings are similar. For example, love for God, the Oversoul or Source of all existence and for other human beings is stressed in most belief systems. Also ethical living, generosity and purity of heart or mind are major components of each religious doctrine. If the teachings are the same, then is it not highly probable that the source of these instructions is one? As Jesus said, when accused of casting out devils in the name of the chief devil Beelzebub, *"...a house divided against itself falleth"* (**Luke 11:17**). Most religious faiths disagree mainly about the execution of cherished rituals and about traditions that often were not started by the original founder. Baird T. Spalding, in Volume 2 of his ***Life and Teaching of the Masters of the Far East*** **(pages 130-132**), described how Christian and Buddhist believers were about to express disagreement through violence when both Jesus and Buddha appeared in the room as bodies of light, arm in arm, and chastised those who were prone to violence. In Volume 3 of the same series (page 121) Spalding describes how one Puriji says: *"Could there be a God of the Hindu, a God of the Mongol, a God of the Jew, and a God of the Christian? There is a true Universal Principle, Infinite and Divine. The central light of that principle is called God. God must enfold all."*

The several faiths were introduced at different times in manners that would appeal to those being taught higher truths and in languages they could understand. The chronological order in which these teachings were enunciated is not as important as the spiritual levels they express. The messengers of God, those seers, prophets, saints and revelators of spiritual truths, taught each culture or group what they could understand and practice at a given time. They each delivered a message that would enable their hearers to take steps upward into greater light. God has equal love and concern for each of his children regardless of the level of moral and cultural development in which each resides. Just as a child in the first grade cannot comprehend lessons being taught in college, those with less spiritual development should not be expected to embrace immediately the most exalted spiritual precepts. Those of each religious persuasion need to have patient love for others with different views. They should understand that God is sending each aspirant a message that he or she can comprehend and practice. Only those on personal ego trips can assume that the doctrines that they have are more important than those cherished by other groups of human beings. The greatest missionary message one can express in the world is the life this person leads. If one is such a radiant example of love, peace and humility that his or her life inspires others to walk in similar footsteps, then this example will be far more convincing than the most eloquent of sermons.

Each person is entitled to judge for himself or herself what is the most appealing and beneficial religious or spiritual practice he or she can perform and endorse. In fact, each individual is obligated to seek the level of inner truth that resonates most beautifully within his or her mind and soul. Then each person must allow every other entity to choose as he or she has chosen and respect that choice.

Chapter 3

SPIRITUALITY, THE INNER ESSENCE

The assertion of Christ that the pure in heart will see God (**Matthew 5:8**) refers to the effects of spiritual living. But what thinking and outer activities lead to this exalted vision of divinity? In order to discern an answer to this question, we may study the lives of those noble luminaries of spirituality who have clearly stated that they have approached ultimate truth and merged into this divine state.

First of all, one is impressed by the obvious devotion demonstrated by these great souls. Most of them performed the most difficult task of all, that of overcoming all negativity of mind and expressing only positive spiritual characteristics. These great ones spent many years in devout prayer and meditation. But instead of praying for material things and fame they simply asked God for God. Then they patiently listened to the reply of the Almighty. There are many types of prayer. Some prayers are of thanksgiving, some are of praise or joy, some are of repentance for past mistakes, and some are petitions for assistance or specific benefits. Certain prayers are nobler than other prayers. For example, a prayer of thanksgiving is far more elevating than a request for some material property. But the finest prayer of all is to petition God for God. If one has access to the Almighty, what else could he or she possibly need?

Prayer and meditation are two distinct forms of devotion. But meditation is a far higher spiritual practice. What is the difference? In prayer one requests something from God or expresses thanks to the giver of life. But in meditation one listens for the reply of God while making an effort to still the mind and emotions so the voice of God can impress the hearer without the interference of one's own mental processes. Various techniques of concentration and stilling of the mind have been used by spiritual teachers. A common procedure is to give the student a mantra or series of names charged by the teacher through his or her meditation. Often these names represent the manifestations of Deity in the various higher planes. By meditating upon these higher names, one moves toward them via the law of "as you think, so you become," and the charging grants a strong boost to the meditator. In the mystical or spiritual experience achieved by meditation, the devotee finally becomes attuned to the will of God and makes this will his or her own after having overcome the obstacles presented by the astral and causal forces.

The higher forms of meditation are by far the most difficult tasks a devotee will ever attempt. This is true because the mind, that we have listened to for so long, must be controlled or stilled so that agencies higher than the mind can speak to a soul that is buried in causal, emotional and physical vestures. Truly speaking, the mind's job is to distract the attention away from anything that will lead beyond it. Since mind gets its energy from the higher soul or spirit, it does not want the latter to rise above it and thus lose a major source of sustenance. Needless to say, the mind does a great job of holding our attention in lower realms by attaching itself to material things and conditions. If the meditator did an equally ardent job of focusing attention without allowing mind to interfere, he or she would accomplish the higher goals easily. But usually this is not the case as mind wins battle after battle and, of course, this adds to the karmic stockpile stored in the causal or celestial plane. This titanic mountain of past karma must be eradicated before the soul can be freed from the realms of the Negative Power. Higher spiritual teachers assist aspirants in a speedy elimination of karmic debts by introducing them to the divine sustaining current or power variously called by such terms as the Word, Nada, Nam, Shabd, Akash Bani, and Kalam-I-Ilahi by the several religious traditions. It should be stressed again that spiritual adepts of the highest order have appeared in every major religious faith to express the same basic truths. No single religion can claim a monopoly on divine revelation. As the Medieval Saint Kabir stated in his poem *"Tethered to Prejudice," "Biased with one view or another, the entire world dwells in delusion. He who adores the Lord without bigotry or bias is the enlightened one."* (**Sethi 1984: 217**).

The most prominent spiritual quality possessed by the highest teachers and by their devoted students is Love. We have already defined Love as a major component of the Divine Source of all. Yes, God is the love with which we love Him and all others. Before we consider this viewpoint in greater detail, let us discuss the several things that Love is not. First of all, it is not to be confused with attachment or infatuation, a strong emotional desire to possess the subject of one's affections. True love promotes freedom, while attachment binds the so-called lover to the smallness of his or her desires. Also, genuine love is not selective or exclusive. When a person says he or she loves a brother or a neighbor but hates someone else, this individual is expressing an emotion, because love and hatred do not reside in the same house. It would be like fire and water existing simultaneously in one place. Real love must be extended to include the worst of sinners and the most egocentric individuals, because they need it the most. Such exposure to love and compassion will help to awaken the divine spark that is deeply buried beneath frozen layers of mental rigidity or immersed in the cauldron of emotional turmoil. If we despise imperfect beings then we promote imperfection. I once heard the highly evolved soul **Millie Prendergast** say: *"you must be too pure to see iniquity in anyone; for if you see it in them, it still exists within you, or you would not recognize it."* Each of us must feed the divinity in every other soul we meet by speaking directly to that divine element and not bolster the imperfections in others and in ourselves. Those who love and bless negative and disdainful human beings and petty patrons of sin because they can see a higher essence within them will be blessed. It is not our job to judge others, only love them. For He who is the light of perfect judgment has only love for you and me. If any of us were judged without patient love and forgiveness, we would not be allowed another breath.

Love is not synonymous with sex, although people with true love for each other may engage in sexual activity. If love and sex were synonymous, then the world would be a marvelously happy place where concern for others would eliminate selfishness and where joyous peace would be universal. Actually, sex is more closely related to an egotistical desire for dominance or for personal physical gratification. Lust often begins as this mental desire for physical control and satisfaction and is connected to procreative animal drives that have been established to perpetuate the human race. People speak of *"making love,"* but lusty mental thoughts coupled with related physical actions cannot create love. If having sex is the closest people ever get to each other, they will forever remain strangers. Sex usually does not instigate love because bodies get in the way and inhibit spiritual expression. John Donne, in his poorly understood poem *"The Ecstasy,"* attempted to explain a height that few physical lovers attain as souls meet and mingle apart from corporeal forms. But even this ecstasy is but a feeble echo of the immaculate wedding that is consummated as perfected spirits coalesce in divine unity.

We must ask ourselves thoughtfully what it is that we love in another. The body, a temporary and often unattractive vehicle, is imperfect at best. Emotions are impersonal diminutions of energy or expressions of desire used by the ego as defensive mechanisms. And mind itself is an instrument of cold analytical reason that is usually a slave to habits and a victim of emotional short-circuits. We may become infatuated with the body or mind of another person, but we never really love either of them. The supreme essence of love already exists at the core of each soul, and blossoms when the divinity in one recognizes the divine in another. As this happens, love unites at an exalted spiritual level and there is a merging into that primal oneness or ocean of love. This is accompanied by an ecstasy that makes the most intense orgasm seem weak and insipid. When scriptures or saints state that God is Love, they obviously are not in reference to the consummation of some sexual act. They are mentioning a state of Divinity that exists above the drama of life and death, a perfection that cannot be broken. As Shakespeare said in Sonnet 116, *"Love is not love which alters when it alteration finds...It is an ever-fixed mark that looks on tempests and is never shaken."* Love makes the heart young, and like a flame it burns away years, fears and tears. Those alive with love join hand in hand, heart in heart and soul in soul, and their flame produces a brilliance that makes hatred, sorrow, and darkness vanish into nothingness. They recognize the One in many. Being forced to break the habits and affections of a lifetime is traumatic but endurable; severing the intensity of love's perfect moment is impossibly tragic, because that moment touches eternity. Only a master of love really comprehends this truth.

The second most prominent characteristic of a saint is natural and unfeigned humility. As the late Saint Kirpal Singh of Delhi, India put it: *"His self has vanished into God, and only God remains"* (**Circular Letter, July 1, 1967**). Those who have glimpsed even a lesser manifestation of the power, glory and endlessness of God sit in humble silence before such an indescribable state of being. Having achieved such a vision, humility comes naturally, because the viewer knows that God is the only real actor. The soul then sees itself as a servant at best, an infinitesimally small drop from the ocean of spirituality. This real humility exists in sharp contrast to the attitude displayed by most mundane or spiritual teachers. Those who are learned and decorated with various university degrees often lecture from a world of vanity. They look down upon others less learned than themselves. True scientists, teachers or scholars are appalled when they realize how little they know in proportion to the totality of potential knowledge. Authority is necessarily graced with humility if it succeeds in accomplishing more than crowing louder than others crow.

Many religious leaders, glorying in their knowledge of certain scriptures and a mastery of pious rituals, dress in ornate robes and wear elaborate headgear to impress those who come to partake of their *"wisdom"*. Preaching from pulpits of self-importance, such purveyors of ritual and dogma usually have deceived themselves into believing that they serve God. As Jesus said, *"When the blind lead the blind, both shall fall into the ditch"* (**Matthew 15:14**). He also said, *"He that is greatest among you shall be a servant"* of all. (**Matthew 23:11**). Did a Saint John of the Cross or a Mother Teresa ever appear in public in ornate splendor? Did they ever pretend to have ultimate wisdom or act as if they were the most important spokes in a Divine wheel? Of course not! They lived on earth to serve others and not to be venerated as religious leaders. And yet such noble souls have more perfectly expressed the love and essence of Christianity than have pontiffs, bishops, priests, and other high church officials dressed in elaborate attire.

Many Oriental teachers have also extolled the virtues of humility. The Chinese sage, Lao Tse, once asked, *"Why is the sea sovereign over all rivers and streams?"* His answer: *"because it lies lower than all of them."* Saint Paltu, a humble 18th Century Indian grocer, spoke out vigorously against religious pride. He stated that Hindu priests, yogis with supernatural powers, and wandering mendicants or ascetics all exhibit pride in some form. The Mahant or Hindu priest delivers sermons to impress the people and win their esteem or veneration. Most yogis and ascetics with ashes smeared upon their bodies long for the praise of those who consider them to be holy men. Paltu concluded that the real Holy Ones transcend desires for name or fame (**Ezekiel 1979:252**). They have, to paraphrase the words of Bulleh Shah, rid themselves of ego and have discovered their true selves (**Puri and Shangari 1986: 264**).

One saturated with selfishness and ego leaves no room for God. Only when one becomes aware of his or her imperfections and is divested of all selfishness can God enter and fill that person with divinity. When a basket is filled with worthless rocks, no one can proceed to fill it with diamonds. In order to approach God the entity must give up all that he or she has and all categories of thinking because these things are less than divine. Only perfection can stand face to face with God. Higher teachers have often said that when an entity puts one foot on the mind in humility and love, the next step takes that soul to God. The injunction of Christ that one needed to become as a little child before he or she could enter heaven reflects the need for humility. Those who approach Him as children will be exalted beyond the gods. Those who try approaching Him as gods will fail to gain exaltation until they become simple and childlike.

As Jesus stated in the Sermon on the Mount (**Matthew 5:8**), *"blessed are the pure in heart: for they shall see God."* Purity and humility go hand in hand and those blessed with these traits certainly see the Divine One; the others see only their concepts of God in the mirrors of their minds. And this is the problem: we allow our minds to mislead us. As Hui-chung told his disciple Ling-chiao, *"Buddahood is attained when there is no mind"* (**Suzuki 1956: 202**). Love, humility and purity enable one to walk through the second death, that of the ego, and reach perfection. No human being can approach the threshold of divinity unaided. He or she must accept the assistance of someone who has crossed the ocean of illusive thought and that empty realm beyond the mind. Such a master of truth has reunited the fragments of original spiritual nature with the Oneness of God. Realizing God is not a process of lighting a candle within the soul but is the act of waking up from the sleep of dreaming among illusions.

Spirituality differs from philosophies, religions or creeds in that it gives you a method of testing the assertions of its teachers. One is not asked to embrace blind faith in some religious doctrine and wait until death to see if you are right. A genuine spiritual teacher helps the devotee experience the higher truths he or she teaches during this lifetime if the devotee develops a pure heart and discrimination. A pure heart opens the door to higher illumination, and discrimination helps one separate higher reality from transient phenomena.

Chapter 4

CHARACTERISTICS OF TRUE SPIRITUAL TEACHERS

Many people will argue that only one teacher, such as Christ, has been sent by God to save mankind or that the last true teacher was a certain revered individual. They insist that we must depend upon the Bible, the Koran or other scriptures for guidance today. God has as much concern for His children living on earth now as he did thousands or hundreds of years ago and makes the same provisions for them at this time as He did in earlier ages. In order to support a position that Jesus Christ was the only perfect master sent to earth, some orthodox Christians will quote **John 14:6** where Jesus is reported to have said, *"I am the way, the truth, and the life: no man cometh unto the Father, but by me."* But these ardent Christians forget that this statement has a historical context. Jesus was speaking to a small group of disciples seated in front of him. And he assured these followers that no one else at that time could show them the Father. This statement of Jesus was written down from memory many years later, so it is easy to see how the words may have been altered slightly. Also, as **Bart Ehrman (2005)** has pointed out in his book *Misquoting Jesus,* poorly educated early scribes often made mistakes when they copied the Gospels by hand. Usually, these mistakes were not intentional, but they did happen. Jesus never said that no other legitimate teacher would ever appear in the world. In fact, he told his disciples that they could do the things he did if they perfected themselves. In **Matthew 5:48** Jesus ordered them to *"be ye therefore perfect, even as your Father which is in heaven is perfect."* Jesus would never have told his disciples to attempt the impossible. According to the biblical record, he stated that the day would come when his disciples would know that Jesus was in the Father, they were in Christ and the Christ in them (**John 14:20**). It is apparent that Jesus, the perfected man, was saying that others could and would be perfect too. And this is what each higher teacher is, a perfected soul. Prophets and seers with various levels of competence are also sent into the world to fulfill the needs of God's children. We should love them all and accept them for what they are.

If salvation can only be conferred by Jesus Christ; then what about the millions of souls that lived on earth before the physical advent of Jesus? Are they forever damned because God placed them in a worldly context where they had no chance to accept or deny Jesus? Also, what about the millions of people who lived and died in remote portions of the world after Jesus was crucified but who never heard the Gospel message? Are they condemned to hell for not being able to accept or reject Christ? Not if the Biblical assertion that "God is Love" is correct (**I John 4:8**). No loving or even thoughtful parent today would be that capricious with his or her children. All would be given an equal chance to achieve salvation. The love of God is greater than human love.

Many Christians quote **John 3:16** that says: *"For God so loved the world, that He gave His only begotten Son, that whosoever believeth in him should not perish, but have everlasting life."* But those who quote this verse usually forget verses 1 through 4 and 14 in the first chapter of John. These verses stress the fact that the Word was the only begotten Son and it was made flesh in the form of Jesus. Perhaps the Word or Logos has assumed other forms when the Christ message has been forgotten. It has remained one Word although several exponents of this divine state have appeared on earth.

An individual manifesting at a specific time in history could never give guidance to all souls even if this personage wrote a book of instructions, and Jesus never wrote a single word in the New Testament. In fact, the Gospel accounts were all written many years after the events they describe had transpired. Whenever a great teacher leaves the world, individuals with various degrees of insight immediately subject his teachings to personal interpretations. And no one can check with the teacher to find out what is really correct. Look at Christianity, for example. Thousands of different denominations base their highly varied beliefs and rituals upon personal interpretations of statements in the Bible. Also, consider Islam. Here we have Shi'ite, Sunni, Sufi and other divisions who do not agree on interpretations of the Koran. None of them can confer with the Prophet to find out what Allah really desires. And then the problems of translation arise. It is quite difficult to translate a scripture from one language to another without losing some of the original meanings. Therefore it is imperative that God send a steady stream of divine personalities into the world to keep spirituality free from erroneous opinions.

The world is full of teachers with various degrees of competence and awareness. These alleged purveyors of knowledge range from outright charlatans with no spiritual attainments to devotees with some or much subjective experience. Deceptive false "*gurus*" often feign mastership as a convenient and easy way to obtain a living from generous but misled followers. Often these self-appointed *"guides"* have much charisma and put on a convincing performance before those without spiritual insight. Since so many people today are really seeking higher truth, anyone with a good act can procure a large group of followers. Unfortunately, some less scrupulous pretenders use suggestion or even hypnosis to convince their disciples that the limited experiences or visions they instill in their minds are genuine and spiritual. Also, certain dubious teachers know fully well that if sensitive devotees truly believe in something or someone, they will *"see"* the objects of their veneration within. This happens because the mind is creative. In fact, if many people believe in and venerate a certain personality, collective mental creativity can cause a form or forms of this so-called entity to appear in both the Causal and Astral planes and even sometimes in the physical world. Jiddu Krishnamurti once told how he was led by founding members of the Theosophical Society to believe in the ascended Master Kuthumi Lal Singh **(Krishnamurti 1989-video)**. Since he was a very pure and sincere seeker, the form of Kuthumi often appeared before him and talked to him. One morning Krishnamurti, in his love and enthusiasm, ran over to embrace the form standing before him. But as his arms touched the space where the form seemed to be, it vanished and he never saw it again. This certainly suggests that the form Krishnamurti saw was not really that of an ascended master. Contrast this with Yogananda's account of how his teacher, Sri Yukteswar, appeared before him physically after he had left his body and how he, Yogananda, threw his arms around the ethereal form and felt it distinctly **(Yogananda 1975:475)**. It did not vanish but continued talking to him.

A certain disciple of a legitimate master once achieved considerable inner experience and traversed the astral subplanes. His ego suggested to him that he pose as a master because, in that capacity, he could help many individuals. So he had an artist prepare depictions of a few alleged masters and then he assumed the role of a "*guru*." He borrowed the teachings of several genuine masters and expounded them as his own. I caught on to this deceit when I read one of his books and recognized that page after page were copied verbatim from a rather obscure work by L. R. Puri and from a volume by Julian Johnson, both disciples of a real Master. Neither of these authors was given credit for the pages extracted from their publications. A genuine teacher would never do this. The part that is most disconcerting to a real seeker is the fact that many of the followers of this "*guru*" began seeing the alleged "*masters*" within after they had meditated upon the artistic depictions. In this case, the "*teacher*" knew enough about the psychology of meditation to be aware that many disciples would be fooled.

On the other hand, a few self-deceived teachers could actually have decent motives. These people may assume that they can help purvey higher instructions even through they have not actually experienced the essence of what they teach as a so-called "*guru*." Such pretenders often do not realize that a substantial penalty is imposed upon those who portray themselves as spiritual leaders but who are actually incompetent. Any way you look at it, teachers who do not have inner experience and who have not been authorized to do the work by a genuine teacher are on ego trips and have deceived themselves. It is dangerous when these so-called "*gurus*" try to lead others because they cannot help their followers avoid all of the pitfalls in the astral and causal planes. Those who intentionally deceive others must pay a most severe penalty in this life or in the future.

Of course, there are some teachers that have actually been appointed by an astral or causal plane power to convey instructions and assume a cosmic responsibility. Seers, reformers and prophets are sent into the world from various positions in the Causal and Astral planes. The mission of these reformers is to promote ethical and moral living and warn those engaged in gross sin that they must reap the results of such actions. The goals of these agents of lesser powers are to reform people and improve conditions in the prison of the world. They do not liberate souls from cells in this prison.

Sometimes truth seems stranger than fiction. We base our fiction upon what we know or think we know, but most people have not experienced higher truths or even things that transpire in the Causal realm. For example, in that dimension one strategy of the Negative Power is to tell a sincere devotee that God is very pleased with his or her devotion and willingness to serve his creation. This disciple is then informed that God is creating a new galaxy in either astral or physical space and many souls will be sent to reside on the several planets to be established in this new environment. The entity is told that because of his or her truthfulness and sincerity, he or she will be placed in charge of the evolution of this new galaxy and will be responsible for bringing the many souls sent there back to the celestial abode of God. What a trap! If the devotee agrees to such a plan, he or she will certainly be responsible for a myriad of souls. Naturally, many of these inexperienced entities will make an abundance of mistakes, and compensation will be required for these errors. Since the *"god of the galaxy"* is ultimately responsible for karmic balance in his or her domain, the payment of such debts may be unpleasant indeed. Only a truly humble and perceptive soul will not fall for such a scheme.

There are always a few highly spiritual Masters of Truth living among us. They reside on earth as directed by the law of supply and demand. In other words, when true seekers cry out to God for guidance, a spiritual adept is sent to assist them. It should be emphasized strongly that a seeker does not find a master even though he or she searches throughout the world. When a sincere longing for God becomes unbearable, the Master he or she is destined to meet finds that seeker and takes this disciple home. Of course, whenever a genuine Saint is sent into the world, the Negative Power does his best to keep devotees within his domain. He does this by sending one or more charismatic teachers with a similar message to mislead the seekers and keep them from escaping to higher realms in the company of the spiritual Master. He also instills doubts in the minds of sincere seekers so they will not accept the teachings of the genuine Saint. But the true Master always can be distinguished from adepts of causal or astral regions by a knowledgeable and sincere seeker. First of all, the teachings of a Master from above the causal plane are always free. We are charged for everything in the causal, astral and physical realms, including our mistakes. But the spiritual Master never charges for teachings, advice, initiations or guidance of any kind. It is certainly legitimate for one to recoup the cost of publications being distributed, but no great amount of profit will be made on these. If a small gain is made from book sales, this profit is never used to personally benefit the instructor. Those who charge for initiations, psychic help, personal guidance or anything else are not true teachers of the highest order. The concern of a genuine Saint is to instruct souls in regard to the higher truth and help them to realize their divine potential. Such a great teacher has no interest in collecting money or other mundane things. He or she has no desire to build great temples or ashrams. Instead, these agents of the Divine live simply upon means that they have personally earned and then help others in spiritual ways.

A true Saint may be recognized by the intense love that radiates from his personality. In the presence of such a divine soul, an aspirant is filled with indescribable elation and peace and time seems to stop entirely. The Saint has love for all people, including those that oppose him and treat him badly, and he instills this love in his genuine disciples. Such evolved souls love even animals and creatures lower on the evolutionary scale. This is one reason why all of the higher teachers encourage vegetarianism. They stress the conviction that animals have souls, and teach that when people deprive them of their life experiences, compensation must be made sooner or later. A venomous snake or a hungry lion will not harm a genuine Saint because these creatures inwardly sense the love and purity of intention these great souls have for them.

The need for love is more basic than the need for food, clothing and shelter. A person may have a superfluous amount of worldly goods and great wealth and still be unhappy and isolated, even in a crowd. With the love instilled by a genuine saint, a disciple may have few worldly things but be filled with inner joy and peace. A saint introduces his followers to the real love of God and it saturates their inner souls.

Those who have been around saintly personages a lot recognize the fact that a Saint can turn off the awesome radiation if there is a reason to do so. He or she also may tersely chide an errant disciple when loving injunctions have not worked. Just as an affectionate parent will discipline a disobedient child, a Saint will also, but all motives will spring from a loving concern for the welfare of the child disciple. The story of Bulleh Shah (1760 – 1810) is a prime example of how a Saint sometimes has to correct an imperfect follower. Bulleh Shah, the son of wealthy and learned Shah Mohammed Dervish, took as his teacher a lowly farmer, Inayat Shah, because he was the only perfected soul that he could find. Of course, he was truly seeking God. The differences in social status between the Saint and his wealthy disciple bothered the latter at first because much emphasis was placed upon the concept of caste in India at that time. In order to teach his egotistical student an important lesson, Inayat Shah sent some of his poorest and most uncouth disciples to invite Bulleh Shah to a wedding. They were poorly received by Bulleh Shah, who wanted to get rid of them as soon as possible, and they reported this poor treatment to the master. Now Bulleh Shah had been getting wonderful results in his meditations, but suddenly the Inner Light and other manifestations were shut off. Bulleh Shah tried pleading with his noble teacher but to no avail. The latter refused to see him. Finally, in desperation, Bulleh Shah learned dancing and singing because he knew that the master often had a certain group of entertainers perform for him. After he had learned the songs and dance steps these entertainers performed, he traded places with one member of the group and performed before his master with a heavy heart. Inayat Shah immediately recognized him and told Bulleh Shah to get out of the dress he was wearing and then he forgave him. Bulleh Shah had learned his lesson and never again let his ego and a lack of love for others separate him from the Inner Light. Ultimately, Bulleh Shah too became a perfect saint.

Much has already been said about the virtue of humility. A real saint gives all credit to his master and to God and considers himself as a servant of all. This writer once heard the late Saint Kirpal Singh (1894-1974) say that he did nothing. He never dreamed that he did anything, he said, and then added that if any good thing came through him, it was from God or his master. An incident from the life of Saint Sawan Singh (1858 – 1948) sheds light upon the humility of saints and expresses the fact that no evolved soul really wants the awesome responsibility of serving as a master. When the great Saint Soami Ji (Seth Shiv Dayal Singh) passed from the earthly scene at Agra, India in 1878, he left behind at least four perfected souls to carry on the spiritual work. One of these was Baba Jaimal Singh (1839 – 1903), a disciple of lofty spiritual attainments. Before Baba Jaimal Singh left the body he authorized Sawan to continue the spiritual work. For over a year the latter did nothing in this regard. Finally he went to Agra to attend a spiritual service being held by Saint Seth Partap Singh, one of the successors of Soami Ji. When Sawan and his group of followers arrived at Agra, Chacha Ji, as Seth Partap Singh was informally called, asked him who was doing the spiritual work at Beas where Sawan lived. One of Sawan's companions replied that Baba Jaimal Singh had authorized Sawan to do the work but that he was not doing it. When asked why he was not following his master's injunctions, Sawan replied that he did not have sufficient power to assume the awesome responsibility of being a master. Upon hearing this honest confession, Saint Partap Singh asked Sawan what he believed him to be. Sawan replied that he considered him to be a perfected soul and one with God. Partap stated that he made no such claims, but added that if Sawan really believed that, he would have to follow his orders too, and he directed him to start his spiritual mission. Partap stated that he also would be responsible for those to whom Sawan taught the higher truths. Then, the ultimate humility descended upon Sawan as the latter replied that he would act like a pipe that delivers water from a source without impeding the flow of that precious liquid (**Munshi Ram 1984:226**). Sawan had finally realized that no genuine saint does anything of his own volition. He simply conveys what he has received to his disciples as an agent and thus escapes the final clutches of ego. This is genuine humility. The average person, and even noble teachers of lesser attainment, do things and are karmically responsible for their actions. But a real saint rises above realms of karma by humbly working in the name of his or her teacher.

The medieval Saint Kabir expressed his humility in several famous couplets (**Sethi 1984:623**). He stated that men laugh at the shortcomings of others but never look at their own faults. To set an example for those given to censure of others, he stated that he once looked for an evil person but could not find one. Then he gazed within himself and decided he was the worst of all. The divine spark at the core of each soul is truly above evil, but human beings are ruled primarily by the mind and this is the origin of all negativity. Kabir did not see the evil in people he met, but he focused upon and nurtured the divine element in each entity. And he counseled *"praise not your own self, nor speak ill of others."* Higher teachers never criticize others or compete with teachers from different schools of thought or with other levels of attainment in order to acquire large numbers of followers. A true saint is more pleased with one devoted disciple than he or she would be with a million casual proselytes.

True masters have spent years in meditation, often six to 12 hours daily, or full time if they have retired from their vocations. Any teacher who has not meditated a lot throughout his life probably is not a genuine saint.

A real spiritual teacher expresses the highest moral and ethical precepts and urges his followers to do the same. If the so-called "*guru*" is not totally honest and truthful, one should leave him or her immediately. A genuine teacher has nothing to hide and operates openly so all can view his actions and understand his intentions. Such a preceptor speaks from personal spiritual experience, not from theory or intellectual comprehension, and this authority permeates his disposition and discourses. A saint speaking from levels of personal attainment never pretends to be more exalted than he is or she is or implies that he or she knows everything. While it is true that a genuine adept can obtain information from inner sources without much difficulty, he or she usually restricts instructions to the scope of a spiritual mission. Some people perhaps feel that if a person is a master he or she should know everything. Yet if you ask a real saint to explain the nature of the weak force in the nucleus of each atom, this person will probably say that he or she does not understand this aspect of physics. A real saint is not sent into the world to master all facets of scientific and philosophical expertise. He or she is ordained to teach spirituality and assist seekers in finding their divine origin.

All genuine saints have overcome lusts of the flesh and have only pure thoughts when they deal with disciples of the opposite sex. They know that there is no comparison between the limited intensity of a sexual orgasm and the ecstatic rapture of higher consciousness. Being above the Causal plane, the source of gender, they see all aspirants as pure souls and are never tempted to indulge in promiscuity. Our concepts of gender do not apply to the Ultimate Source of Being. Certainly many saints have been married householders and have had children, but they limited any sexual involvement to that necessary for procreation. Adepts do not look upon sex as something dirty or obscene but as a natural biological function like eating or sleeping. Excessive indulgence in food consumption, sleeping or sexual activity should be avoided so higher faculties can develop properly.

In their teachings, saints recommend faithfulness to one partner as well as moral purity. In an age when sexuality has been reduced to a bedroom sport involving multiple partners and erotic variety devoid of love, all higher teachers set an example by transmuting their procreative energies into spiritual channels. The benefits of doing this include more robust physical vigor, sharper mental acuity, enhanced creativity, developed intuition and deeper spiritual perception. The procreative urge is so strong that it cannot be repressed safely. It must either be expressed or transmuted. Another advantage of energy transmutation is the development of deeper insight into the attainments and motives of others. Those that are pure in heart are not fooled easily by self-appointed "*gurus*" and religious charlatans. Also, they are not influenced by medical advice or prescriptions recommended by traditional physicians who are dominated by passion themselves. Moral purity also has the advantage of keeping the individual free from such sexually transmitted diseases as AIDS, syphilis and gonorrhea. Teachers of the highest order are never addicted to illicit drugs, including alcohol, and they encourage their students to abstain from any form of substance abuse, addictive materials or addictive behaviors since these dull the higher senses and diminish spiritual progress.

All spiritual teachers of the highest caliber earn their own livings via honest and beneficial labor. Some saints have been farmers, others have been weavers or clothing manufacturers, a few have been merchants and several have even been government employees. Baba Jaimal Singh had a military career because, as a farmer, caste tradition in India required him to marry. Since he was not inclined toward matrimony, he became a soldier, although he never took human life during his years in the service. Defending one's country can be looked upon as a beneficial activity, although no nation should ever instigate hostilities as an aggressor. The adept or teacher that solicits donations from the public or accepts a living from his disciples is not a saint of the highest order. Any money contributed to a saint will be used to benefit others; he or she will keep nothing for personal use. Contributions given to higher spiritual teachers usually are used to provide food in free kitchens or spent to help the poor or infirm people of the areas in which they live. All genuine saints of the highest order require their disciples to earn their own livings by honest and ethical means. They suggest that whatever work one does to make a living actually benefit society. A person can produce useful goods of high quality or perform a service to the best of his or her ability. Although a pyramid scheme where an idea of questionable merit is sold could be legal, such a strategy may be of little benefit to people other than the originator. Therefore it would be better to produce food, clothing or shelter for others or provide a service such as health maintenance or building repair at a reasonable fee.

Higher laws can be used to circumvent physical situations or perform feats that the average person cannot accomplish. According to the biblical record, Jesus walked upon water and fed a multitude with a few loaves of bread. While the disciples around him looked upon such actions as miracles, Jesus was actually using laws that are not understood by most people. Modern saints of the highest order do not openly perform miracles although they certainly have the power to do so. However, in private they will promote remarkable events in order to help others. During the life of Saint Sawan Singh of Beas, India, a group of several hundred men who opposed him came to his free kitchen after the usual group of disciples had eaten and demanded to be fed. They hoped to embarrass him because they felt that there would not be enough food left after the normal meal had been served. Sawan told a chief disciple to put a few pieces of bread in a covered basket and serve from that basket. He did so and provided bread for all of the people present. No open display was allowed. On another occasion a disciple of Saint Kirpal Singh of New Delhi, India was in a terrible hurricane in Florida. Her car was about to be blown from the road. The disciple thought of Saint Kirpal and immediately a wonderful calm surrounded the car and rain ceased to fall upon it. She looked in the seat beside her and there sat Saint Kirpal. She was able to drive to safety under this circumstance. Although the lady was told not to divulge what had happened, the account did leak out. Saints do not feel that they attract true seekers by doing so-called "miracles" in public. Also, an open display of so-called miraculous powers does not harmonize with the humility expressed by saints. Many people will go to see a magician perform his illusive deceptions, but very few in the audience actually aspire to become magicians. If a person is a true seeker, he or she will not demand or expect to see higher laws of energy manipulation utilized in this physical world. Any yogi or disciplined meditator can perform remarkable feats because this person has sharpened powers of concentration and has gained control over certain material or subtle natural forces. But such power is no guarantee that the practitioner has achieved a high spiritual status.

Forms of spiritual practice or meditation vary from one teacher to another. As recently as the 18th Century, higher adepts often started disciples on a probationary schedule of breath control, repetition of a holy word or words to promote concentration, and dietetic, ethical and moral constraints. When they had demonstrated sincerity in these practices and habits, these disciples were introduced to the main spiritual methods. More recently, most higher teachers have ceased to use prana or breath control as an introductory procedure. They have chosen techniques that lead one past the lower astral subplanes and introduce students to levels where temptation is less severe. It often takes longer for this method to produce significant inner vision than did the older methods, but this procedure is much safer. Often the limited light seen by a practitioner of certain forms of yoga is simply the light present or reflected in a lower chakra. While this gives the student something to look at, this light does not elevate the soul in the way that higher spiritual light pulls it upward. Also, the higher saints of today usually grant two initiations at one time. They give the disciple a charged mantra to promote mind control and then add ethical, moral and dietetic instructions as a first step. Simultaneously, they link the inner faculties to the Word, Shabd, Nada or Creative Current that sustains all existence. In earlier times only the first initiation was given, and then, after the student had progressed adequately in meditation, he or she was given the link to the inner Word. Unfortunately, sometimes a student would not progress rapidly for various reasons and the Saint would leave the physical body before the higher spiritual connection could be made. To prevent this from happening, modern adepts give both initiations at once.

Some saints have encouraged categories of visualization, usually of the form of a holy person or a respected symbol, to assist in mind control. If the teacher is present to monitor the process, this can be beneficial. But the mind is extremely creative, as is the Negative Power, and either can produce a form or symbol before the gaze. Usually the student is given a means of challenging any form or vision that appears during meditation, but some devotees, desirous of seeing *something* within, do not execute the challenge properly and end up being fooled. Saint Kirpal Singh did not advocate any form of visualization. He would say: *"Don't imagine anything. Just patiently wait and see what appears of itself. Then challenge the form or forms as you have been taught. If something or someone stands before the challenge, this one will help you and you can trust this entity.* That loving disciple of Sawan Singh, Ishwar Puri recommends an effective process of ignoring the mind while focusing the higher attention on the Word or Divine Light that comes from above the mind. If one fights the mind, his or her attention will be on the battle and the mind will win. Therefore, one should focus loving attention upon the positive or divine state within at the core of one's being. If attention is placed upon things outside of our ultimate nature, we become involved in illusions.

The Negative Power or Universal Mind as well as the individual mind can create forms that are visible in the ethereal physical dimension as well as in the astral plane. Unless the devotee has been warned and practices acute discrimination, it is only a matter of time until these crystallized thought forms mislead him or her. There are many gross and subtle distractions in the astral dimension that can impede spiritual progress. For example, there are schools where one can learn the history of the cosmos or that of the world from a perspective that is not totally reliable. Of course such classes fascinate the mind. There are teachers that will offer to assist you in reading the akashic records or help you study your past. You will meet men that are godlike physical wonders and women that are exotic goddesses. Although these entities seem to radiate light, they may have no greater moral development than the average person does on the physical dimension. Any activity that can be done on earth can be performed in the astral, so if one has a weakness in the physical world, God help that person in the astral dimension. Very few can view all astral temptations without succumbing to one or more of them. And they always attack the weakest link in your moral chain. But that is their job. As it says in **Revelation 21:7** *"He that overcometh shall inherit all things; and I will be his God, and he shall be my son."* Note that those who fall under temptation do not inherit spiritual status until they stand up and overcome. Many spiritual adepts do not let their students wake up in the astral dimension until they are sure that these pupils can withstand all of the temptations afforded there. Often they escort them through the astral subplanes personally or wake them up in the higher causal plane when they are pure enough to maintain consciousness there. After they have observed the greater light of causal plane phenomena, astral entities or conditions no longer tempt them.

The sincere seeker should be informed that testing of the soul does not end when one has risen above the astral dimension. The Causal Plane has seven subplanes. When an entity enters the lowest causal subplane, he or she is exposed to one of the most difficult of all learning experiences. If one is a believer in Jesus Christ, the *master* appears before him or her in a form that he or she finds most wonderful and convincing. This apparent personage then proceeds to tell the enraptured devotee exactly what he or she wants to hear. The listener will be told that God is very pleased with his or her devotion and that it has been accepted and that entry into paradise is ensured. If the devotee has been a follower of Buddha, then a radiant buddhic form will meet his or her gaze and the apparent Buddha will praise the devotion of this disciple. Obviously the visitor will be enthralled and overjoyed to be in such a holy presence. If one has been a devotee of some other noble teacher, his or her form will seem to appear before the probationer as he or she enters the Causal Plane. And the seeker will stay there worshipping the image before him or her until the realization arrives that this visage is not the real Jesus Christ, Buddha or other respected teacher. This image is a product of the devotee's creative mind. In other words, the devotee is seeing what he or she most wants to see. Pure and focused thought is extremely creative in mental or causal realms, and the mind can produce an image of a loved one, that of a saint or divine personage or even fashion a paradise or heaven in which the soul can dwell for a time. Such forms are allowed to manifest because they teach discrimination. Until one rises above the Causal Plane and the deceptive mind, one can never totally trust what seems to be valid.

The Divine Word, Logos, Shabd, Nada, Naam, Bani or Voice of God is the central unifying theme in all higher spiritual teachings, although some perfectly valid teachers do not immediately introduce their disciples to the Word. The different adepts that have appeared in the several religious traditions have given many names to this creative and sustaining current. And almost all religions have produced examples of genuine saints. Several of these great teachers will be discussed in later chapters of this book. In fact many religious scriptures refer to this Primal Creative Current. In the Bible it is referred to as The Word. *"In the beginning was the Word, and the Word was with God and the Word was God. All things were made by Him."* (**John 1:1-3**). In the Gnostic Gospel of John, we are told that *"Christ, the self-produced God, created everything by the Word."* (**Meyer 1986:61**). This creative power is often referred to as a current of sound because it can be heard. In sections 33-34 of the Nad Bind Upanishad of the Rig-Veda (**Puri 1940:217**), we have these words: *"In the beginning of practice many sounds are heard. Gradually they increase in pitch, and are heard more and more subtly. The sound at first is like that of the ocean, (then) drums and cataracts. In the middle stage one hears bell and trumpet."* These latter sounds, especially the big bell, draw the attention into higher realms. As **Saint Bahadur Jagat Singh (1982:105)** put it, *"the function of Maya is to draw our attention outwards and downwards and that of Naam inwards and upwards."*

The Creative Current that emanated from the Absolute State of God exhibited two qualities, light and sound. These manifestations are two aspects of the one Primal Current. All dimensions, universes, planets and forms of life were brought into being via this Primal Expression of God. This spiritual light diminishes as it permeates the lower dimensions at a distance from its source. For example, in realms above the Causal Plane it is far more brilliant than it is in the astral or physical dimensions. The soul, being a drop from the ocean of divine light, has the brilliance of 12 physical suns in Parbrahm and the light of 16 suns at a higher spiritual level. The higher one penetrates within during meditation the greater the brilliance he or she sees and the more brilliant is this soul.

The sound portion of the creative current permeates all higher spiritual planes. Due to dimensional differences, the sound varies from one level to another. Although there are many sounds heard in the various dimensions, some higher teachers have spoken of five important sounds because these are the key sounds that lead the listener from one dimension to the next. For example, as one enters the Astral Plane, he or she may hear the sounds of birds, small bells, symphonic music, the roar of a conch shell and finally the sound of a big bell. It is the big bell sound that carries the soul over into the Causal Plane. This is the long forgotten reason why many churches at one time rang a big bell before services commenced. Originally, the ringing bell symbolized entry of the soul into the Causal Plane and into the divine presence there. But now most people will tell you that they use the ringing bell simply to call people to worship services.

The sound of thunder is heard in the Causal Plane along with pounding drums. In Parbrahm the enchanting sound of a lute permeates this pure atmosphere and in the next dimension the plaintive music of a spiritual flute inspires the soul. Of course these sounds are far superior to music produced by physical instruments. Saints who have heard these sounds admit that such comparisons are totally inadequate, but these are the closest approximations that can be made to sounds emerging from musical instruments. **L.R. Puri (1940)** describes these sounds in detail in Chapter 2 of his book, although anyone who goes within can experience them.

The aspirant who is searching for a true spiritual guide can evaluate most potential teachers using the criteria presented in this chapter. In summary, the teachings and guidance should be free. The teacher should be authorized to do the work by his or her master. Love and humility should radiate from the spiritual leader. He or she should practice and promote the highest moral and ethical teachings and have earned and be earning his or her own living by honest and useful means. The teacher should not ask you to accept a doctrine upon faith alone. If you will eliminate all flaws of character and practice spiritual meditation as prescribed, you will actually see and hear the higher truths in realms above this physical dimension. You will explore realms far grander and more inspiring than any vista or condition on earth. You will travel beyond the most wonderful heavens of your wildest imagination and enter into states where death, pain and change do not exist. The old adage, *"Seeing is believing."* is appropriate to emphasize here; however, it should also be emphasized that the disciple should test the status of every entity and everything he or she encounters within in order to determine the validity and helpfulness of this encounter. A genuine spiritual guide will give you a method of checking the authenticity of everything on this pathway to God. Remember too that a saint will not openly perform miracles in order to attract disciples. And finally, the guru should expound upon and give you a contact with the Primal Current whether it is called the Word, Nada, Bani, Shabd or some other name. If the teacher does not do all of these things, you can be assured that he or she is not from the highest source. If he or she does meet these guidelines, you should still take a deep and careful look before you leap upon any bandwagon because ego trips can be extremely subtle. A few so-called "*gurus*" may even give free teachings, feign love and humility, earn an honest living and teach about the Word or Divine Current because he or she relishes basking in the spotlight of devoted attention. As Saint Partap Singh once said, *"there is a plethora of gurus in this world who are all aspiring to wealth and fame. From among* (all potential candidates), *to recognize and select the true and perfect guru is very difficult"* **(Jaimal Singh 1998:267-268)**. Only a truly sincere and pure seeker can see behind the mask worn by a charismatic teacher.

Chapter 5

THE WESTERN SPIRITUAL TRADITION

Although Spiritual Adepts of the highest order may have appeared first in the Far East or Middle East because they could find more true seekers in those areas, they have manifested in all parts of the world and in every major religious tradition. In fact, spiritual teachers have expressed different levels of spiritual achievement in all of the regions where they have appeared. Some have reached the Ultimate State, others have awakened in slightly lower spiritual planes, and certain teachers have evolved to Par-Brahm or some state above the mind. All of these saints or sages have been given important work to accomplish, and all of them must be respected. In this chapter we will consider a few of those great souls who have taught in Europe, England and, via literature, in America. The Greco-Roman mystic philosophers, such as Pythagoras, Plato, Socrates, Plotinus and Epictectus will not be considered in this chapter, and we will omit the little-known Celtic seers as well as the enigmatic Quetzalcoatl of Aztec legend.

Meister Eckhart

Meister Eckhart (C 1260-1329)

The humble need not beg God so much as to bid Him, for the heights of divinity can disregard everything else but the depths of humility.

With its highest faculties the Soul touches eternity, with its lowest it is in touch with time.

Meister Eckhart

Probably the greatest European exponent of Spirituality was Meister Eckhart of Hochheim (c 1260 – 1329). He was born in the province of Thuringia, Germany about A.D. 1260. He joined the Dominican Order at Erfurt as a young man and received the traditional training for a Dominican preacher: two years of the Office and Constitutions of the Order, five years of philosophy, and three years of theology. Then Eckhart attended the *stadium generale* for advanced studies. After completing his academic training, Eckhart served as prior at Erfurt and vicar of Thuringia. In 1302 he was given the chair that Thomas Aquinas had occupied in Paris. From 1314 until his death in 1329 Eckhart served as prior, professor and preacher at Strasburg and Cologne. Fortunately, followers using shorthand recorded his sermons verbatim, so we now have a good record of his teachings. It is clear that Eckhart received much higher spiritual training than that offered by the church of his day. Whether he encountered and learned from a higher teacher in his youth or was born into this world as a perfect Saint is not clear, but he certainly expressed the spiritual teachings given by all higher masters of the east and west. Translations of his sermons into English by **Matthew Fox (1980)** and by **Maurice O'Connell Walshe (1998)** were used in this study.

In 1326, while Eckhart was in Cologne, the Franciscan Archbishop of that city raised charges of heresy against him. Upon his request, Eckhart was granted the opportunity of a trial before a papal court at Avignon. He died in 1329 before a papal bull condemned seventeen of his concepts and labeled nine others heretical. The penalty for heresy at that time was death, usually at the stake. Ironically, the headquarters of the church that tried Eckhart was a citadel of corruption and decadence. As Saint Birgitta lamented: *"fear of God is thrown away and in its place is found a bottomless bag of money."* In fact, Avignon was a temporal state of sumptuous pomp where everything the church possessed, be it an office, a Cardinal's hat or a holy relic, was for sale to anyone with sufficient money. The wardrobe of Pope John XXII cost 7,500 florins annually, and the prices paid for elaborate church furnishings perpetually impoverished a populace that was already subjected to excessive taxation by immoral despots, one of which was Philip IV, king of France between 1285 and 1314. Thus a decadent church condemned as heretical one of the few men in Christendom who was truly spiritual. As an honest and God-realized man, Eckhart had no real fear of the church because those blind religious bigots could not in any way punish or diminish his soul. The condemnation of Eckhart was in essence a self-announced condemnation by a corrupt priesthood that could not tolerate a higher truth that pinched the conscience.

The denunciation of Eckhart did not prevent his teachings from influencing such contemporaries as Henry Suso and John Tauler. Fifteenth Century Nicholas of Cusa as well as Martin Luther (1483 – 1546) and Jakob Boehme, the Lutheran mystic, (1575 – 1629) were all indebted to the spiritual concepts of Eckhart. The anonymous English author of *The Cloud of Unknowing*, Walter Hilton and Julian of Norwich are English mystics who were influenced by Meister Eckhart. The Polish poet-mystic Angelus Silesius, Flemish mystic Jan van Ruysbroeck and Teresa of Avila drew heavily upon the sermons of Eckhart. The Spanish saint, Juan de Yepes, better known as John of the Cross (1542 – 1591), was quite aware of Eckhart's concepts.

Nineteenth Century scholars and philosophers such as Friedrich Schelling and Georg Hegel; Marxist thinkers like Erich Fromm and Ernst Bloch; and modern philosophers such as Martin Heidegger and D. T. Suzuki admit being indebted to Eckhart. Thomas Merton agreed with the Japanese scholar S. Ueda when he said, *"whatever (Whatever) Zen may be, however you define it, it is somehow there in Eckhart."* Quaker mystic Rufus Jones, psychologist C. G. Jung and such writers as John Updike, Saul Bellow, Alan Watts and Annie Dillard have all admired Eckhart.

Matthew Fox, a Dominican priest and perhaps the most perceptive scholar of the sermons of Eckhart, has demonstrated that the medieval master was not affiliated with either Aristotelian or Platonistic thought but was an acute and independent spiritual thinker. Modern Christian scholars and believers have misunderstood him because they are unaware of the mystical creation-centered spirituality taught by many Old Testament prophets and by Jesus himself. Eckhart's obvious congruence with Zen, Sufi and Sikh doctrines simply accentuates the fact that no single religion, philosophy or way of life has a monopoly on higher truth.

Before we look briefly at the teachings of the Meister, we will consider an esoteric connotation to the name "*Eckhart*." The Indian word *Eckankar*, often shortened to Eck, means the one supreme God. The expression "*hart*" suggests an obvious meaning. By this interpretation the word Eckhart would mean *"one whose heart is the supreme God."* The sermons of Eckhart make it extremely clear that the Divinity he knew existed beyond time and space and that access to this State of Oneness could only be achieved by inwardly hearing the Word of God.

It is clear when one studies the sermons of Eckhart that he expounded two aspects of God. The first was the concept of God Absolute or a condition of total oneness where observer and observed do not exist separately and where there is neither light nor the Word. As Eckhart said in **Sermon 13**, *"I cannot see what is one."* The Biblical statement that no man had seen God at any time, apparently contradicted by assertions that Moses and other prophets saw God, may refer to an absolute divine state. The second concept of God was God-into-Expression or the creative Word. We will consider briefly each of these spiritual aspects.

Throughout the sermons of Eckhart the reader finds references to a state above the Godhead and even above being. In this Divine State there is neither light nor the Word, a viewer and something viewed. In **Sermon 7** Eckhart states that *"in God there is neither time nor space."* Of such a difficult to describe condition Eckhart declares: *"So totally one and simple is this State, and so elevated above all modes and powers, that not even God him-*

self can gaze into it. And He has never gazed into it insofar as He exists in the way and attributes of His Person. This power is without a way and is devoid of attributes. This state is neither Father, Son nor the Holy Spirit" (**Sermon 20**). In Sermon 28 he restates this concept in these words: *"The pure divine being is above the Trinity."*

One is reminded of Zen teachings in a paraphrased statement from **Sermon 12**: "God is nameless nothingness. A pagan teacher says that what we can know or express about the First Cause is more than anything else what we are than anything that the First Cause might be, for it is beyond all expression and understanding. If I were to say that God is good, I would be wrong. It would be more correct to say that I am good and God is not good, because whatever is good can become better and what is better can become best. For all of these terms (good-better; wise-wiser; or even *"being"*) are far from God's reality. So be silent and do not flap your gums about God, for to the extent that you flap your gums about God, you lie and commit sin. A teacher says: *"If I had a God whom I was able to know, I would never be able to regard Him as God.' With this business of knowing about God you run into a complete lack of knowledge, and through ignorance fall into a beastlike state."* Later in the same sermon Eckhart implies that we should love God not as an image or person or even as mind but as a pure and clear state of Oneness and we should sink eternally from something into nothing and then into this One.

In **Sermon 15** Eckhart relates the spirit of each human entity to this state of oneness. He says: *"I pray God to rid me of* (my conception of) *God; for my essential being is above God insofar as we consider God to be the origin of creatures."* Saint Kirpal Singh (1894 – 1974) often expressed a similar sentiment when he referred to *"the God beyond God."*

The Absolute State of God was the source of all souls and all existence in Eckhart's view. All souls originally were part of and sprang from the Supreme Oneness and each one may ultimately awaken in this state. In **Sermon 3** he asserted: *"When I was still in the source of the Godhead, no one asked me where I wanted to go or what I was doing. There was no one present who might have put such a question to me. But when I flowed out, all creatures called out to God and asked (me) 'when did you leave the house?' Everything in the Source is Unity."* As Eckhart explains in **Sermon 7**, *"With its highest faculties the soul touches eternity, with its lowest it is in touch with time."*

The second spiritual aspect discussed by Eckhart was the Divine Word or God into Expression. It is clear even to a casual reader of his sermons that Eckhart considers the Word of God to be a transcendent creative force and not something synonymous with the accepted scriptures. He is even more specific than was the author of the Gospel of John in his first chapter. In **Sermon 8** Eckhart quotes this scripture and comments as follows: *"Saint John said: 'In the beginning was the Word, and the Word was with God, and the Word was God.' Now whoever will hear this Word in the Father must be cut off from all images and forms. Indeed, such people must conduct themselves so faithfully toward God that all things can cause them neither delight nor dismay."* Then he emphasizes in **Sermon 17**: *"The True Word of Eternity will be spoken only in solitude, where people are made desolate and estranged from themselves and all multiplicity."*

Eckhart stresses to the reader that the Divine Word is something one hears within. He is not simply employing a familiar figure of speech in a conventional way. Consider this utterance from **Sermon 18**: *"Whenever the Word is heard, it must occur in stillness and silence. There we can hear it and understand it correctly."* Elsewhere in the same sermon he asserts: *"A master of the spiritual life says the power of hearing is much more noble than the power of sight, for we learn more wisdom through hearing than through seeing. We shall be much happier in the Eternal Life thanks to our hearing than our sight."*

How does one hear the Eternal Word and where does this hearing take place? Eckhart declares that one hears this transcendent Voice after purifying and stilling the mind and listening with the inner soul in the pure silence. He says in **Sermon 21**: *"The soul in which this birth is to take place must remain very pure and live in a way that is noble and very collected* (concentrated) *and very spiritual. The soul must not flow out through the five senses into the multiplicity of creatures. It must remain quite inward and collected in its purest state."* It is clear that this rebirth spoken of by Eckhart is not synonymous with the *"born-again"* concept of orthodox Christians. Eckhart refers to an eternal birth and comments upon it in Sermon 21 as follows: *"Now we talk about this birth, and how it takes place within us and is accomplished in the good soul whenever God the Father declares His Eternal Word in the perfect soul."* The last two words are important for the soul is to be perfected. Jesus, in Matthew 5:48 declared: *"Be ye perfect as the Father in Heaven is perfect."*

Higher teachers in all religious traditions have praised the Word. Hindu sages have called it Naad (or Nad) or Akash Bani (Song from the heavens), Muslim Sufis have referred to it as Sultan-ul-azkar (king of prayers), the Sikhs have named it Naam (or Nam) and Theosophists have called it *"The Voice of the Silence."* This does not mean that most traditional religionists have understood or accepted the concept of the Word. In fact, all too often they have ridiculed and persecuted those who taught this divine practice of hearing the inner Word. The central thesis of this book is the fact that religion deals with outer rituals, while spirituality emphasizes contacting the Divine through the Word. Of course, as previously stated, religion has its function, and that is to prepare the way for the higher teachings by inculcating ethical precepts and endorsing pure living. It is not an end in itself.

We will now consider Eckhart's teachings on several other topics. First of all, the Meister stressed that our concepts of time and space are illusions in an eternal present. In **Sermon 2** he says that God is creating this entire world in the present now. In other words, God sustains this world and creates the entire cosmos in and from the region of the soul. It is obvious that Eckhart goes beyond the concept held by several religious groups that all things are created spiritually before they come into objective form. These groups believe that the germ of all outer manifestation springs from the Causal realm. But Eckhart is speaking about something beyond the Causal State when he says, in **Sermon 9**, *"If the soul is to recognize God, it must do so beyond time and space."* In **Sermon 6** he states that *"God is a power in the Eternal now."* Referring to conditions above the Universal Mind and the accompanying time and space, Eckhart teaches that attention and will are qualities of the soul and transcend mental realms. In Sermon 8 he says: *"The soul is as young as when it was created* (separated from Oneness). *Old age concerns only the soul's use of bodily senses."* Then he adds: *"Indeed, it is even younger!"*

Eckhart says much about spiritual and practical living. So many mystics of lesser stature are caught up in a spiritual experience that overwhelms them, and they hardly have their feet on mundane soil. But Eckhart is a practical man with transcendent vision and he considers all realms with clear insight. He is especially concerned with human motives as these words in **Sermon 14** suggest: *"I emphatically state that, so long as you accomplish your deeds for heaven's sake or for God's sake or for your eternal happiness, you are not doing things properly for yourself."* In other words you should love others because of the divinity in them and act accordingly out of love and not be scheming for a grander place in heaven. He implies that if one thinks a person can gain more by religious activities or even by devout worship than one can by working in a stable or by serving others unselfishly, this individual is deluding himself or herself. In **Luke 10:27** we are told that one should love the Lord thy God with all thy heart, soul, and strength, and thy neighbor as thyself. Eckhart quotes this and then adds in **Sermon 37**, *"Love your neighbor as you love yourself, not as you hate yourself."* He continues: *"He who knows how to love himself loves God"* because the soul essentially is a part of God. This means that one must love every other person because all souls have the same source. Then Eckhart goes to the heart of the matter when he quotes **John 13:34**: *"A new commandment I give to you, that you love one another as I have loved you."* Eckhart says that the words *"as I have loved you"* tell us that we should love God and others with the same purity and intensity with which God loves us. If we can do this, we will not have to worry about transgressing either divine or human laws.

Saint Augustine is reputed to have said that there are three ways to heaven: humility, humility and humility. Eckhart is even more explicit in **Sermon 11** when he says: *"The humble need not beg God so much as bid Him, for the heights of divinity can disregard everything else but the depths of humility, for the humble person and God are one and not two. If a humble person were in hell, God would be impelled to join that person there and hell itself would be for such a person like heaven."* In **Sermon 15**, when commenting upon Jesus' statement in **Matthew 5:3** that *"blessed are the poor in spirit,"* Eckhart defines this level of humility. He says: *"He is a poor person who wills nothing, knows nothing, and has nothing. So long as one has a personal wish to fulfill, even God's will, or has a desire for eternity or God, to this extent he is not properly poor."* Few writers or speakers have ever been this profound.

Closed minds are doors that block the pathway to God. We must open all locked doors by pure living, thinking only loving thoughts and by meditating so deeply that we forget ourselves. The soul has scattered itself throughout the mind, emotional nature and bodily organs and is focused outward. In **Sermon 18**, Eckhart expresses this clearly: *"The soul has scattered itself through its powers outside itself, each power through its own activity: the power of seeing into the eyes, the power of hearing into the ears, the power of taste into the tongue. As a result, the soul's inner powers for effective deeds are all the weaker, for every divided power is incomplete. If the soul wishes to be effective inside itself, it must recall all its powers and gather them together to an internal activity."* This reuniting of powers is done through real meditation where the mind is stilled and the attention focused at one inner point. As Eckhart says in **Sermon 21**, *"If God is to speak His Word within the Soul, it must be in peace and at rest."* Of course it is diffi-cult in the beginning to separate oneself from the mind and outer things. But when we make a feeble effort to take a step in God's direction, the Divine One will take a thousand steps to give us aid.

Saintly spiritual teachers cannot relegate techniques of meditation to print because personal guidance is essential. Since spiritual practices lead the student through vast dimensions, planes and subplanes, populated by imperfect and vain entities, well-meaning or deceitful guides almost certainly will attempt to mislead the novice practitioner. That is why it is imperative that a genuine seeker find a perfect saint who can direct the soul in all astral, causal and spiritual planes. In **Sermon 1**, Eckhart apparently hints at part of his meditation procedure when he says: *"We can find no name that we dare to give God. Nevertheless, we are allowed those names which the saints have named Him, and which God has dedicated in their hearts and permeated with Divine Light."* This strongly suggests that Eckhart gave his students a series of charged names that relate to Divine manifestations on the several levels of being. Modern saints employ this procedure, and saints of the highest order do exist in each age. In Sermon 2, Eckhart probably startled his audience when he said: *"People think that God only became a human being in the historical incarnation of Jesus, but that is not so; for God is here in this very place just as much incarnate as in a human long ago. And this is why He has become a human being: that He might give birth to you as His Only Begotten Son, and no less."* Those who believe in the efficacy of only one perfected personage and insist that this Saint or Son of God is a savior for all times are seriously mistaken. God is as concerned for people living today as He was for individuals living a thousand or more years ago. And when it comes to traveling the lengthy and difficult way back to the Source of All, seekers need levels of guidance that cannot be obtained from scriptures, even those written by a Saint.

St. John of the Cross

St. John of the Cross (1542-1591)

Love lends grace, beauty and freshness to the white garment of faith…for without love no virtue is pleasing in the sight of God.

The more memory relies on the mind, the further it departs from God, because God is above our thoughts.

John of the Cross

Another mystic who obviously had great inner awareness was St. John of the Cross. Juan de Yepes was born near Avila, Spain in 1542. Deeply spiritual at a time when most priests led superficial and often sensual lives, John was incarcerated by local church authorities for being excessively devout. He was locked in a ten-foot by six-foot cell with no window. The only light entered via a small hole in the wall from an adjacent corridor. For nine months he was fed bread and water once a day, occasionally beaten, and was not allowed to change his clothing. While in this prison cell, he wrote some of his most admired spiritual works (**Peers 1950:189**). John's unfeigned devotion provided a great contrast between his piety and the worldliness of the Catholic Church of his day. After escaping from Toledo prison on August 15, 1578 when a guard forgot to lock the door, John joined the order of Calced Carmelites. However, he found that the residents of this convent lacked true devotion, simplicity of life and serious sincerity, so he left it intending to unite with the Carthusians. When St. Teresa told him that the Carmelite friars were about to be reformed, John changed his mind and became the first discalced or barefoot friar of this order. The inspiring film *John of the Cross*, available from Ignatius Press (1 800 651 1531) beautifully depicts the saintly John and Teresa of Avila as they try to reform a corrupt church. Leonardo Defilippis portrays the great Spanish saint and poet and his wife Patti plays the spiritual Teresa in this highly recommended film. St. John of the Cross wrote such inspired works as *Dark Night of the Soul, The Spiritual Canticle and The Living Flame of Love.* These works do not attempt to describe the indescribable, but they do explain that the way back to God is through right living and spiritual meditation. The teachings of John of the Cross are now divided into several categories for convenience although they are often amalgamated in his writings.

St. John of the Cross looked upon literally *"Nothingness, Nothingness, Nothingness"*. Interestingly, in India the word Nada is often defined as an ocean of fire or love. He enunciated the famous doctrine of *"Nada, Nada, Nada"*. *"Nad"* or *"Nada"* refers to the Divine Word or Shabd. While John did not speak as much about God as did Eckhart, he shared Eckhart's view that the Word was a Divine Expression of God and not a printed book. In **Maxim 284 (St. John of the Cross 1912:234)**, he was most explicit: *"The Father uttered one Word; that Word is His Son; and He utters Him forever in everlasting silence. In silence the soul has to hear it."* In *The Dark Night of the Soul*, he said: *"The gentle touch of the Word, the Son of God, does penetrate the very substance of my soul and absorbs it wholly in a divine sweetness not 'heard in the land of Canaan' nor 'seen in Teman.'"* The word *"Teman"* is found in **Habakkuk 3:3**, a verse that says, *"God came from Teman,* *and the Holy One from mount Paran."* While Habakkuk does not stipulate where these locations may be found, the prophet does say that Teman is a place where God's glory covers the heavens. In this same work, John is very clear when he says: *"If we would listen to the Voice of God with due reverence, the soul must stand upright and not lean on the affections of sense for support. I cast off desires and cease from reflections of sense that I may behold and understand what God will speak to me. Out of this night springs first the knowledge of one's self and on that is built up the knowledge of God."* In his poem *"Song of the Soul and its Bridegroom"* **(St. John of the Cross 1912:257)**, John says:

My beloved fills the silent tranquil night before the morn;
Ere the ruddy dawn approaches and another day is born.
He is Music that is Soundless; in the wilderness a Voice,
And the supper that refresheth, making hearts that love rejoice.

Those who try to unite with the Word will encounter both worldly and satanic opposition. St. John says (St. John of the Cross 1912:102-103): *"Satan stations himself with great cunning on the frontiers between sense and spirit; there he deludes the soul, feeds the senses, and prevents the soul from escaping out of his hands. These devices most easily deceive the soul, for it knows of nothing better. It looks upon the sense worlds and outer things as a great gain and accepts the suggestions of the evil one gladly thinking he is God."* In another passage John says that Satan hates to see the soul commune with the Holy Ghost or Word because this enables it to fly beyond his reach and become adorned with the permanent wealth of God. He would prefer for it to focus its attention upon the riches of the world and transitory sensual sweetness. Satan, or the Negative Power, utilizes our minds to lead us astray, and St. John advises us to keep our attention continually upon God. **St. John of the**

Cross (1909:184) tells us that *"Satan is in great fear of that soul who has attained to perfection."*

Christ and all saints of higher order have stressed that God is Love in the ultimate sense and that love for God and for all life arises with true awakening. In his maxim, Prayer of the Enamored Soul **(St. John of the Cross 1912:249)**, he says, *"O Lord, my God, whoever seeks you with pure and single love will find you greatly; for you make the advance and go about to meet those who love you."* Then he adds, *"He that is on fire with love divinely touched of God receives a taste so new that all his own are gone."* Such love consumes the lower nature and merges the pure soul into God. Love yields discernible results in the attitude and actions of the lover. In the words of **St. John of the Cross (1909:301)**, *"Love is like a fine robe of many colors, which lends grace, beauty, and freshness to the white garment of faith, the vesture of hope, and to all the virtues; for without love no virtue is pleasing in the sight of God."* He relates love and the Word in the following way: *"The Holy Ghost envelops the soul in a flame of Love. O how the soul marvels at the visions it has. Who can describe them? The soul is profoundly immersed in the waters of divine splendors where the Everlasting Father is pouring forth the irrigating streams with a bounteous hand. These streams penetrate soul and body."*

Love involves a selfless giving to all people in the world. In the words of **St. John of the Cross (1912:134)**, *"Preserve an equal love for all, whether relatives or not. Do not love one person more than another, for if you do you will fall into error. It is true that He whom God loves is most worthy of love; but you do not know who he is."* So, to escape from error, love all equally.

Real love results in enlightened conduct wherein the lover never sees or advertises the weaknesses of others. **St. John of the Cross (1912:206)** advised: *"Never listen to accounts of the frailties of others; and if anyone should complain to you of another, humbly ask this person not to speak except in compassion. Suspect no evil in your brother, for that takes away purity of heart."* And then he adds **(1912:202)**: *"Purity of heart is nothing less than the love and grace of God. Hence our Lord says: 'blessed are the pure in heart,' that is those who love; for blessedness is given to nothing less than love. Wisdom enters by love, silence, and humility; so the soul who is in love with God is a gentle, meek, humble and patient soul."*

A difficult concept for many to entertain is the fact that all imperfect things or people must die, for God will sentence no soul to everlasting imperfection. Some people say they love someone as they are and try to perpetuate their concept of that individual, but this is possessive infatuation speaking and not love. God wants all souls to gain perfection and sets this divine state as the goal. *"Be you perfect as the Father in Heaven is perfect"* **(Matthew 5:48)**. The real lover of others sees the pure state of perfection in each soul and feeds that divine state with love.

When the fruit of humility grows abundantly upon the tree of life, the laden branches hang close to the soil of divinity. In his ***Jiwat Mritak***, the Medieval Saint Dadu said, *"When a person has abandoned false pride, arrogance, and vain glory, when he has become humble and meek, then does he find true bliss."* St. John of the Cross, speaking from a similar level of development, said (in ***The Dark Night of the Soul***): *"Amid the aridities and emptiness of this night of the desires, the soul acquires spiritual humility, which is the opposite virtue of the first capital sin, spiritual pride or ego. The humility acquired by self-knowledge purifies* *the soul from all imperfections. Now it does not think for a moment it is better than others, or that it has outstripped them on the spiritual road as it did before. On the contrary, it acknowledges that all others are better. Out of this grows love of our neighbor."* Then he adds, *"Strive with all of your heart after humility in thought, word, and deed, taking more pleasure in others than in yourself. Always be more ready to receive instructions than to give them, even from the least knowledgeable of your brethren."* St. John of the Cross further urged, *"Practice virtues. Do all for God's sake without regard for the pleasure, displeasure, or reward a work yields. The servant should always strive for others to be preferred to him in everything that is pleasant, putting himself in the lowest place and that with all his heart. As God tells us in the Gospel: 'He that humbles himself shall be exalted'* **(Luke 14:11)." St. John of the Cross (1912:318)** in Maxim 318 reiterates in these words: *"The communications that come from God have this property, that they humble and exalt the soul at the same time."*

Most of us place more emphasis upon physical labor than upon meditation because it is easier to perform hard work in the objective world than to meditate correctly with a silent mind. Stilling and subduing the mind is the most difficult task anyone will ever undertake in life. St. John of the Cross says (in ***The Dark Night of the Soul***): *"Some insist upon continuous physical labor, and thus God finds no opportunity for doing His work. How precious in His sight is a calm annihilation of the senses."* He is not saying that one should neglect important physical labor in earning an honest living, but he is asserting that one should live a balanced life where meditation is given proper priority. He emphasizes the proper attitude in these words: *"At no time or season, when once the soul has begun to enter into this pure and restful state of contemplation, must it seek to gather to itself (thoughts), neither must* *it desire to find help in spiritual sweetness or delight, but it must stand in complete detachment above all this and the spirit (should) be freed from it."* **(Peers: 1950:189)**.

To many people in the Western world, *"meditation"* is a synonym for thinking deeply about something. But St. John of the Cross, in his ***Dark Night of the Soul***, emphasized the fact that spiritual meditation only takes place when all thinking is stilled. He said, *"To contemplate is to receive, and it is impossible to receive the highest wisdom otherwise than in a silent spirit detached from all thoughts."* He went on to say, *"Neither are we to be distressed when the memory is emptied of all forms and thoughts; for, as God is formless, the memory is safe when empty and draws nearer to God. The more memory relies on the mind, the further it departs from God, because God is above our thoughts."* **St. John of the Cross (1912:221)** then adds, *"Let the soul be quiet and at rest. Although one may think that he is doing nothing and losing time, he will do enough if he keeps patience and perseveres in meditation, keeping the soul free from all thoughts and knowledge. One should simply direct his attention lovingly and calmly toward God, without anxiety or effort or even a desire to feel or taste His presence."*

Genuine meditation is progressive in nature, and success comes surely to the pure in heart. St. John of the Cross says (in ***Dark Night of the Soul***), *"Finally, as the soul is purified from all sensual affections and desires, it attains to liberty of spirit, wherein the twelve fruits of the Holy Ghost are had. So sally forth from this mortal life and reach the center of the spirit, the perfect life in Christ. The visions of the glory of God to which the soul is now admitted are more continuous than they used to be, more perfect and stable. But in the life to come they will be most perfect, unchanging and uninterrupted. There too the soul will see clearly how God moves not at all."* Echoes of Eckhart seem apparent in this statement: *"Inner tranquility and self forgetfulness are ever attended with a certain interior absorption. Therefore under no circumstances whatever, either of time or place, is it lawful for the soul, now that it has begun to enter the state of contemplation, to recur to its previous meditation or cleave to past spiritual sweetness. It must detach itself from all spiritual sweetness and rise above it in the freedom of the spirit."* Meditation, according to St. John of the Cross, elevates the attention above the physical body and all creation, above natural actions and thoughts, and allows the attention to enter into an awareness of the Unchanging Divinity.

Spiritual laziness is one of the worst enemies of a person who desires to approach God. **St. John of the Cross (1912:47-48)** drives home this point in these words: *"Why do so few attain the Divine State? The reason is because so many are weak and shrink from trouble, and are unwilling to undergo the least discomfort or to labor with constant patience. If you get out of breath when running with footmen, how can you contend with horses? If the ordinary trials of life are too great a burden for you, how can you venture out of common trials into a life of greater difficulty? If you are unwilling to make war against your own desire for worldly peace, comfort, pleasures, and your own sensuality, how will you stand against the rushing waters of tribulation in the more intense interior trials of the spirit? Oh souls that seek only ease and comfort, if you knew how necessary this suffering and hard work are for attaining great blessings, you would take up the cross with vinegar and gall and never seek for comfort anywhere."*

Those who wish to understand their true natures and return to the Divine Presence must be permeated by love, work steadfastly at meditation, and overcome all lower desires. In **Maxim 155 (1912:211)**, St. John of the Cross states that if people knew how many blessings they are losing because they do not raise their desires above trifles, they would be amazed. He, like all other divinely inspired teachers, advises us to ask God for God and nothing else.

Jacob Boehme (1575-1624)

Jacob Boehme (1575-1624)

The virtue of Love is nothing and all: its power is through all things; its height is as high as God.

God must become man; man must become God.

Jacob Boehme

Jacob Boehme was born in Old Seidenburg, a small market town in upper Lusatia, in 1575. Since his father was a farmer, Jacob first served as a shepherd. Later he became a shoemaker's apprentice and learned the cobbling trade, a vocation he practiced until shortly before his death.

Reared as a Lutheran, Jacob was simple, sincere and very devout. William Law, himself a noted Western mystic in later life, described what apparently was an initiatory experience for Jacob while he was still a cobbler's apprentice. Law said that a poorly dressed but grave and reverend man entered the shop while the master shoemaker was out. After buying a pair of shoes, he called Jacob by name and had the boy follow him to a secluded place where he told him that he was to become a great man at whom the world should wonder. He added: *"Therefore be pious, fear God and reverence His Word. Read diligently the Holy Scriptures wherein you have comfort and instruction. For thou must endure much misery and poverty and suffer persecution. But be courageous and persevere for God loves and is gracious to thee."* Then the stranger pressed his hand, gazed upon Jacob, and departed **(Law 1938)**. Apparently he transferred power through his eyes to Jacob. Boehme had a second illumination in 1600, and later a third and even more enlightening one, although these were not described in detail.

Jacob's first mystical work, ***Aurora*** **(1612)**, aroused opposition from the local Lutheran pastor, so the municipal authorities forbade Boehme to write additional works. The pastor denounced Jacob's views that the universe was a manifestation of God, and that evil was a reflection of God's power (untempered by divine love). Between 1618 and 1623, Jacob wrote a series of devotional works called ***The Way of Christ***. Since Lutheran authorities still opposed him, Boehme left Gorlitz and moved to Dresden. Later he went to Silesia. He died in 1624 and most of his works were published posthumously.

As a man of inner realization, Boehme claimed that his writings told only what he learned in person from divine revelations. This assertion is supported by the fact that the sincere writings of Boehme do not closely resemble the wordings of such earlier mystics as Eckhart or the anonymous author of ***The Cloud of Unknowing*** although certain ideas are similar. Like William Blake, the nineteenth-century artist and mystical poet of England, Boehme deliberately obscured many of his ideas in symbolic and alchemical imagery. This was done to prevent accusations of heresy, a "*crime*" that was punishable by death in those days. However, some passages are very clear and require no deciphering to be understood. These are the ones that will be quoted in this study.

Jacob Boehme had a profound influence on such German Romantics as Schelling and Hegel; and his writings strongly impressed George Fox (founder of the Quakers), the Cambridge Platonists, and the well-known mystical writer William Law.

Boehme does not dwell as extensively on the Absolute concept of God as did Eckhart, but there are clear references to this State in his works. In the following passage from page 14 of ***The Signature of All Things***, he refers to an Absolute State as The Nothing: *"We understand that without (or beyond) nature there is an eternal stillness and rest, viz. The Nothing; and then we understand that an eternal will arises in The Nothing to introduce The Nothing into something that the will might find, feel, and behold itself. For in The Nothing the will would not be manifest to itself. The will must be in the darkness in its contrariety, and it conceives in itself another will to go out from the darkness again into the Liberty or The Nothing. Therefore the will must enter inwards, and yet there is no separation."* On page 58 of this same work, Boehme adds, *"For whatever hungers after the Eternal Nothing (will find) the quiet, meek liberty of God."*

While these statements suggest the much misunderstood Buddhist concept of the Nothing or Great Void of Parbrahm, the Nothing here apparently refers to the state of God Absolute. Instead of the Western interpretation of total annihilation or non-existence, the word *Nothing* is clearer if divided into the words *"no thing."* To Boehme *"thing"* includes mental thoughts as well as Astral and physical objects.

In his ***Confessions*** Boehme states that a deep melancholy and heavy sadness fell over him when he saw the great deep of the world with love and anger mixed in all life from stones to stars, beasts to men. The wicked seemed to do as well as the pious. In this affliction he raised his spirit to God with whole heart and mind and *"broke through"* the gates of hell into the *"innermost moving of the deity, and there I was embraced in love as a bridegroom embraces his dearly beloved bride."* It was like a resurrection from the dead. *"My spirit suddenly saw through all and knew that God was in creatures, herbs, and grass. It knew His nature and His will. But because I could not comprehend the movings of God in my reason, almost twelve years passed before the exact understanding was given me. The spirit comprehends it well but the animal man attains only a glimpse thereof* (by the Holy Ghost). *The true heaven is everywhere, even in the very place where you stand. So when the spirit passes through the fleshly and astral and apprehends the innermost moving of God, then it is clearly in heaven."*

Here Boehme makes it clear that in the purely spiritual realm he comprehended the working of God in all dimensions, but he did not understand it mentally for twelve years because he had to purify the mind and allow the spirit to dominate his consciousness. Boehme realized that God was at the core or inner essence of all life and that even stones were alive in the sense that they too were crystallized energy.

Also in his ***Confessions***, Boehme says that in the astral (or emotional zone) love and wrath strive with one another, but that the Holy Ghost or Word is also there. The upper Astral is where one first contacts the uplifting resonance of the Word that enables the attention to enter the Causal subplanes. Above the Causal, the third clear and holy heaven unites one with the heart of God, which is distinct from and above all heavens. Apparently Boehme considered the upper Astral as the first heaven, the Causal

Plane the second, and Parbrahm (Empty realm of Buddhists) the third. But, he notes, God is above all of these everywhere in His innermost working. In ***The Way to Christ*** Boehme says that time is in eternity and eternity is in time. In other words, the outer human is in time, but the inner soul or attention is in eternity. When the two unite, this is true self-realization. The next step is union with the divine source of all.

When one reads the works of Boehme, it is clear that he refers to the Word as a divine creative expression of the Absolute God and is not in reference to a scriptural text. This passage from page 29 of ***The Signature of All Things*** is quite specific: *"Understand it right; all things proceed from the Word or heart of God in the birth of the Holy Trinity and manifest themselves in and through God's wisdom. And they again do eagerly force and press out of the egress, in and towards His heart and power, and vehemently long after it; all creatures groan and pant to be delivered from ego."*

In ***Mysterium Magnum*** **(Law, Vol. III, pp. 34-35)** Boehme stresses the role of the Word in this way: *"For whatsoever has life, liveth in the speaking Word; the angels in the Eternal Speaking and the temporal spirits in the… echoing forth of the formings of time out of the sound or breath of time, and the angels out of the Sound of Eternity… or the voice of the manifested Word of God. And therefore they bear the names of the several degrees in the manifested voice of God. And one degree is more holy in the power than another."*

Much emphasis was placed upon the auditory pleasantness of the Divine Word. On page 22 of the same text, Boehme said, *"In the light of God which is called the kingdom of heaven, the sound is wholly soft, pleasant, lovely, pure, and thin. It is a stillness in comparison to the outer gross shrillness in pronouncing, speaking, sounding, singing, and chanting as if the mind did play and melodize in a kingdom of joy within itself, and did hear in a most entire inward manner such a sweet and pleasing melody."*

In another comparison with objective sounds, Boehme, in ***The Aurora***, says this of the Word: *"If you should in this world bring many thousand sorts of musical instruments together, and all should be tuned in the best manner… and the most skillful masters of music should play on them in concert together, all would be no more than the howlings and barkings of dogs in comparison to the Divine Music… which rises from eternity to eternity."* **(Law, Vol. I, p. 43)**.

In ***The Signature of All Things*** Boehme calls the Word the signature with which God signs the document of life. He speaks simply, eloquently and symbolically in these words on page 9: *"All that is spoken or written of God without knowledge of the Signature is dumb and void of understanding. But if the spirit opens to one the Signature, then he understands how the spirit has manifested and revealed itself (out of the Essence through the principle) in the Sound with the Voice. For though I see one speak, teach, preach, and write of God, and though I hear and read the same, yet this is not sufficient for me to understand Him. But if his sound and spirit out of his signature and similitude enter into my own similitude and imprint his similitude into mine, then I may understand him…if he has the hammer that can strike my bell."*

The relationship between the Word and the five levels of manifestation seem to be expressed clearly in the following passage. Although there are five manifestations of deity in the five planes, Boehme assures us that only one Power is involved. He says in ***Mysterium Mag-***

***num* (Law, Vol. III, pp. 193-4)** that *"these five names figure out and set forth as in a type the five head speeches of the spiritual tongue through the formed Word, proceeding from the High Name of God…For the spirit does also under the names point at the kingdoms and dominions, and they are God's, who with His Name does order, govern, guide and lead every kingdom according the property of His Name…Not that there is more than one God (but) God gives Himself forth in His manifestation in or via the formed Word."*

Boehme taught that the Word was responsible for manifestation of the heavens, Causal and Astral, and the earth. He explained the creation this way: *"In the beginning the world was created out of inward properties. The devil has only the wrath's part in possession* (that is, will predominates; love is not dominant). *After the creation of the highest spirits, God created this visible world* (universe) *with the stars and elements as an external birth out of the mother of all essences—all of which proceeded out of the external beginning into time. Afterwards God formed the earth."* **(Law, Vol. 3, p. 29)**. Clearly Boehme had an awareness of the fragmentation of basic spiritual values into separate qualities since he recognized that ego-saturated Satan is dominated by power or will and not by love.

It was obviously difficult for Boehme to explain how crystallized energy was organized into physical forms because the science of physics had not evolved. Even with our present knowledge of how energy can congeal and be transmuted, scientists are still grouping in the darkness of uncertainty in their search for a correct understanding of how the universe came into its present state. Boehme makes it clear that God exists above time, space and all mundane elements. The *"highest spirits"* may refer to denizens of the Causal and Astral states, both of which were established before the objective universe came into existence.

All mystic or spiritual teachers have stressed the concept that each human entity is a microcosmic expression of a greater macrocosm. In other words, the spiritual counterpart of each soul is essentially a drop from the ocean of God. In fact each human being has within him or her vestures that correspond to the several planes of life and a spiritual essence that is a part of God. Boehme **(Law, Vol. 3, p. 10)** tells us that: *"Man has indeed all of the forms of the three worlds lying within him; for he is a complete image of God or the Being of all Beings. . . Everything as it is inwardly, so it is outwardly signed."* "The "three worlds" mentioned above refers to the Physical, Astral and Causal dimensions in all spiritual literature. This suggests the widely held belief that each objective manifestation has causal and astral counterparts that serve to connect the spirit or higher attention with each physical expression. Boehme (Law, Vol. 3, p. 44) clearly states it in these words: *"Man was created good and perfect . . . and above the three worlds, as an image of Deity, in whom God dwells."*

Boehme frequently refers to the mechanics of human physical evolution and return to God. His concept of this process was clearly and simply stated: *"God must become man; man must become God."* **(Law, Vol. 3, p. 121)**. On page 60 he is even more specific: *"The self will makes a form according to its innate nature. However, the eternal model, as it was known in the glass of God's wisdom before the times of this world, influences the evolution of the form. But no selfish form with its own ego can inherit the only Eternal Being; for where there are two wills, there is enmity."* The late Saint Kirpal Singh often echoed this concept when he stated that each person must become *"a conscious coworker with the Divine Plan."* The potential to do this is latent in each individual and is not the destiny of one or a few great souls. Boehme said: *"Whatever Jesus has done through the Christ, viz., through his and my humanity, the same he does yet today in me and in all my fellow members . . . Thus now I live in God and my self-hood does not know it."* **(Law, Vol. IV, *Signatura Rerum*, p.99).** Remember that Jesus said **(John 14:12)**: *"The works that I do shall you do also, and greater things than these shall you do because I go unto the Father."* Oneness was certainly implied when Jesus said: *"At that day you shall know that I am in my Father, and ye in me, and I in you."* **(John 14:20)**. The divine potential is latent in each individual, but most people are lazy; they want someone else to do the basic work for them and liberate them without effort on their parts. It does not work this way. Certainly it is easy to simply believe something and say you have faith, but to practice a disciplined meditation and style of living requires sustained effort, but it can be done.

Generally the human response to living in this physical world has been one of two extremes. Either the person has looked upon the material world as the only reality and has tried to gather as much mundane property as possible, or the individual has considered the world to be an illusion and has retired to some remote desert, cave or jungle to seek a spiritual goal. Boehme, as have all masters of a higher order, advocated a balanced development because they knew that physical seclusion with an active mind was no more conducive to spirituality than was living in a typical social order with an active mentality. Boehme **(Law, Vol. 3, p. 246)** said: *"Indeed it is a treasure to be possessed by the light of God and nature, operating in higher spheres; and to have both the eyes of time and eternity at once open together, and yet not to interfere with each other is the goal."* The Teutonic master realized that we were in the world for a reason, and he advocated that we master both the mundane and the spiritual. In other words we should place as much or more emphasis upon the inner spiritual growth as we do on material achievements.

Those who assert that there is only one master are in a sense correct. Each higher teacher has emphasized that the Divine Word (also called Logos, Shabd, Naad, Kalma, Saut-I-Sarmadi, etc.) is the true master and that the teacher on the physical plane simply expresses what this Divine Word stresses through him or her. He or she acts as a mouthpiece or channel for the Word. The objective master assumes the human form and physical limitations in order to teach those human beings that are ready to accept higher truth. In Volume 4 of ***Signatura Rerum*** **(Law, p. 60)** Boehme says: *"Now we will come to the process of Christ, and go with him out of eternity into time, and then out of time into eternity. Christ came into this world in the shut-up human form; he came into the world as a pilgrim in our poor form. He became ours that he might tincture us in himself. Did he behave like a Lord? No; he entered into death, and died, and quickened our essence with the divine, that our essence may enter again with its will into the Divine Essence."*

The roles of the Word and master are succinctly stated in these words from the *Signatura Rerum* **(Law, Vol. 4, p. 9)**: *"The signature or the (physical) form is not (absolute) spirit, but the receptacle or cabinet of the spirit; for the signature stands in the essence as a lute that lieth still and dumb until played upon. Then its form and tune is understood. In the human mind the signature lies most artificially composed, according to the essence of all essences; and man wants nothing but the wise master that can strike his instrument, which is the true spirit of eternity. If that be quickened in man, that it stirs and acts in the center of the mind, then it plays on the instrument of the human form with the* *sound of the Word. The inward manifests itself in the sound of the Word."* In the *Mysterium Magnum* **(Law, Vol. 3, p. 235)** Boehme stresses: *"So God has sent his officer, viz. His Holy Word, by His servant in the world to the true man, and He causes His servants to sit down by the fountain of his Holy Word with command that they should in their office and charge committed to them call upon God and pray and teach His Word till God draws the virgin's heart and brings her to the fountain of His Word."*

Boehme approaches the eloquence and depth of Eckhart when he discusses love. In *Mysterium Magnum* **(Law, Vol. 3, p. 240)** he uses these words: *"The virtue of love is Nothing and All; its power is through all things; its height is as high as God. Its virtue is the principle of all principles; its power supports the heavens and upholds the earth. Its height is higher than the highest heavens; and its greatness is even greater than the very manifestation of the Godhead in the glorious light of the Divine Essence, as being infinitely capable of greater and greater manifestations in all eternity. What more can I say? Love is higher than the highest . . . yea, it is in a certain sense greater than God: while in the highest sense of all God is Love and Love is God. Love being the highest principle is the virtue by which all virtues flow. Love is the power of all powers from which the wonders of God have been wrought by the hands of His elect servants in their generations successively. Whoever finds it finds nothing and all things . . . It infinitely transcends all that human sense and reason can reach . . . For love enters into that where the Godhead is not manifested in the glorious light."*

The Lutheran mystic often praised *"the sweet love of the Lord Christ"* because Jesus practiced in the world the love he realized with the Father. The implication is that we also must radiate a similar love toward all forms of life before we can merge into the Great Love of God. Boehme said: *"For man's salvation consists in this, that he has in him a true desire for God, and out of that desire springs forth the love that overcomes anger and death. Then that desire receives the meekness of God into itself and immerses itself in the meekness and becomes essential. And therein the soul's spirit (which lay shut up in anger and death) does again arise in the love of God"* **(Boehme 1969: 30)**.

William Blake, himself a noted mystic as well as a great author and artist, once said that without contraries there is no progression. In other words, we must experience a lesser condition in order to realize the value of a greater one. There must be contrast between states of consciousness if we are to appreciate the noblest conditions. **Boehme (1969:234)** puts it this way: *"If love dwelt not in trouble, it could have nothing to love. But the poor soul, being in trouble and pain, . it delivers . . . so itself by it may be loved again. No one would know what love is if there were no hatred; or what friendship is if there were no foe."*

Most religious teachers today are saturated with egotism. Boehme looked upon a similar condition in his day and thundered: *"Ye rabbis and masters! That you could understand...you have been a long time blind, the cause of which is your pride."* **(1969:24)**. He then added **(Boehme 1969: 230)**.: *"The way is childlike. 'Except ye become as little children, ye shall not enter into the kingdom of heaven.' There is no shorter way than this; neither can a better way be found...If thou wilt be like God, thou must forsake all things or turn your desire away from them all, and not desire or hanker after any of them. For as soon as thou takest something into thy desire, and receive it as thy own, then this very something is the same with thyself; and this worketh with thee in thy will, and thou are bound to take care of it. But if thou* *dost receive nothing into thy desire, then thou are free from all things, and rulest over them as a prince of God."*

The above quotation clearly relates ego with a desire for things and for dominion over others, for the ego likes to assert itself and dominate others. Even great angelic beings fell from glory after the initial sin of pride placed karmic weights upon their shoulders. As Boehme states **(1969:58)**: *"Both Lucifer and Adam lost the oil of divine meekness. They and man were corrupted by imagination and pride. Man must learn to hunger after the eternal Nothing, the quiet meek liberty of God."*

The fact cannot be overstressed that controlling the mind is the most difficult task a person will ever face. In his ***Dialogue between a Scholar and His Master Concerning the Supersensual Life*** **(Boehme 1969: 245)**, the scholar or disciple complains: *"There is still a partition wall in me which beats back the heavenly sounds in their passage, and obstructs the passage of that light." The master then says: "This is the creaturely will* (ego) *in thee which can be broken by nothing but the grace of self denial...and conformity with the Divine Will."*

It must be emphasized that overcoming the ego relates more to realization than it does to annihilation of this mental trait. The soul realizes its true nature, a harmonic oneness with God, and ceases making excursions into the surrealistic labyrinth of vanity. **Boehme (1969:156)** explains in these words: *"Thus now I live in God, and my selfhood does not know it for it lives not in God but in self. God is indeed in it but self does not apprehend Him...Now if anything be freed from this selfhood, viz., from the wrathful death, and again be brought into the universal highest perfection, then it must die to its selfhood and enter into the stillness."*

Meditation was a very important teaching of Boehme. The aphorism "as one thinks, so he or she becomes," was clearly stressed. By keeping the attention on the objective world, the average person identifies with material things, mundane goals, and with political or secular realities. Jacob Boehme described the two directions through which the attention could flow. The inner eye looked into eternity, while the outer eye gazed outward into time. He said **(1969:249)**: *"Be on thy watch... give not thy mind leave to enter into that which is without thee; neither look thou backward upon thyself...let not the outer eye deceive thee, but bring the eye of time into the eye of eternity."* Elsewhere **(1969: 254)** he adds: *"Delay not to enter in by this gate, which if thou seest in the spirit, as some highly favored souls have seen it, thou seest in the supersensual ground all that God is."*

This gateway that Boehme mentions is that of meditation or concentration of the attention inwardly, as the following selection **(1969:247-248)** stresses: *"Seek the fountain of light, waiting in the deep ground of thy soul for the rising there of the sun of righteousness. Cease from thy own activity, steadfastly fixing thine eye upon one point, and with a strong purpose relying upon the promised grace of God in Christ, to bring thee out of thy darkness into His marvelous light. For this end gather in all thy thoughts, and by faith press into the center, laying hold upon the Word of God, which is infallible. Be silent before the Lord, sitting with Him alone in thy inmost hidden cell.* (Then) *shall light break forth as the morning; and after the redness thereof has passed, the sun shall rise unto thee."* Then he adds: *"it will be necessary, my child, in the first place to wait and attend the true east, which is the center of paradise; and in great might breaking forth out of the darkness within thee,* (go) *through a pillar of fire and thunder clouds."*

Interestingly, William Blake, a mystic and artist who will be considered later, stated that in the higher worlds the direction "*east*" was within. Boehme seems to imply the same thing. Of course the symbolism of the fire and thunder can be found in many mystical and religious texts. We can conclude this brief study with the assertion that Jacob Boehme was a teacher of high order who appeared in the Protestant Christian tradition and stressed the age-old truth of spirituality. He is more difficult than some mystical writers to understand because conditions of his time forced him to write in obscure alchemical terms that would not be considered heretical. In the Seventeenth Century heresy was a crime still punishable by death.

William Law

William Law (1688-1761)

Poor sinner! Consider the treasure thou hast within thee. The Eternal Word of God lies hid in thee as a spark of the divine flame

Where all of God is known and felt, there is a fire of love, a pure disinterested love that begins and ends in God.

William Law

William Law was born at King's Cliffe, Northamptonshire, England in 1688 and was educated at Emmanuel College, University of Cambridge. In 1711 he was ordained in the Church of England and elected a fellow. Law refused to swear allegiance to George I and was dismissed from Cambridge. He then became a private tutor until 1740 when he retired at King's Cliffe.

In 1728 he wrote his most popular book, ***A Serious Call to a Devout and Holy Life***. The beautiful style, simple language and profound thought of this book influenced Dr. Samuel Johnson during his student days at Oxford. He said **(Day 1963:141)**: *"I took up Law's Serious Call to a Holy Life expecting to find it a dull book* (as such books generally are). . . *But I found Law quite an overmatch for me; and this was the first occasion of my thinking in earnest of religion."* John and Charles Wesley frequently visited Law before 1740, but broke with him after this when his writings became very mystical. These later mystical works had some influence upon William Blake.

Law stated that his first reading of Boehme put him into *"a perfect sweat"* as it gripped his attention **(Day 1963:141)**. It is difficult to state what parts of Law's concepts were derived from Boehme and what parts were based upon his own inner experiences. However, it seems quite apparent that Law had gained much spiritual illumination. Law praised Boehme strongly and frequently in **"The Way to Divine Knowledge."** However, Law did not resort to alchemical language as did Boehme, but instead expressed his ideas in a mystical or spiritual Christian context. Like Boehme, Law stressed the basic unity of all existence and asserted that what men consider to be good or evil are but expressions of God's love and power separated from the primal oneness. The Blakean concept that without contraries there is no progression is certainly present in the writings of Law. He asserted that the *"Fall of Man"* was the first assertion of human selfhood and separation from the great unity. As Law put it in ***The Spirit of Prayer,*** page 98: *"the loss of (Divine) love was the fall of man, as it opened in him a kingdom of the self in which Satan, the world and flesh (senses) could all bring forth their works. If man is to rise from his fall and return to his life in God, there is an absolute necessity that self, with all its brood of gross affections be deposed."* The objective of life is to gain experience in lower worlds, develop reason and then overcome or rise above it, reunite the separated powers, and return to the state of oneness. ***The Spirit of Prayer*** **(1749)** and ***The Spirit of Love*** **(1752)** are examples of Law's mystical writings. Much repetition of concept can be found in Law's writings.

The essential role of the Word (*Logos, Nada, Naam,* etc.) is not stressed as strongly and as frequently in the writings of Law as it was in Eckhart or even Boehme. But it is acknowledged as the creative power mentioned in the first chapter of John in the Bible. In ***The Spirit of Prayer*** **(Law 1938:79)** he says: *"But if thou wouldst know how the birth of Christ is to be effected in thee…*(know) *that this great work is already begun in every one of us. The savior and new life of the soul that is to raise thee out of the darkness of death into the light of life and give thee power to become a son of God is already within thee…calling, knocking at the door of thy heart. For the Eternal Word or Son of God did not first begin to be the savior of the world when He was born in Bethlehem of Judea; but that Word which became a man in* (via) *the Virgin Mary did from the beginning of the world enter as a Word of Life. Hence Christ said to his disciples 'The Kingdom of God is within you;' That is, the Divine Nature is within you."* Here it is clear that Law considered the man Jesus to be a physical expression of the Word that had existed from before the inception of the world.

Law is even more specific in this passage: *"Poor sinner! Consider the treasure thou hast within thee; …the Eternal Word of God lies hid in thee as a spark of the Divine Nature.* (Turn within) *and thy heart will find its savior, its God within itself. This turning to the light and spirit of God within thee is thy only true turning to God…For though God be everywhere present, yet He is only present to thee in the deepest most central part of thy soul."* Then he adds: *"Nothing can give the soul rest but the infinity of God."* **(Law 1938:81-82)**.

Elsewhere in ***The Spirit of Prayer*** **(Law 1938:87)** he says: *"Thou needest not run here or there saying 'where is Christ?' Behold the Word, which is the wisdom of God, is in thy heart."* While it is clear that Law considered Jesus the

Christ to be an expression of the Word or an incarnation of it in the world, he also believed that this Word was a transcendent reality that was more than any one physical expression. Nowhere does he suggest that the incarnation Jesus was the only possible manifestation of the Word. Certainly Law had read in scripture the assertions of Jesus that He considered everyone to be a child of God who could do everything that He did if he or she perfected or purified the inner nature. Law does not clearly state that the Word is a reality that can be heard by the pure ear as did Eckhart, John of the Cross or Boehme. But he clearly was familiar with this transcendent reality.

Meditation was implied more than stressed by Law. In ***The Spirit of Prayer*** **(Law 1938:83)** he asserts: *"For God cannot be truly found by any worshippers but those who worship Him in spirit and truth, so this light and spirit, though always with us, cannot be found and enjoyed but by those whose whole spirit* (or attention) *is turned to it."* Later (on page 89 of this same work) Law says: *"Accustom thyself to the Holy Service of this inward temple. In the midst of it is a fountain of living water of which thou mayest drink and live forever...There...the bread that came down from Heaven (is found)."*

Those who meditate correctly know that this directing of attention inwardly is indeed a difficult task. Law suggests a high mark for meditation in these words: *"keep the soul* (or inner attention) *fixed and continually turned toward God in faith, prayer, desire and resignation to Him... The soul thus turned to God must be always receiving from Him."* This is actually a very good definition of higher meditation, but one that is rarely attained except by a few pure souls.

In both *The Spirit of Prayer* and *The Spirit of Love* Law stresses both the nature of and the importance of love. It is apparent that he considers it to be a central or basic tenant in his spiritual doctrine. Page after page is devoted to love and its applications in our lives. In ***The Spirit of Prayer*** **(Law 1938:97)** Law says: *"This spirit of love, born of that Celestial fire with which Christ baptizes His true disciples is above that spirit which can enter into heaven."* This seems to imply that love is a divine state that transcends all of the heavens, a concept that higher teachers have stressed. And yet that love must be offered to every person one meets. Law suggests that we must love the divinity within each creature and not the apparent outer shell of the physical nature. In ***The Spirit of Prayer*** **(Law 1938:97-98)** he asserts: *"I am to love myself as I love my neighbor or any other created being, that is, only in and for God...as God's work, image and delight. This is loving it in God."*

Law repeatedly stresses that real love unites one with God. In ***The Spirit of Prayer*** **(page101-102)** he says: *"Where this All of God is truly known and felt, there is a fire of love, a pure disinterested love that begins and ends in God. And where this love is born in any creature, there a seraphic life is born along with it. For this pure love introduces the creature into the All of God...it is united with God."* By *"disinterested love"* Law probably means love that is free from emotional attachment. On page 109 Law tells us that real religion is the spirit of love and that all divine gifts and graces are those of love. He says: *"Nothing changes death into life, earth into heaven and men into angels but love alone. Love breathes the Spirit of God; its words and works are the inspiration of God. It speaketh not of itself, but the Word. All that Love speaketh, God speaketh, because God is Love."* He adds in **The Spirit**

of Love (page 142): *"For as Love is the God that created all things, so love is the purity, the perfection, and blessing of all created things; and nothing can live in God but as it lives in love. Look at every vice, pain and disorder in human nature. It is nothing else but the spirit of the creature turned* (away) *from the Universality of love."* Similar statements can be found in page after page of Law's later writings.

Law also stresses humility. A prime example from **page 101** of ***The Spirit of Prayer*** asserts: *"By thus knowing and owning our own nothingness and inability, that we have no other capacity for good but that of receiving it from God alone, self is wholly denied, its kingdom destroyed; no room is left for spiritual pride, (and) we are saved from a Pharisaical 'holiness'...and a multitude of errors."*

Most Christian churches have deviated far from the loving and spiritual teachings found in **Matthew 5, 6 and 7** (The Sermon on the Mount). In his ***Address to the Clergy*** Law says: *"Look now at warring Christendom. What smallest drop of pity toward sinners is to be found in it? You further see the fall of the Universal Church from being led by the spirit of Christ to be guided by the inspiration of the great fiery dragon."* He then continues: *"Look at European Christendom sailing around the globe with fire and sword and every murdering art of war to seize the possessions and kill the inhabitants of both the Indies."* Of course, this indictment by Law of so-called Christianity still can be applied to many modern religious and political institutions.

Law recognized but one universal method of salvation for all people. In ***The Spirit of Prayer*** **(Law 1938: 102)** he stated that *"God has but one design or intent towards all people and that is to introduce or generate His own Life, Light, and Spirit in them."* He then adds: *"There is but one possible way for man to attain this salvation or* *life of God in the soul. There is not one way for the Jew, another way for a Christian and a third for (others). No; God is one, human nature is one, salvation is one, and the way to it is one."*

William Blake

William Blake (1757-1827)

He who loves the best of men loves the
Father of men;
for where is the Father of men to be seen but
in the most perfect of His children.

It is the God in all that is our companion and
friend, for our God Himself says,
"You are my brother, my sister and my mother.
Who so dwelleth in love dwelleth in God."

William Blake

William Blake was England's greatest mystic-visionary and one of its most inspired artists in both literary and visual media. This man of rare talent and imagination possessed great spiritual insight. His wife once told a visitor that her husband spent more time in the higher worlds than he did in this one. Blake was not impressed with orthodox religious opinions, and he rebelled against the rationalistic philosophies of men such as Locke, Bacon and Newton. He was saddened and disturbed by human blindness and by the bigotry that led to inhuman acts in the names of religion and philosophy. A poet, painter, printer and prophetic visionary with the simple complexity of Blake is difficult to explain in a lengthy volume, so this brief resume of his life and thought is, at best, an introduction. Many full volume studies of Blake exist, but most of them reflect the philosophies and interests of their writers much more than they explain Blake.

The son of a London shopkeeper, Blake was born on November 28, 1757. At the age of ten he was sent to a drawing school and at fourteen was apprenticed to an engraver. He mastered the art of engraving and for the rest of his life earned a meager living by this trade. The enigmatic mystic artist educated himself by reading a wide variety of books. Often he would assert his independent judgment by annotating the margins of these volumes with his opinions.

As a child William Blake had visions of angels, Jesus and the apostles, and the prophet Ezekiel as well as various devic entities (nature spirits). He started writing poetry when he was twelve years of age and continued to do so for the rest of his life. His earliest writings were disarmingly simple lyrics with deep inherent significance. His later mature works, such as ***Milton, America, Vala or the Four Zoas*** and ***Jerusalem,*** are highly symbolic visions of the fall of humanity into realms of experience and an ultimate return to the Divine Source. The vision of Blake did not change from his early years through his later ones, but the mature prophetic works explain in a more integrated manner and in dramatic and cohesive language what was expressed in piecemeal fashion in the simpler early lyrics. Since heresy and political dissent were still serious offenses in Blake's day, the poet disguised his concepts in symbolic and allegorical poetry that seemed meaningless to his contemporaries. In 1811 the poet Robert Southy described *Jerusalem* as a *"perfectly mad poem."* Even in the late nineteenth century Swinburne, who felt the work was rich and subtle, found the mythological plan strange and tortuous. In fact, as recently as 1948 a catalog describing a Philadelphia exhibit of Blake's works commented on page 72: *"Reading* ***Jerusalem****, and rare is the hardy soul who finishes it, one is antagonized and exhausted by the nearly unintelligible parade of eternals who create and are created, who disappear, divide themselves into characters of the opposite sexes and reunite themselves in sexless wholes. Familiar names here and there seem to offer a refuge in the chaos, but the miracle is a mirage: the names are used symbolically."* Only in recent years have a few scholars partially understood the mature works of Blake, and this enhanced awareness has contributed much to his soaring reputation. Blake passed away on August 12, 1827 in a most unorthodox manner: singing as loudly as he could!

Poetical Sketches, a book of youthful verse, was the only volume by Blake printed with traditional type. In later volumes, the author combined engraved illustrations with his handwritten verbal art. Marvelous pictures, printed from engraved plates and carefully colored by hand, illuminated the text. Thus each mature expression of Blake is a synthesis of poetry with lyric or dramatic verbal music and remarkable visual beauty. Although Blake had difficulty in selling any of his illustrated poetic utterances during his lifetime, these unique works are extremely valuable today.

The mystic poet encouraged young writers, painters and sculptors to abandon veneration for classical models and contemporary "authorities" and develop imagination and intuition. He believed that reform in art would be accompanied by comparable reforms in social and political fields. But, as is usually the case with visionaries and original thinkers, Blake had little influence upon the concepts of his time. His only one-man show, a modest art exhibit at his brother's shop in 1809, attracted little public attention and was reviewed in the *Examiner* as the work of a lunatic. The ***Descriptive Catalog*** of the exhibition explained Blake's artistic concepts in competent prose, but it was totally ignored by contemporary writers and critics. Today the *Descriptive Catalog* is much appreciated and often quoted.

Since we are mainly interested in Blake's spiritual concepts, we will only mention his poetic volumes. ***Songs of Innocence* (1789)** considers the introduction of the naïve soul into the vast realms of living experience. And ***Songs of Experience* (1794)** considers the contrary states, such as birth and death, war and peace, and love and hate that the soul progresses through in its return to a primal state. Blake understood that without difficulty and challenge there could be no progression, and explained that untested innocence is not holiness. The latter occurs when souls see sin for what it is, usually through hard experience, and choose a higher and purer way of life. This attitude is clearly stipulated in **Revelation 21:7** of the Bible where it says that the person who overcomes will inherit all (spiritual) things.

A long series of prophetic books follow the early songs. These culminate in Blake's masterpiece, ***Jerusalem,*** an epic that is far more original and encompassing than ***Milton's Paradise Lost***. In this four-part epic, with its complex structure of interfolded growth, Blake traces the fall of man into an earthly "*Ulro*" where he is given law and learns to recognize sin. Then, man moves to Judaism (or any childhood religion of law and fear). Next, he progresses through Deism and into a rejuvenated Christianity of faith and love. Finally, the experienced soul overcomes all lower tendencies and rises consciously into the New Jerusalem, a state of consciousness that is established spiritually in every land. Since Blake was reared in a Christian context and apparently was not well versed in other religious traditions, he explained things in biblical language. But much of what he said in his own way could be applied to other religious or spiritual paths.

Now we will consider Blake's views of the roles of what he termed Beulah *(upper Astral)*, Generation *(lower Astral)* and Ulro *(the dense material world)* as human souls descend into illusion and matter. The values of struggle, self expression and overcoming in realms of sleep and death will lead to the personal erection of a New Jerusalem where the soul can unite with God in the focus of eternity. According to Blake, this is the purpose behind the soul's excursion into the darkness of Ulro.

This writer must admit to having been influenced by the Blakean concept of God as being a unity of four basic qualities. However, there are slight differences between the views of Blake and those presented in Chapter 1 of this book. Blake believed that God was a union of four forces: Power, Love, Perception and Imagination. Perhaps we are dealing with semantics more than actual opinions, but Imagination seems to be more of a mental quality than a synonym for the Creative Word or Logos. Power, Love, and Perception (or consciousness) are the same as stipulated in Chapter 1. From this Absolute Unity came the Celestial Eden where a state of oneness no longer existed, and where egos could fall into lower realms of crystallized energy, illusion and darkness (or Ulro). Blake definitely had a vision that included at least one state of being above the Celestial realm, but it is difficult to determine how far up the spiritual ladder that he was able to climb. However, his familiarity with the Causal and Astral realms was second to none.

William Blake suggests that the biblical account of the fall of man was highly symbolic. In the Blakean view,

Eden was a Causal Plane expression that existed on the Celestial counterpart of earth. He believed that all things were created spiritually before they came into physical manifestation. In other words, every physical form, from insect to planet or sun, connects to a spiritual counterpart that is a divine expression. The forbidden fruit was the ego or self-assertion. The fall, a result of cause and effect or karmic factors on the part of entities with free will, carried souls from the Causal Eden through Beulah *(upper Astral)* and Generation *(lower Astral)* into the single vision of Ulro (physical world). Now the soul must gain experience, overcome lower tendencies of mind and emotions, and return to the source from which it emanated.

There is no conflict between Blake's stages of Albion (souls in a collective sense) and the planes of existence taught by other spiritual exponents. Human beings are now in Ulro, a world of single vision and *"Newton's sleep"* where Satan, the father of natural religion and materialistic science, reigns. Blake questioned the efficacy of Newton's methods of scientific investigation in order to understand physical phenomena. He felt that one had to soar into higher realms in order to understand the lower ones because energy flows from above into lower dimensions. In other words, scientists work from the mundane toward the unknown, while Blake viewed things from the spiritual into objective form. While he certainly believed that experience was an essential ingredient in progress, he was not sympathetic toward certain rational or scientific approaches to gaining experience. Blake did not seem to realize that higher insight is often preceded by scientific education. He trusted the poetic imagination and spiritual insight more than he did the inductive reasoning and the deductive inferences of science because he believed that many rational assumptions were false. Blake did not understand that training in logical thinking and scientific methods could help elevate the thinker above those levels of gross superstition and emotional fear taught by many religious institutions. It is often necessary for one to learn the value of many things through experience, and rational thinking can be of value in discriminating between certain lower levels of reality. But he was correct in believing that intuitive insight was superior to scientific evaluation.

Some spiritual teachers have commented upon the actions of corrupt and misguided political leaders in spite of the fact that these teachers' main missions were supposed to be spiritual ones. Blake made it clear that he did not approve of the English monarchy, mainly because he considered it harsh and unenlightened. The establishment of a democratic society in the United States after the American Revolution pleased him, but he apparently foresaw some of the problems that could evolve even in a democracy. In a public address given about 1810, he said: *"Empires flourish till they become commercial, and then they are scattered abroad to the four winds."* In an annotation to Bacon's political essay "Of Seditions and Troubles" Blake wrote: *"The increase of a state, as of a man, is from internal improvement."* It is clear that Blake thought that a government would prosper and be beneficial as long as it adhered to high ethical and moral standards and served the public unselfishly. But it will fall from the weight of its own corruption when it becomes strictly commercial and selfish or allows big business to dictate the terms of government.

Modern linguistic research suggests the existence at one time of what is called the Indo-European language, a parent base for most of the languages of India, Russia, the Mediterranean area and Western Europe. Scholars of religion are amazed at the similarities between all of the major faiths and many of the minor ones when culturally induced rituals are stripped away and one studies basic concepts. Perhaps they too had a common primal source. Blake makes a comment that is relevant to this probability in his ***Descriptive Catalog,* Number V**: *"The antiquities of every nation under heaven is no less sacred than that of the Jews. All had originally one language and one religion: the religion of Jesus, the Everlasting Gospel."* In the course of time, this primal faith became distorted by political and cultural traditions as each group tried to justify its actions as divinely inspired because, in its opinion, it possessed the *"correct faith."* Such egotistical rationalizations emerged at the expense of spirituality. As Blake continued in his catalog: *"The Bible, exclusive of conscience, is that abomination."*

Blake became quite specific regarding the origin of this primal religion in his ***"All Religions Are One,"*** which was etched about 1788. He said: *"All sects of philosophy are from the Poetic Genius adapted to the weaknesses of every individual. The religions of all nations are derived from each nation's different reception of the Poetic Genius. The True Man is the source, he being the Poetic Genius."* To be more specific, all religions sprang from the inner Christ Consciousness, Creative Imagination or Poetic Genius. This is why so many exponents of spiritual concepts have been poets.

Blake believed that true spirituality was continually being given to humanity in all nations. On **page 9 of his annotations on Watson**, he said of revelation: *"It is strange that God should speak to man formerly and not now: it is not true! Every man may converse with God and be a king and priest in his own house."*

Although spirituality is constantly being reintroduced into the world, unenlightened opinions, political precepts and rituals always change it into a vehicle for vanity, hypocrisy and repression. *"State Religion,"* said Blake in his **annotations on Watson, p.25**, "is the source of all cruelty." In his *"Proverbs of Hell"* the poet adds: *"Prisons are built with stones of law, brothels with bricks of religion."* Such an amalgamation of corruption and faith caused Blake to exclaim: "Who is really righteous? It is all pretension." **(Blake 1969:396, Annotations on Watson, pp.118-119).**

In many places Blake expounded his ideas of spiritual worship. In an **annotation to Swedenborg's *Divine Love,*** he said: *"Essence is not identity, but from essence proceeds identity and from one essence may proceed many identities. That there is but one Omnipotent, uncreated God I agree, but that there is but one Infinite I do not; for if all but God is not infinite, they shall come to an end, which God forbid."* This suggests that Blake believed that all spirits were eternal drops from the ocean of all consciousness. The inner essence remains forever although the imperfect personality will not endure. Death affects physical bodies, emotional natures and even all aspects of mind, but it does not eliminate the core essence of each entity. In his *"Proverbs of Heaven and Hell"* the poet says: *"men forgot that all deities reside in the human breast."* Then he added: *"If the doors of perception were cleansed, everything would appear to man as it is, infinite. But man has closed himself up, till he sees all things through the narrow chinks of his cavern."* In an **annotation to Lavater's Aphorism 630**, Blake says: *"It is the God in all that is our companion and friend, for our God himself says: 'you are my brother, my sister and my mother.'* St John says: *'Whoso dwelleth in love dwelleth in God and God in him," and such a one cannot judge of any but in love. Creation is God descending according to* *the weakness of man, for our Lord is the Word of God and in its essence is God."* Notice that Blake recognizes *"our Lord"* as the Divine Word and asserts that it is responsible for all life. In an **alteration of Lavater's Aphorism 549** Blake changed the writing to read: *"He who loves the wisest and best of men loves the father of men; for where is the father of men to be seen but in the most perfect of his children? This is true worship!"* All higher spiritual teachers have expressed these sentiments in their own words.

The role of art in the development of nations and civilizations was emphasized strongly by Blake, because the source of inspired art is the higher consciousness. Blake saw the suppression of higher art as well as decadence in art as examples of the tyranny of Satan. In an annotation on the title page of Sir Joshua Reynolds' discourses, Blake wrote: *"The foundation of empire is art and science. Remove them or degrade them, and the empire is no more. Empire follows art and not visa versa as Englishmen suppose."* While it is true that great art can transform society, apparently Blake did not realize that such a transformation is often slow to manifest. In his perceptive book ***Music, its Secret Influence Throughout the Ages***, composer Cyril Scott pointed out how such great composers as Bach, Beethoven, Chopin, Wagner and others greatly influenced the cultures that heard their works, but these changes were not always immediate. Music and visual arts first affect the mental and emotional natures of people before their effects filter down into physical consciousness. Blake believed that an individual's attitude toward great art reflected the inner state of that person.

In his own visual art, Blake demonstrated a remarkable exuberance and imagination. In fact in his **1810 public address**, he stated that *"imagination is my world."* Only a few artists, such as Michelangelo and Raphael, possessed his ability to depict the human form, and probably no artist in the western world expressed comparable vision, imagination and execution in as many media. In Blake's case his art included poetry, engraving, and painting. In his ***Descriptive Catalog,* Number II**, he stated: *"The artist having been taken in vision into the ancient republics…has seen these wonderful originals…which were sculptured and painted on walls of temples, towers, cities, palaces. The artist has endeavored to emulate the grandeur of those seen in his vision."* Ancient art was often spontaneous and intuitive depictions of the essence of particular subjects, whereas modern art is often unduly influenced by *"rules"* postulated by so called authorities. Thus the Artistic Genius of Blake is overruled by mental strictures.

Blake's contemporary, William Wordsworth, said (in his poem "Tintern Abbey") that he found in nature "the anchor of my purest thoughts…the guide, the guardian of my heart." On the contrary, Blake (in an annotation to Boyd's Dante, pp. 56-57) wrote: "Nature teaches nothing of spiritual life but only of natural life." Whereas Wordsworth in his youth essentially worshipped nature as a reflection of the Divine, Blake even as a youth had a different view. Although he believed that God permeated all life in a spiritual sense, in Jerusalem 91:8-10 Blake said: "The worship of God is honoring His gifts in men." In other words, one recognizes those who are divinely inspired and spiritually developed. One might add that Wordsworth in his later life altered his views of nature when he became acutely aware of the fangs and thorns hiding within what seemed to be a placid landscape. Blake never changed his views because they were based upon the deep visions he first knew as a child.

On page 196 of **Swedenborg's *Divine Love*** Blake wrote: *"Study sciences till you are blind, study intellectuals* *till you are cold, yet science cannot teach intellect. Much less can science teach affection."* Believing that love was one part of ultimate Divinity, Blake distinguished between emotional attachment and genuine love. He stressed that real love was selfless, involving mutual giving and concern for each other. In this world most people are traders, not lovers, because they want something in return for being nice to you. But love, an unlimited repository of giving, has no strings attached. Love also promotes an awesome endurance as Henry David Thoreau once stated. He commented that during severe Massachusetts winter storms local farmers, woodsmen, philosophers and others stayed at home. Only a poet traveled through this inclement weather to visit him. In the words of **Thoreau (1969:202):** *"...nothing can deter a poet, for he is actuated by pure love."*

Blake believed that all natural functions, including sex, can be holy, and he scorned puritanical views of chastity because they result in feelings of guilt. He understood that sex was the only close relationship known by many people in a world that emphasized sexual activity, and he knew that suppression and guilt could produce insanity. In his opinion, physical sex could be involved in either perversity or sublimity depending upon the motives and views of the individuals involved. He understood that physical sex must be involved with love on the Causal Plane or it leads to bondage. He once said that people do not love physical bodies any more than they love rocks and clouds. It is the indweller or inner nature that makes higher spiritual love possible just as it is a mental attitude that promotes lust. In ***Milton* 26:24-29** Blake describes the sons of Los *"around the lake of Udan-Adan...where souls incessant wail, being piteous passions and desires; for such alone sleepers remain, meer passion and appetite."* These graphic and powerful words depict the fate of those dominated by unfulfilled desires and passions that are never satisfied. Of course, Blake recognized the role of desire in human development. It should serve as a teacher and not form a perpetual bondage. He annotated Bacon's essay "Of Empire" with these words: *"He who has few things to desire cannot have many to fear."* The American philosopher and author Henry David Thoreau echoed similar sentiments when he said, *"A man is rich in proportion to the number of things he can afford to leave alone."* This lesson, so important in Buddhism, is learned only through much experience.

All higher spiritual exponents have stressed the importance of humility. Blake could easily be misunderstood because much of his writing suggests boundless energy and powerful self-assertion. In such annotations as *"Damn him!"* or *"A dog! Get a stick to him!"* the poet expresses the emotional side of his nature because he disagrees with certain writers. But he balances such assertions in ***Poetical Sketches*** with these words: *"Oh man, slave of every moment, Lord of Eternity! O what an humble garb true joy puts on! Those who want happiness must stoop to find it; it is a flower that grows in every vale. Foolish man that roams on lofty rocks, where 'cause his garments are swoln with wind, he fancies he is grown into a giant! Humility, take it, and wear it in thine heart."* Blake understood that real humility is natural and spontaneous. The truly humble person is unaware that he or she is humble.

Most human beings fear death more than any other phenomena because to them it is the greatest unknown. Blake obviously had no fear of death because he had passed through it regularly since youth. In his **"Dedication of Illustrations to Blair's Grave"** the poet wrote:

The door of death is made of gold
that mortal eyes cannot behold;
But when the mortal eyes are closed...
The soul awakes and wond'ring sees...
The grave is heaven's Golden Gate.

Blake understood that death existed in all of the lower states of Albion (Causal, Astral, and physical dimensions) and believed that these states and death were essential for the progressing soul. One abandons the old when he or she finds something better or when the old wears out. Apparently Blake knew where he was going, because, as was stated previously, the poet died singing as loudly as he could.

The Celtic Renaissance

It is repeatedly pointed out in this book that most geographical areas of the world, indeed most nationalities, have cultural roots deeply immersed in mystical soils. In the surviving folklore of ancient Celtic peoples of Northern Europe (the now extinct continental group) as well as the insular Brythonic (British) and Goidelic (Gaelic) Celtic divisions, one finds mystical concepts of ancient parentage. Early in the 20th Century a group of Irish writers, representing what has been called the Celtic Renaissance, began drawing upon this amazingly fertile spiritual heritage. We find the great Poet William Butler Yeats (1865-1939) tapping into what he felt was the deeper roots of elemental mystic nature than could be found in the churches of his day. In such volumes as ***The Wanderings of Oisin,*** Yeats has the ancient bard recount to St. Patrick an extensive residence in a devic fairyland with the brilliant goddess Niamh (pronounced 'Neeve'). In youth he dwelt on the Island of Love, later he resided on the Island of Maturity, and, in old age, he lived on the Island of Contemplation. Haunting symbols and ethereal magic permeate such early writings of Yeats. Even in dramatic compositions Yeats explored the Celtic mystic tradition. A good example is his 1902 play ***Where There is Nothing***. Here the main thesis is that humanity recedes from divine intuitive joy and love to a society that considers objective things more valuable than spiritual faith or even life itself. He stresses that we must eradicate from our attention the world and everything that features law and duality, for where there is nothing, there is God.

During his *"Mask Period"* (1910-1925), Yeats enunciated an intricate cosmological system in such works as ***The Wild Swans at Coole***. The swans symbolize beauty and immortality. In eastern *spirituality* one also notices the swan symbol (here called *Hansa*) representing one who has achieved the spiritual realms above the mind. The poetry of this volume expounds how in youth the body is emphasized especially, while in old age the soul is stressed. However, in the Yeatsian view, the wise seek a harmonious compound of body and soul: in the words of Blake, a balancing of Zoas.

Literary authorities consider the creative outburst of Yeats between 1925 and his death in 1939 to represent a "Prophetic Period." His system of cosmology becomes quite elaborate and difficult to follow. The extensively revised ***A Vision* (1937)** is a prose enunciation of the Yeatsian system. Life is seen as patterned after a great wheel with twenty-eight spokes or phases. Each soul and culture passes through all twenty-eight phases. Each historical revolution of the wheel takes 2,000 years, and each successive revolution carries humanity upward toward the Great Year. This Yeatsian wheel reminds one of the giant *Wheel of Life and Death* found in Eastern cosmology.

Yeats also believed that each individual and nation was composed of warring elements or gyres of internal and external orientations. Although not synonymous with Four Zoas of Blake, Yeats' 'gyres" certainly remind one of Blakean concepts.

Another exponent of the Celtic rebirth was James Stephens (1880-1950). Via imaginative verse forms and prose fantasies Stephens explored the doctrines of subjective truth. Believing that the soul creates its own good and evil, and thus directs its own fate, this Irish writer depicted the battle between the sensual and divine parts of each entity. Perhaps Stephens' best-known work is the delightful fantasy, ***The Crock of Gold*** **(1912)**.

George William Russell (or AE)

George William Russell (or AE)

(1867 – 1935)

Eternal joy becomes love, changing into desire, and is lead on to earthly passion and forgetfulness of its own divinity.

Fear not the stillness; for doubt and despair cease with the gentle voices guiding us to peace.

George William Russell

Although Lord Dunsany (1878-1957), John Millington Synge (1871-1909), and Padraic Column (1881-1972) also drew upon the imaginative folklore of Ireland to represent their views of illusion and reality, it was George William Russell (1867-1935) who obviously had the deepest spiritual experiences among the writers of the Celtic Renaissance. The name of Russell is poorly known, partly because he signed his work AE and partly because the same themes were repeated from his earliest to his latest works. Also, there is the factor of a pervasive optimism and sweetness that is rejected by many modern readers because this optimism does not reflect the life they know. Few critics today consider Russell to have been a great poet. As a result the literary reputation of AE has dwindled in recent years. But regardless of how one views the literary merits of Russell's work, any unbiased reader must recognize that it is based upon genuine mystical experience.

Rebelling against an orthodox Protestant upbringing, Russell studied art and oriental mysticism. He was a schoolmate and lifelong friend of Yeats. Although he painted extensively, he made his living as a minor clerk and as an organizer of agricultural cooperatives. Russell promoted Irish nationalism as editor of the Irish Homestead and later as editor of the Irish Statesman. He died in England in 1935.

Considering the name "Russell" to represent the objective side of his nature, the author signed his initial work AEON, to symbolize his spiritual nature. However the printer could make out only the AE and thus his pseudonym was established. Later, Russell stated that the AEON represented the circular passage of the soul from revolt against God through successive experiences of life, ultimately returning to the Divine Source. The word Aeon is a Gnostic term that Russell must have encountered through his extensive reading. We will now consider the spiritual concepts of AE in some detail.

It is well known that AE read the Bible as well as Theosophical and eastern mystical literature. However, his own poetic and prose writings are not syntheses of his considerable reading. They seem to reflect a strong element of personal experience. Like his contemporary, Yeats, Russell believed that traditional Christianity had lost the inner spark of visionary experience known by ancient seers and was now little more than a social order that used fear to induce conformity. Yeats, in his poem **"The Second Coming,"** saw emerging from the world mind a beastly and dim-witted combination of lion and man *"slouching toward Bethlehem to be born."* AE was more optimistic than Yeats, but he obviously thought that orthodox religion was blindly misused. In his poem **"Outcast,"** he says of men:

They crucify the Mystery with words of good cheer.
When love and life are over, the flight's at an end,
On the outcast majesty they lean as a friend.

Neither Yeats nor Russell considered Christianity to be the only valid religion. AE even believed that mythology often reflected higher truth because many old myths were originally based upon personal experience. In ***The Candle of Vision*** (p. 149) he wrote: *"In our Gaelic wonder tales I often find a vision which is, I think, authentic, and we can, I believe, learn from these voyages to the Heaven-world more of the geography of the spirit and the many mansions in the Being of the Father than we can from the greatest of our sightless philosophers. Our Gaelic ancestors had the gift of seership."*

Russell obviously believed that great literary geniuses, such as Milton and Dante, based their works more upon fanciful interpretations of orthodox theology than upon personal experience. In ***The Avatars*** he says that such treatises as ***Paradise Lost and The Inferno*** "detract us in another way from the true, for they send the imagination outward, whereas the aim of all (true) religion (or spirituality) is to throw the imagination inward toward being."

This leads us to the role of meditation in the life of AE. In a short poem **"The Silence of Love,"** he writes:

Fear not the stillness; for doubt and despair cease
with the gentle voices guiding us into peace.

It is apparent too that he considered meditation to be an internal exercise of the attention, for in his poem **"Shadows and Lights"** he expressed these thoughts:

Ah, let us for a little while abate
The outward roving eye, and seek within
Where spirit unto spirit is allied;
There in our inmost being, we may win
The joyful vision of the heavenly wise.

Experiences realized in meditation are contingent upon such things as past spiritual background, purity of mind, ability to concentrate and childlike simplicity. AE realized that experiences would vary from one person to another. In his ***The Candle of Vision*** (p. 151), he says: *"I think that meditation is beginning anew... To some there come starling flashes of vision, while others (only) feel a hand of power touching them."*

In his own meditations Russell saw several worlds or planes of life. His visionary trips into the higher planes were, by his own admission, rare. But he often saw into the elemental or devic world. In ***The Candle of Vision*** (p. 156) he describes one such experience in these words: *"I was drawn to meditate beside a deep pool amid woods. As I gazed into the dark waters, consciousness seemed to sink beneath them and I found myself in another world. It was more luminous than this, and I found one there who seemed like an elemental king. The figure was of a brilliant blue and gold opalescence...and a golden light seemed to pervade it."* This certainly was an excursion into a devic realm or place of ethereal nature spirits.

Some of AE's visions were of a higher order. In ***The Candle of Vision*** (p. 147) he described an experience that overwhelmed him in these words: *"Out of what sphere came that being, taller and mightier than human, whose body* *seemed wrought out of flame and whose eyes had the stillness of an immortal. It was so lofty and above humanity that I seemed to myself less than an insect, though something in me cried out to it in brotherhood. I knew not whether I had fallen from its height, or was a lost comrade lagging far behind in time who should have been equal, but was too feeble to rise to such majesty."* The description of this flame-like entity certainly suggests that AE had an Upper Astral experience. His description reminds one of the Jyoti mentioned by Guru Nanak, Gobind Singh and other Sikh teachers and of the Jehovah of the Old Testament and the Book of Revelation (**Exodus 3:2-4; Revelation 1:12-16**).

Russell wondered why scientists and philosophers did not mention or explain the visionary excursions that he, Blake and others had experienced. He concluded that *"I have not found in latter day philosophical writers the explanation of my own experiences, and think that is because there has been an over-development of intellect and few have cultivated vision."* Then he adds: *"It is only when I turn to the literature of vision and intuition, to the sacred books, poets and seers that I find a grandiose conception of nature in which every spiritual experience is* (explained). *I have not entered the paradises they entered, but what little I know finds its place in the universe of their vision. Whether they are of Syrian, Greek, Egyptian, or Hindu backgrounds, the writers of the sacred books seem to me as men who had all gazed upon the same august vision."* (***The Candle of Vision,* p. 149)**.

In ***The Living Torch*** (p. 116) AE was most expressive regarding the visions of William Blake. He said: *"In William Blake there was, perhaps, more of the element of infinity than in any of his contemporaries. Byron and Scott, the great ostensibles, were exhausted by their own generation. Only Blake, the most obscure of the great writers of his time, can still excite us spiritually, for he speaks of truths to which* *the world has yet to travel. His mind has not been completely charted. Nor can it be charted until our psychology becomes more profound."*

In order to avoid controversy, many writers on religious and mystical themes either avoid the subject of reincarnation or refer to it symbolically. Since AE was most explicit on this topic, one must consider it when his writings are explained. While some will argue that Russell was introduced to the concept by his studies of Oriental mystical writings, that is not necessarily the case. Many western writers who may not been exposed to Eastern thought also believed in reincarnation. To mention a few of them: Henry Moore (1614-1687), Thomas Vaughan (1621-1665), David Hume (1711-1776), Thomas Carlyle (1795-1881), Charles Dickens (1812-1870), Edward Carpenter (1844-1929), H. G. Wells (1866-1946), Somerset Maugham (1874-1965) and John Middleton Murray (1889-1957) among prose writers. Space here does not allow a listing of all of the English and American poets who have believed in this concept. A few English poets include Alfred, Lord Tennyson (1809-1892), Robert Browning (1812-1889), Matthew Arnold (1822-1888), Dante G. Rosetti (1828-1882) and John Masefield (1878-1967). American poets include Oliver Wendell Holmes (1809-1894), Walt Whitman (1819-1892), James Russell Lowell (1819-1891), Emily Dickinson (1830-1886) and Robert Frost (1874-1963). The reader is invited to consider the book ***Reincarnation, an East-West Anthology*** **(edited by Head and Cranston, 2000)** for documentation of these writers' opinions and a thorough list of famous people who believed in rebirth. This work quotes over 400 western thinkers and religious writers of the world. Whether the reader believes or disbelieves in reincarnation, he or she must acknowledge that many brilliant and intuitive people have been convinced that it is true.

In ***The Candle of Vision*** (pp. 144-145) AE is quite explicit on this topic. He says: *"From long pondering I have come to believe in the eternity of the spirit and that it is an inhabitant of many spheres. I think our dreams and visions often come in all completeness into our sphere out of other spheres of being and are not built up* (solely) *from memories of earth. I see breaking in upon the images of this world forms of I know not what antiquity. Are they not, I ask myself, memories of the spirit incarnated many times?"*

AE does not mention having an objective teacher, so he may have garnered many concepts from extensive reading. However, he does refer to actual entities that meet and offer to guide one in the astral and causal planes. With more insight than many who follow their own mental creations, Russell offers these words from ***The Candle of Vision*** (p. 148): *"There are few whose intent will has tried to scale the heavens who have not been met by messages from the gods…who are, I think, our selves beyond this mirage of time and space by which we are enchanted."* Apparently AE did not believe that all "guides" in higher planes were self-created, because he suggests that Christ or some other higher power sometimes send angelic agents to assist the awakening soul.

Every spiritual writer throughout history has written or uttered eloquent words about love. AE describes the transformation of eternal or Divine Love to worldly attachment in these words from ***The Candle of Vision*** (p. 157): *"The eternal joy becomes* (lesser) *love when it has first merged itself in form, and images of a divine beauty dance before it and lure it afar."* He then continues: *"Eternal joy becomes love, changing into desire, and is led on to earthly passion and forgetfulness of its own divinity."Similar sentiments express the effect of "Time, more murderous than death" on love. These lines are from the poem "Time":*

Time has buried love alive
In the heart, and day by day
O'er the piteous image casts
Shovelfulls of airy clay.

Finally the divine love becomes so covered and externalized that only the discerning visionary detects its germinal presence. In ***The Candle of Vision*** (p. 158) AE references Whitman in these words: *"Whitman writes of the earth that is rude and incomprehensible at first. 'But I swear to you,' he cries, 'that there are divine things well hidden.' Yet they are not so concealed that the lover may not discern them."* This is why many intuitive poets have eulogized love and its relationships to higher levels of being in lines of intense beauty. As Shelley in his **"A Defense of Poetry"** said: *"Poetry is indeed something divine. It is at once the centre and circumference of knowledge."*

Gradually the lover graduates by experience from attachment to things and infatuation for imperfect peo--ple to the love that means freedom for both lover and beloved. In his poem **"On the Waters"** AE says:

They thrill me not, I know not how,
The lips but late so sweetly kissed.
A love more ancient draws me now
To keep some immemorial tryst.

The higher union is beautifully described in Russell's poem **"Mirage."** He said:

The Peace as deep as being passed beyond sight or sound,
Where lover and beloved are in each other drowned.
Fullness unto the utter most, a deep that has no bound.

These latter lines express ideas that Eckhart would have approved. While there is no evidence to suggest that AE had achieved the higher consciousness of Eckhart, there are often indications that inspired poets sometimes tap into levels of their own nature that exist beyond their conscious awareness.

Russell concluded that the inner significance of revealed scripture was not understood by most of those who professed religious faith. Many of them did not think deeply, and very few churchgoers cultivated the intuitive faculties. They preferred the *"easy way"* of simply believing in what they were told instead of applying a rigorous and concentrated mental appraisal to the ideas they had heard since childhood. He would have agreed with **Tolstoy (1984: 50)** when he wrote:*"The significance of the Gospel is hidden from believers by the church, from unbelievers by science."* We can conclude this brief consideration of Russell by stating that he believed we are on earth to grow intimate with it and love mountains, rocks, trees, birds, beasts, and spirits of nature and recognize our kinship with all of them. Then our primal essence, or soul, which has always existed and maintained a connection to God, shall return as a prodigal to the primal Father-Being and consciously become one with this Infinitude. In other words, the spiritual drop shall return to the divine ocean and merge with it. This is a fitting termination to each excursion in space and time since each unit of consciousness is a fragment of the Divine Source.

Mildred Bruner Prendergast, Mother Millie

Mildred Bruner Prendergast
Mother Millie
(1900 – 1987)

You cannot use the mind in meditation because the mind
In the end will trap you in ego.

There is a difference between human affection and Divine love. The latter sets you free while human infatuation entangles you more deeply in karmic relationships.

Mother Millie

Every true master is a saint, but not every saint has been authorized to serve as a master or satguru. In the East, where many spiritual luminaries have appeared, masters have been divided into several categories depending upon the spiritual levels attained. First, there is a Param Satguru or Saint, one who has returned to the primal oneness or Ultimate Source of all. Then there is the Satguru, an adept who has risen to the stable spiritual realm often called Sach Khand (or True Home). Then there is the Sadh Guru, a Saint who has traversed beyond the mental region of Brahm into what is known as Parbrahm (above Brahm). Buddhist adepts have referred to this stage as the *"empty realm"* of nothing (no things). The term *"Sadh"* may also refer to one who has crossed the Maha Sunna or region of darkness above Parbrahm and entered the next spiritual state, a region of amazing grandeur and light. No words can describe it. It is important to stress that initiation by a Sadh Guru is just as valid as that of a Satguru if his master is a perfect Satguru, because he or she will have total devotion to the master who guided them to their present state. This love will enable them to take their disciples wherever they go as they expand in love for God. Yes, real spiritual love is the ticket that allows one to return to the Divine Source. But the guide who leads one must have been authorized, and usually they have been ordered, to serve as a master. No one in his or her right mind would want to function as a guru because the responsibility is awesome and the task extremely difficult. As Saint Sawan Singh, who is considered later, said: *"it is like volunteering to be crucified."* All masters act out of pure love for God, their masters and their disciples and serve unselfishly in spite of the extreme difficulty of this demanding role.

A great soul, Mildred Bruner Prendergast (1900 – 1987) became a saint because her awesome love propelled her toward God. Her master once stated that it was her love, not intellectual knowledge or even faith, which would take her home. She was assigned the task of going to groups of disciples that were having degrees of discord and promoting love. *"I was terrified,"* she told me, *"but I had to go."* It was especially difficult for Mother Millie since she was inclined toward a life of inner introspection or meditation in her later life. *"But,"* she said, *"Master would come and take over and everything would become beautiful."* Those of us who knew her personally loved her deeply because she found the light of love in each soul and fed it until it grew into a flame that consumed all negativity.

Mother Millie, as she was called by many who knew her, was born Mildred Bruner on October 19, 1900 and was reared on a ranch in South Dakota. She was sent to a convent school by her father because she was constantly trying to deliver spiritual instructions to the ranch hands. Also, she was fond of riding horses and engaging in outdoor activities, and her father thought that convent school would change her into a dignified lady. After completing her training at the convent school, she met a Boston attorney named Michael Prendergast. At this time, in 1923, she won the Miss Boston beauty contest and in September of that year won the third Miss America Contest held at Atlantic City. She was disqualified from being Miss America because she had just married the Boston attorney. Miss Alaska was disqualified also since she was married.

During the first twenty years of a difficult marriage she gave birth to three sons, one of whom died in his 20's. After many arduous years of marriage, her husband changed, becoming kind to her and allowing her to visit her master. After her husband passed away, she lost all of her possessions, even her home, as partners in her husband's law firm claimed the property. Alone on the street with only a suitcase she felt great fear until a Jewish man stopped his car and took her to his home. It turned out that he was an attorney and he succeeded in regaining some of her property, such as her house and some furnishings, and a small amount of money.

I met Mother Millie at Glenwood Springs, Colorado in July of 1980 while I was attending a spiritual retreat being held under the direction of Saint Ajaib Singh, an initiate of Mother Millie's master. Many disciples were standing on one side of a street waiting for Saint Ji, as he was called, to walk up from the cottage where he was staying. I looked across the street and was amazed to see, standing by herself, the most radiant woman I had ever observed. Light literally sprang out from her slender form. Immediately, I walked across the street, introduced myself and thus became acquainted with Mother Millie. She visited my home in Arkansas on several occasions and inspired all of those who were present with her love and wisdom. Whenever word got out that she was visiting my home, people drove for hundreds of miles and from several nearby states to be present with her. In fact my house could hardly accommodate all of them.

Mother Millie also traveled to Texas where she was loved by many spiritually oriented people. On one occasion, she visited a home in Dallas. The organizer of this retreat had invited a group of street kids to come and meet Millie. All of them had either been kicked out of their homes or abandoned by parents. One of these kids looked like he was about five years old. The oldest teenager, probably all of 16 years of age, served as a sort of guardian for the younger children. Anyhow, they entered the room as a group of street-hardened young people wearing icy attitudes like masks on their faces. They had to adopt such outer displays in order to survive on the streets of Dallas. The five year old took one look at Mother Millie and with tears in his eyes jumped into her lap. She caressed him as all of the others sat at her feet on the floor. She told all of them that they were children of a God that loved them and wanted to help them. Mother Millie saw the divine potential in each of these children and fed this inner divinity with her spiritual love. The group of children left the house looking like little angels with radiant faces. Such was her effect upon others. In fact when she walked down a street, total strangers often would run up to her and embrace her.

Between 1980 and 1986, Mother Millie and I had many lengthy talks in private. She said that her master had authorized her to tell certain inner experiences to bolster the faith of others. Usually one is asked to keep inner experiences to oneself, but she was actually ordered to tell them. She told me of meeting Jesus and many other saints in the higher realms, and she was allowed to visit her mother and others whom she loved on occasion even though they had passed away years before. She told me that she had passed through the Astral realm, the Causal plane and Parbrahm, but she was having trouble crossing the vast dark region known as Maha Sunna. After she had removed the last vestiges of subtle emotional attachments to certain people, her master came and guided her across this region. She had to learn, as all of us do, that love is not an emotion but a component of divinity and that true love has no strings attached: it allows perfect freedom to all others. Needless to say, she rapidly passed through the remaining expanse and reached the True Home. In her last communication with me she stated that she had made it home and urged me to get on the ball and finish my meditations *"so we can all be together."*

Mother Millie did not write books or even pamphlets, but she did deliver many informal talks that were recorded by various people. I obtained several of these audio cassettes years ago and listen to them frequently. The quotations below were taken from these tapes as I played them recently. I also recall her many words of encouragement to groups of seekers. Here are a few of Mother Millie's comments derived from her taped talks delivered in Boston, Arkansas and elsewhere.

> *"God oversees our thoughts and knows our desires, so you must realize this and desire the right things."*

> *"Don't try to bind anyone to yourself* (emotionally). *It's not going to last anyhow. We come into the world alone and go alone. You think your case will be different, but it never is."*

> *"We get stuck in the middle of our desires when we forget God. In order to free a soul from desires that are burning it, you must use the divine impulse given to you by the master."*

> *"Masters come and go of their own free will to benefit mankind with their life impulse. If your soul is near the master, you have nothing more to worry about."*

> *"God himself comes in the garb of man to lead the souls out of the tentacles of the Negative Power. Some of us are closing in on or concluding our probationary period in the world and are attuning to more divine and beautiful vibrations. Sit quietly in front of Him and enjoy the romance with the Naam* (or word)*."*

> *"If people are suffering, walk along with them and let them know that suffering is a blessing that purifies them."*

Mother Millie had much to say about meditation. Here are a few quotes:

> *"Dare to find out who you are in the stillness. Remember, you cannot use the mind in meditation because mind in the end will trap you in ego. The mind is never going to help you get through anything."*

"When you are alone with God, the Divine One will instruct you. It won't be like reading a book, because God will enlighten you without words. There is a beautiful freedom in closeness to God."

"We have been separated from the ocean of bliss and are imprisoned in body and mind. Now we have a chance to escape this prison. If we did as we are told by the master, we would go home so fast. We would get so much grace that we would be amazed."

"A longing for true awareness exists within each person and he or she cannot be satisfied until the mystery of life is solved. The question remains, how to withdraw from outside in order to receive the higher impulse from within? The master tells us how to do this and he will appear to you when you are listening to Naam (or Word).*"*

"Meditation is the hardest but finest practice of all as we travel the road to God. Listen to the Naam or Word within and it will take you upward. There is a wisdom that comes from knowing God that balances everything you do. If you can maintain a very intense meditation, you will find healing for body and mind in it."

"You have to tune yourself higher now. Don't let your mind drop into habitual patterns of neglect."

Mother Millie often cautioned her listeners about wasting time. She was especially concerned about the habit of watching television many hours each day. She believed that watching news was all right because this enabled one to know what was happening in the world. But she felt that most TV programs were a waste of time and instilled improper ideas and a calloused attitude toward violence in many people. She said: *"I have a button that turns it off."* And apparently she used this button or remote control wisely and regularly.

Mother Millie's master once told a certain lady on the West Coast that if she had spent as much time in meditation as she had watching soap operas, she would already be in the True Home. One initiate told me that watching sports events was important to him, especially football games. I asked him who won the Super Bowl in 1998. He could not tell me. I then asked him why he did not remember this if it was so very important. He had no response, but I think that he got the point. It is our attention that makes anything significant to us. If our attention is focused upon God or higher truth, things of the lower worlds lose their importance and we see things as they really are.

Many of her most profound statements were about love.

> *"If you are tired, go into the silence and look into the eyes of your master. Energy then comes in. Love is a great energy; in fact you can get young on love. You can help others if you let it flow from you."*

> *"All real Love is eternal. Infatuation, lust and possessive emotion all die. There is a difference between human affection and Divine Love. The latter sets you free, while human infatuation entangles people more deeply in karmic relationships."*

> *"That little atom of light and love is within you. If you are Love, you can walk down the street and attract so much love that you can hardly carry it home. Only divine love will lead you through avenues of service."*

Mother Millie distributed the love she received from her master in a humble way. She often commented upon how incapable she was, but these assertions were not convincing to her admirers. What was convincing and so very real was her amazing love for everyone.

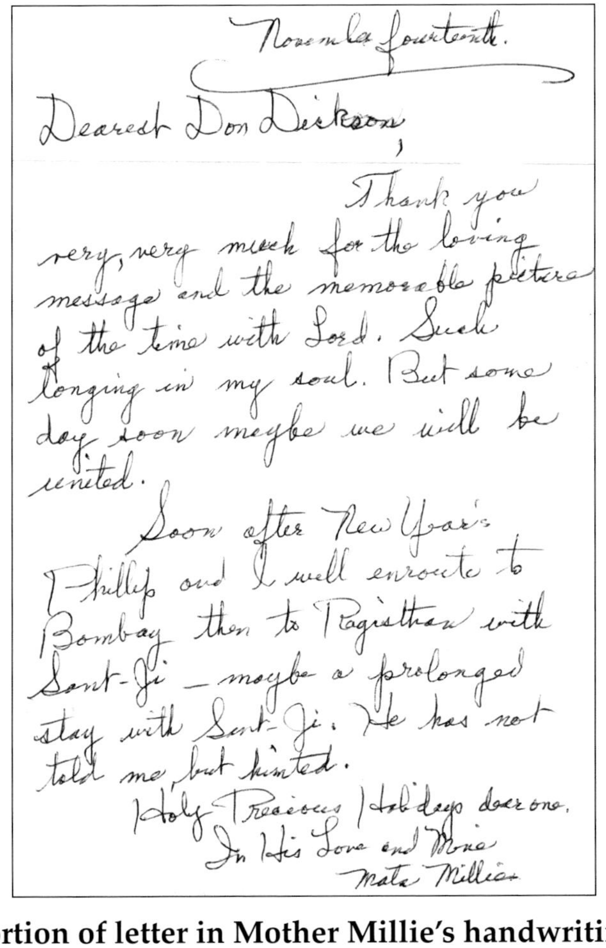

November fourteenth.

Dearest Don Dickson,

Thank you very, very much for the loving message and the memorable picture of the time with Lord. Such longing in my soul. But some day soon maybe we will be united.

Soon after New Year's Phillip and I will enroute to Bombay then to Ragisthan with Sant-Ji — maybe a prolonged stay with Sant-Ji. He has not told me, but hinted.

Holy Precious Holidays dear one.

In His Love and Mine

Mata Millie

Portion of letter in Mother Millie's handwriting.

Chapter 6

THE EASTERN SPIRITUAL TRADITION

In this chapter we will only consider a few of the more outstanding spiritual exponents from the Middle East and from the Far East. No one volume could thoroughly examine the teachings of the hundreds of great spiritual luminaries that lived and taught in these vast areas across the centuries. Greater numbers of the highest spiritual teachers have appeared in eastern contexts than in the western world, probably because many people in these regions were not as materialistic as the typical westerner and many true seekers resided in those areas. Humility and childlike simplicity are extremely common in eastern cultures. It is true that much superstition and many rituals of questionable merit permeate the intense devotion found in these nations, but it is often easier to eradicate such undesirable traits than it is to get rid of the blatant materialism and sensuality that so dominate western countries.

Whenever someone in America considers the lives and teachings of many great eastern saints, he or she faces the problem of a scarcity of competent books in English regarding them. A writer cannot adequately document the teachings of many eastern saints, and interested readers cannot easily find copies of existing publications in English. One major problem is the fact that some of the available publications were written from the perspectives of specific schools of thought and may not accurately reflect the actual teachings of the subjects that they consider. Generally religions evolve from the spiritual instructions given out by saintly souls. After a few centuries or even decades of interpretation and mythic development, such vehicles of belief assume characteristics that the founders would scarcely recognize. W. G. Orr excellently documented this fact in his fine book ***A Sixteenth Century Indian Mystic, Dadu and His Followers***. Mr. Orr contrasted the beliefs of modern followers of Dadu with the teachings expressed in his *Bani* and in early manuscripts compiled by his disciples and noted definite changes in attitude. Whereas Dadu taught love for all and endorsed peace and nonviolence, many members of the Dadu Panth, or followers of Dadu, later became armed ascetics or professional fighters. The rituals observed in the modern Dadu temples consist of several formal prostrations followed by the *Arati* or recitations from the *Bani* or holy writings of Dadu. Apparently Dadu did not endorse rites and rituals but encouraged his immediate followers to meditate, rise above the ego and maintain good will for all creatures. Rituals observed in the modern Dadu temples were formulated by his followers years after he left the physical world. The life and teachings of Dadu will be considered later in this chapter.

As we found in a consideration of the Western Spiritual Traditions, there will be much repetition of the basic ideas expressed by the several noble souls who taught those willing to listen. This is to be expected since all of them arrived to teach the same essential truths. This repetition may be considered valuable since it reinforces in our minds certain thoughts that we really need to imbibe deeply. A genuine seeker never tires of hearing words expressing Love, Peace and Truth. Such a holy conceptual mantra is of immeasurable value in instilling in each of us a desire to discover what these words really mean in realms where such concepts permeate all life.

Before we consider the lives and teachings of a few of the great spiritual luminaries of the Middle East and Far East, we will briefly appraise arguments against and for reincarnation since this concept is widely accepted in these areas. And almost all of the eastern teachers to be considered taught this precept in some detail. Certainly several of the great spiritual masters of the west did not refer to it much, if at all, probably because the subject of rebirth was not openly taught in accepted scriptures and it was not widely believed except by certain writers and poets. However, since all of the other precepts, as well as the cosmology, have been the same for spiritual teachers east or west, the subject of reincarnation deserves thoughtful consideration.

First of all, the arguments against reincarnation usually hinge upon two issues. The first is the fact that most intelligent people cannot remember having lived before; so they assume that this present life is the only one they have experienced. Of course this can be countered by asking the skeptic if he or she only believes what they personally remember. If this persons answers in the affirmative, then ask if he or she remembers being born. *"Do you recall the moment you emerged from the womb?"* Of course the person will say, *"no."* Then you reply, *"Is this evidence that you were never born, that you have always been here?"* Naturally this individual will respond that others, such as parents, were present and saw the birth, so one can prove that it happened. They may further say that it is common knowledge that every living mammal enters the world via birth. But such reasoning does not eliminate the possibility that one has lived before. Of course witnesses to such alleged past events are not easily found today because few living people claim to remember a past life, and even fewer can speak knowingly about the lives of others.

Common knowledge has never been a reliable criterion. History demonstrates that many precepts universally accepted centuries ago were inaccurate. For example, it was "*obvious*" to most people in the year 1000 that the earth was flat and that the sun moved around this earth on a regular basis. Today everyone knows that this is not true. At this same time it was commonly believed that Bubonic Plague and other diseases were caused by "*humors in the blood*" or by dangerous "*night air.*" Now we know that bacteria, viruses, fungi, parasites and harmful habits are involved in such maladies and that improper sanitation and insect or animal hosts are responsible for spreading most of these pathogens. Many biologists and bacteriologists in the Nineteenth Century believed in the spontaneous generation of microorganisms even after Louis Pasteur presented evidence that they were wrong. A fierce debate ensued between Pasteur and the French biologist Felix Pouchet (1800-1872) and the English bacteriologist Henry Bastion (1837-1915). Pouchet and Bastion maintained that instances of spontaneous generation of bacteria could be found, while Pasteur argued that they were mistaken (**Funk and Wagnalls 1986: 189**). So it is easy to see that a consensus of opinion at a given time is no guarantee of accuracy. In fact we are probably wrong in regard to many of our cherished beliefs today. The fact that reincarnation is commonly accepted in modern Buddhist, Hindu, Sikh and other belief systems or ways of life does not prove it is true either. One must move beyond culturally induced opinions to a higher level of probability. The great scientist Thomas H. Huxley (1825-1895) once said that only a hasty thinker would denounce reincarnation on the grounds of inherent absurdity **(Head and Cranston** 2000:369). And he added: *"Like the doctrine of evolution itself, that of transmigration has its roots in the world of reality; and it may claim such support as the great argument from analogy is capable of supplying."* While Huxley may not have believed personally in rebirth, he was a sufficiently deep thinker to acknowledge that the concept was rational. David Darling in his book ***Zen Physics*** **(1996)** was quite specific when he said: *"some form of reincarnation is logically inescapable."*

The second argument against reincarnation, at least by Christians, Jews and Moslems, is that their scriptures do not teach this doctrine. Scriptures in other religions certainly do. But we sometimes forget that scriptures are not scientific textbooks and that all of them are open to various interpretations. That is why so many divisions exist in each of the major religions. While all scriptures should be respected, each of us should be aware of what they were intended to accomplish in the areas where they were introduced. God sent each group of people doctrines that they could understand and accept at a given time.

Let us consider the Bible first. We will appraise the several references to be mentioned in the order in which they appear in the scripture. Many of the Old Testament prophets were sent into the world with the mission of warning sinners and encouraging repentance. These messengers were not obliged to teach cosmology or refined spiritual precepts. However, the story in **Ezekiel 37** of the prophet in the valley of dry bones suggests both resurrection and rebirth. Ezekiel was shown a valley full of very dry bones, apparently from the bodies of once living people of the house of Israel. He was told to prophesy to these bones that the Lord was going to enrobe them in flesh again and cause them to live once more. He would thus rescue them from the grave of death. Also, a verse such as **Malachi 4:5** seems to suggest that Elijah would live more than once. The verse says: *"Behold, I will send you Elijah the prophet before the great and terrible day of the Lord come."* Since Elijah (or Elias) had already lived among the Jews, this could only mean rebirth of this entity. Jesus implies the same connotation in Matthew 11:11-15 when he says: *"For all the prophets and the law prophesied until John. And if ye will receive it, this* (John) *is Elias which was for to come. He that hath ears to hear, let him hear."* This is further affirmed in **Matthew 17:9-13** where Jesus makes it absolutely clear that John the Baptist was the Old Testament Prophet Elijah (or Elias). Since the scribes of Jesus' time taught that Elijah would reappear before the Messiah (or Son of Man) was revealed, Jesus wanted it to be understood that John was the reborn Elijah and that He Jesus was the true Messiah. To interpret this passage otherwise is to assert that the prophecies of the Bible were unreliable or that Jesus was not the Messiah. Although John denied being Elijah when questioned by the Jews (**John 1:21-27**), in his life as John he was not that prophet since he was acting in a different capacity. It is also possible that he simply did not remember his life as Elijah, but Jesus knew that John had been this prophet and stated so with great clarity.

In **Matthew 16:13-14** (also **Mark 8:27**), Jesus came into the coasts of Caesarea Phillipi where he asked his disciples *"Who do men say that I the Son of man am?"* They replied, *"Some say that thou art John the Baptist, some Elias, and others Jeremias or one of the prophets."* This is clear evidence that many people of Jesus' day believed in rebirth. In fact some rabbis taught it. Rabbi Manassa, in his book ***Nishmath Hayem*** wrote: *"The belief in transmigration of souls is a firm and infallible dogma accepted by the whole assemblage of our church with one accord."* Of course all Jewish peoples did not agree with the opinions of certain rabbis.

St. Paul, in **Romans 9:10-13**, refers to Jacob and Esau, saying that the Lord loved one and hated the other before they were born into the world. If God is impartial, and if the souls were just created, how could He hate one and love another? There would have to be a reason for this, otherwise one must believe that the deity mentioned in the Bible is capricious and unfair. Some form of pre-existence must have taken place for the Lord to consider Jacob and Esau so differently.

In **Ephesians 1:4** the Apostle Paul states that the Disciples of Christ had been blessed with spiritual blessings in heavenly places before the foundation of the world so they would be holy and blameless as disciples. Upon what basis was this predestination formulated? God had to have had a logical reason for choosing these souls, and what would be more sensible than basing His choice upon their earlier life experiences. He knew that they were pure because they had lived noble or pure lives in the past.

Some fundamentalists use **Hebrew 9:27** to refute reincarnation. This verse says, *"It is appointed unto men once to die, but after this the judgment."* But this scripture does not state what happens after the judgment. Certainly many believers assume that the judged soul is sent either to heaven or hell. But it is also possible that the soul is prepared for another life on earth or elsewhere. Dr. Newton in his book ***Journey of Souls*** **(2002)** offers evidence that this certainly can take place. Using the Bible as a reference, a person cannot disprove the concept of reincarnation.

In **Revelation 3:12** one finds: *"Him that overcometh will I make a pillar in the temple of my God, and he shall go out no more."* How could one "go out," and where would the soul go, unless this was into another life experience?

Revelation 13:10 states the law of cause and effect concisely in these words: *"He that leadeth into captivity shall go into captivity: he that killeth with the sword must be killed with the sword. Here is the patience and faith of the saints."* This would be difficult to happen if each person only lived one time, because it is obvious that some people who have killed in this life did not face death in the same manner. And of course a sword even in some hell could not kill the spirit. The only way that this verse can be true is for one to reincarnate in some place where physical death is possible.

Many scholars believe that certain biblical teachings were changed or removed by early Roman leaders (such as Helena or Theodora, wives of Constantius I, or even by Constantine the Great) when very few copies of the Gospels were available. The book of Revelation was not altered because of the curse in **Revelation 22:19** on anyone who modified the book. At the time of Constantine (A.D. 313-335) the Christian faith was divided between Arianism, favored in the East, and Orthodox Catholicism, promoted in the West. Enthusiastic theologians and bishops in both traditions offered differing interpretations of Christian doctrines, causing fragmentation of the church (**Vagi 1999:457**). In his monumental ***The History of the Church from Christ to Constantine,*** the early historian **Eusebius (1995:108-109)** indicated that there was much disagreement among the early church fathers regarding which epistles were authentic and which were spurious. Personal opinion dictated the attitude each authority had regarding these many religious manuscripts. Eusebius attributes most of the generally accepted Christian concepts to the writings of the Apostle Paul.

Just as many contemporaries of Jesus accepted the concept of reincarnation, many early Christian leaders of the Fifth and Sixth Centuries apparently believed it too. If this were not so, why did the Emperor Justinian declare belief in reincarnation to be a heresy at the Council of Constantinople in A.D. 553? **(Head and Cranston 2000:51)**.

The Koran was written to warn people to avoid idolatry, live righteous lives and follow the injunctions given by Allah through the Prophet Mohammed. In **Surah III** it is clear that Allah will punish wrongdoers in the world and hereafter. **Surah XXXIX** speaks of the day of resurrection, but this seems to be a reference to a judgment day when the good are rewarded and evil sinners are punished. Simply put, the Koran seems to be a message sent via the Prophet Mohammed to warn sinners about the effects of negative thoughts and bad deeds. Its message, like much of the Old Testament in the Bible, does not include reincarnation. On the other hand, it does not explicitly say it cannot happen.

Some of the Sufi saints and poets certainly are very specific in endorsing reincarnation. Such Sufi mystics as Jalalu 'D-Din Rumi and Sharf-U'Din Maneri are clear on this subject **(Head and Cranston 2000:74-75)**. Of course orthodox Muslims do not accept the concepts of Sufi poets and teachers any more than the Catholic Church embraces all of the precepts of St. John of the Cross or Meister Eckhart. Writings of the great poet Rumi will be considered later in this book.

Reincarnation does offer a rational explanation for much of life as we find it. If all people are *"created"* equal at conception or at birth, then all should be born the same way and be given comparable opportunities in this world. The Bible assures us that God is no respecter of persons and tells us that God is Love. If these statements are true, then why is one person born in opulence as a member of a wealthy family while another is barely able to keep body and soul together due to abject poverty? Why does one individual have good health over a lifetime of maybe 90 or more years while another is sickly and in misery throughout the 20 years that he or she resides in a deformed body? Why are some people born in a place where God's truth is allegedly taught, while another person is reared in a nation where superstition abounds? And of course why does one individual seem to thrive in spite of living a wicked and dissolute life, while a saintly individual with high moral and ethical standards faces one tragedy after another? These things are simply not explained by asserting that *"it is the will of God that they happen."* The verse already quoted in Revelation 13:10 as well as the assertion *"as ye sow so shall ye reap,"* imply that God is fair and that people in all worldly conditions are reaping what they have sown somewhere and at some time. Reincarnation may logically explain why some apparently innocent people suffer a great deal in this life.

It is certainly possible that some individuals now living on earth have never incarnated here before. But they have lived somewhere, because souls were not created at birth. People could have resided on other planets in this physical dimension, or they could have had one or more incarnations in the astral or causal planes before being born into this world. Also, there is the factor of the angelic (or devic) evolution. Frequently, a soul may move from the angelic or devic evolutionary track to the human pathway for a different range of experiences. Laws of cause and effect operate in causal, astral and physical dimensions and regulate both human and angelic conditions.

We often wonder why victims of wars and natural disasters, such as hurricanes, earthquakes, tsunamis and other severe floods have to face death or a loss of property. Although these tragedies usually occur under the laws of cause and effect, it is probably best that we do not know why each effect takes place the way it does because this knowledge might cause us to rationalize *"they deserved it"* or *"it is a karmically induced event."* This is a wrong attitude for any of us to have. We should maintain compassion and love for all people regardless of any past mistakes that they have made, for a callous attitude would be a flaw on our part. It is safe to say that each of us has erred many times, so none of us is in a position to judge the faults of others. But each of us does have an obligation to forgive and forget the blunders or poor judgments of the people that we meet and hope that those who know us are willing to disregard our mistakes.

Certain people will argue that it is unfair if many individuals cannot remember why they are being punished. The answer is that forgetfulness is a characteristic of this lower world and the Negative Power does not want people to remember their past lives so he can keep them in his domain. Of course the higher nature, the real person, does recall all past experiences and knows why a certain crop is being reaped at a given time. **Dr. Michael Newton (2002:68)** writes: *"Our eternal identity never leaves us alone in the bodies we choose, despite our current status. In reflection, meditation, or prayer, the memories of who we really are do filter down to us in selective thought each day. In* *small intuitive ways—through the cloud of amnesia—we are given clues for the justification of our being."*

It can be emphatically stated that the higher levels of mind never forget anything as long as an entity employs the mind. For example, if you use hypnotic regression to ask an adult what he or she was doing at 3:14 PM on his or her third birthday, the one under hypnosis can tell you exactly what occurred. If older adults who remember the birthday party are present, they may verify that the recollection is correct. The one under hypnosis remembers such events because all thoughts and recollections are stored in subconscious levels of mind and the hypnotic state allows the attention to retrieve this data. Certainly some hypnotists allegedly have used regression procedures to enable various subjects to recall past life experiences. Dr. Michael Newton in his book ***Journey of Souls*** **(2002)** presents a series of case studies of earlier lives apparently remembered via regression and even tells of experiences souls had between lives.

While regression therapy unquestionably can be of value in treating problems related to this present life, such as trauma experienced in childhood, one must be careful even in dealing with childhood situations to prevent the hypnotist from unintentionally suggesting certain things that may then seem real to the patient. A critical evaluation of all regression procedures is in order. The astute student should neither gullibly accept such data without question, nor should this person blatantly relate it to the realm of superstition without thoughtful study. The assertion by some fundamentalists that Satan induces all of these experiences and memories is not rational since any poorly understood phenomena could be attributed to a negative source. Humanity would never progress if it refused to assess things it did not understand for fear that it might be of the devil. While I certainly agree that a Negative Power does exist, such an entity is all too often a scapegoat for our own weaknesses, and we do not place the blame where it actually belongs. As the cartoon character Pogo once said: *"We have met the enemy and he is us."* While the sentence is grammatically incorrect, the inherent concept is quite true. We seldom blame ourselves for our own weaknesses but try to dredge up an excuse for our actions. A commonly expressed reason for negative behavior is *"the Devil made me do it."* But we tend to forget that no negative power can deceive a pure heart and loving soul who sincerely seeks the truth. Fear only leads us into bondage and despair. Remember the words of **II Timothy 1:7:** *"God hath not given us the spirit of fear; but of power, and of love, and of a sound mind."* As it says in I John 4:18, *"Perfect love casts out fear."* So we can all order Satan to take a walk out of our lives.

Maulana Rumi

Maulana Rumi (1207-1273)

Why should I seek? I am the same as He. His essence speaks through me. I have been looking for myself.

If you put your heart against the earth with me, in serving every creature, our Beloved will enter you from our sacred realm and we will be so happy.

Maulana Rumi

The great mystic poet Rumi was born in Balkh, Afghanistan September 30, 1207. When he was about ten years of age, Rumi's parents fled from the invading Mongol armies and immigrated to Konya, Turkey. His father, Bahauddin Walad, was a mystically oriented theologian who had unusual visionary experiences. Apparently he had a former student, Buranuddin Mahaqqiq, instruct Rumi in the mystical precepts that he followed. After his father passed away, Rumi became a sheikh in the dervish community at Konya. At this time he lived the typical life of a religious scholar and teacher until 1244 when he met the wandering dervish, Shams of Tabriz, and became enraptured with his deep spiritual nature. They spent months together in ecstatic communication and deep meditation until Shams suddenly disappeared. It is then that Rumi became a mystical poet (**Barks 1997**, introduction).

When Rumi heard that Shams was in Damascus, he sent his son, Sultan Velad, to Syria to ask Shams to return. He did and stayed for some time in Rumi's home until December 5, 1248 when he again vanished. Rumi searched for him, even traveling to Damascus. It was there that he realized their unity and wrote (as translated by **Barks 1997**):

Why should I seek? I am the same as he.
His essence speaks through me.
I have been looking for myself.

Rumi then titled the collection of his odes and quatrains T***he Works of Shams of Tabriz*** **(Barks 1997,** introduction).

After Shams of Tabriz passed on, Rumi addressed many of his poems to a close friend Saladin Zarkub, and when Saladin died, Husam Chelebi became the close associate of Rumi. The latter dictated the six volumes of his masterpiece *Mathnawi (*or *Masnavi)* to Husam, whom Rumi claimed was the only living person that understood it. The great mystic poet died on December 17, 1273. (**Barks 1997**, introduction).

The importance of Rumi as a poet is widely acknowledged throughout the east and in the western world also. Those who understand his symbolism and unique use of metaphor also recognize his spiritual stature. In Persia (now Iran) and in Afghanistan Maulana Rumi is known as "Jelaluddin Balkhi."

Many of those who have inquired into the life of Rumi have misunderstood his intense relationship with Shams of Tabriz. Actually it is a classic example of the spiritual love that exists between a great spiritual master and a devoted disciple. This love was a force beyond the physical, emotional and even mental worlds; it was a union of spirit far above realms of gender and emotion. Only one who has been guided by a genuine Saint and has realized the greatness of his mentor can understand the relationship that existed between Shams of Tabriz and his devoted disciple Maulana Rumi.

The poetry of Rumi was a spontaneous outpouring from an inner source as is all truly inspired verse. Rumi said that he never knew what he was going to say and didn't plan it. His lines simply gushed forth in highly symbolic words. Often he used mundane situations to symbolize spiritual truths. For example, the tavern was often looked upon as a divine center where the wine of spirituality intoxicated the seeker. He often spoke of being so drunk with a divine elixir that he forgot who he was and where he belonged. Early in his career Rumi pondered the question of his real identity in these words:

"All day I think about it, then at night I say it.
Where did I come from and what am I supposed to be doing?
I have no idea. My soul is from elsewhere, I'm sure of that,
And I intend to end up there. . .
Who looks out through my eyes? What is the soul?
I cannot stop asking. . .
I didn't come here of my own accord, and I can't leave that way.
Whoever brought me here will have to take me home."

(Barks 1997:2)

Several scholars have translated the works of Rumi into English. Reynold Nicholson translated ***The***

Mathnawi of Jalaluddin Rumi in eight volumes (1925-1940). A.J. Arberry translated his ***Mystical Poems of Rumi*** as part of the Persian Heritage Series (no. 23) and also translated part of the Rubaiyat in his 1949 work, ***The Rubaiyat of Jalal al-din Rumi: Select Translations into English Verse***. Coleman Barks consulted the translations of John Moyne and others to produce his work, ***The Essential Rumi* (1997)**. Later he translated more of Rumi's poetry into English in ***The Soul of Rumi* (2001)**. Lekh R. Puri (1940) translated short passages from Rumi in his book, ***Mysticism, the Spiritual Path***. Puri first states the passage in the original Persian and beneath this places his translation. This enables a scholar conversant with Persian to see what words were translated as well as the translation.

The free style translations of Barks (after Moyne) have been used in this consideration of Rumi more than any other available versions of his works. This is because the Barks' translations seem to depict the imagery and essence of Rumi's spiritual expressions quite favorably. Since it is so difficult to reproduce the poetical and musical qualities of Rumi's verse and retain a close approximation of his original meaning, as some have tried, this writer chooses accuracy of translation over poetic expression. Of course the reason for this is the fact that this work is attempting to show that the basic essence of all mystical writing, east or west, is the same. In the case of Rumi, one has to dig through a mass of juxtaposed ideas to sort out specific themes. And one has to be very perceptive because many of Rumi's concepts are expressed symbolically.

Unlike other master teachers who have written extensively about the nature of the Supreme Being, Rumi says little about the highest spiritual essence, although he mentions the word *"God"* often. The reader has to search diligently for the occasional reference to the divine nature. More than anything else he associates God with Love. Rumi suggests that God is the sky that his spirit soars in, the love inside of love, and the place of true resurrection. These concepts are expressed in the poem *"I Have Five Things to Say"* **(Barks 1997:9)**. In this same poem Rumi says that he has been searching for God ever since he was separated from Him. Just as the famous female mystic, Rabia of Basra (d. A.D. 801) sought for God while shedding tears, Rumi sought the divine as he wept and cried out in poetic lines. A persistent metaphor in Rumi is the tavern of God where divine love is imbibed. This quality of God opens up the vast inner nature of the lover who becomes so intoxicated that he or she dances in perpetual delight. Rumi concluded that God was Love and the way to God was via Love. In fact, Love was Rumi's formula for vanishing into God. He insisted that lovers have no fear because *"Love is a quality of God."* Fear dominates those who think that they serve the Divine but who are preoccupied with sex and other worldly things that they inwardly sense will soon end (**Barks 1997:179**). *"Love so needs to love that it will endure almost anything, even abuse, just to flicker for a moment"* (**Ladinsky 2002:76**). If love that has plunged into time is so ecstatic, what can one say about the divine love that reigns beyond time and space? Rumi states that such a love has taken away his (spiritual) practices and filled him with poetry, and so he has to dance and sing. He then adds that *"Love is the reality and poetry is the drum that calls us to that."* (**Barks 1997:104**). Many saints have expressed themselves poetically because such utterances have great effect upon pure and sensitive souls. One can relate Rumi's assertions to higher reality because many mystics have mentioned that the sounds of drum and thunder resound in the Causal Plane around the sun of Brahm. According to Rumi, enlightened poetry makes one sensitive to the Divine Word or creative sound and light. He then added: *"Behold thou the midnight Sun, then shall I speak to thee. In that dawn there is no difference between day and night."* (**Puri 1940:44**). Love enables one to experience these sounds and sights.

Rumi alludes to the Word or Voice of God, so praised by other mystics, in many of his lines. However, a reader must be conversant with the cosmology stated by most spiritual adepts in order to recognize these allusions. For example, a flute-like sound is said to permeate the realm Moslem mystics call Anahu (Sohang among Sikh gurus). **Puri (1940:57)** states that Rumi begins his **Masnavi** from this stage and translates the first few lines as:

Oh listen what story the flute narrateth,
of separation doth it complain.
Ever since from the reeds was I cut off,
men and women have wailed.

On the other hand, Barks (1997:17) translates these same lines as *"The Reed Flute's Song"* in these words:

Listen to the story told by the reed
of being separated.
"Since I was cut from the reedbed,
I have made this crying sound."

Elsewhere in this poem as translated by Barks, Rumi states that few can hear the secrets hidden within the flute notes or hear the love-fire tangled within them. The one who secretly hears the song of this flute dwells above senses and swims in an awesome ocean of grace. In the poem *"Each Note"* (**Barks 1997:103**) Rumi tells us what causes this song of the flute. He says, *"God picks up the reed-flute world and blows."* In other words this song is a musical expression of God that can be heard in the mosque of the body. This mosque is not built of stone but via wisdom and intelligent action. Solomon (the wise man) goes there every morning and gives guidance with words and musical harmonies. (See **Barks 1997:191**, *"The Far Mosque"*). But one must rise above the physical consciousness to hear the internal Word. Rumi put it this way: *"Bring the firmament under thy feet, oh brave man, and listen to the melodious song coming from above"* (**Puri 1940:149**). In this way one dies to the world and awakens in the Divine. Says Rumi, *"I placed one foot on the wide plain of death, and some grand immensity sounded on the emptiness. I have felt nothing ever like the wonder of that moment"* **(Barks 2001:96)**. In another place he said, *"See into the region beyond phenomena, and all of the questions you ask will dissolve into love within love"* **(Barks 2001:343)**.

The importance of the Master Teacher was stressed by the way Rumi associated with his teacher Shams of Tabriz. In the words of Rumi, translated by ***Barks*** **(1997: 254)** as *"A Basket of Bread,"* Rumi asks if one can do good work without a teacher. Then he continues by adding that one needs the presence of a Master. *"Even the lowest livelihood requires some instruction."* And whenever one meets a genuine spiritual teacher, the seeker should be gentle, polite and eager to obtain answers. It matters not if the Master wears threadbare clothing, because that does not diminish his mastery. Let me tell you *"Lovers of God,"* he asserted, *"a human being becomes a way for grace to come through"* **(Barks 1997:188)**. And he associated his human teacher with the wonderful creative sounds that permeate higher worlds. Rumi suggests that we rarely hear the inner music, but nevertheless we dance to its strains as directed by our teacher, the music master. The effects of the Master-disciple relationship were eloquently expressed. Rumi stated that when he was with Shams of Tabriz they stayed up all night, and when Shams was away, he could not sleep. He continued with the couplet: *"Praise God for these two insomnias and the difference between them!"* **(Barks 1997:106)**. Like God, the real teacher works without hands or feet in spiritual realms, and "without speaking he gives lessons to his disciples" **(Puri 1940:212)**.

Rumi tells us that we should search for a genuine spiritual teacher and then put away all pride of learning, position, and wealth. Talking a lot, reading books and even practicing difficult disciplines by themselves will not help us. We should *"put on humble clothes"* and become friends with a Master (sheikh) if we want spiritual poverty or emptiness and inner illumination **(Barks 1997:255)**. Rumi said that all of us are prisoners (in the body) awaiting death except for that brave soul (or Master) whose body is in prison but whose conscious soul is in heaven **(Puri 1940:369)**.

The importance of meditation is a theme postulated by all spiritual masters. Rumi suggests that one should meditate with steadfastness and clarity and *"let those be the wings that lift and soar through the celestial spheres"* **(Barks 1997:185)**. Of course meditation is a job that the mind does not relish, but we should do it regularly. As Rumi put it, *"We should always ask for discipline because those who have no self-control will not receive grace from the Master."* **(Barks 1997:227)**. We should seek to expand our love and meditate upon the light revealed by our awareness of love. *"Close your eyes and surrender. Find yourself in the city of God"* **(Barks 2001:227)**.

Although Rumi resided in a region where the Muslim faith was the dominant religious view, he often spoke of Jesus (who is mentioned in the Koran). He said that the miracle of the son of Mary was not what he said or did but what he was. Apparently Rumi distinguished between Jesus the man and the Christ Power that permeated him. *"Christ is the population of the world,"* he stated. The implication here seems to be that every person is potentially a *"Christ"* in his or her inner nature. Rumi implies that Jesus could not understand why some did not respond, but remained cold and indifferent, when he spoke the Great Name lovingly to them **(Barks 1997:204)**.

Rumi often used what seem to be crude and sensual metaphors to shock the reader into thinking. Clearly he did not consider the normal activities of human nature to be lewd or wicked. Such actions as eating, sleeping or sexual involvement were in themselves not vulgar or sinful. It was the abuse of such activities that was wrong. Eating too much, sleeping an excessive amount or putting too much attention upon sexual indulgence was undesirable. In one instance he described a caliph's sensual actions with a woman in spite of the whisperings of his conscience. Physically this caliph was a strong and virile individual, but he was not mature in the eyes of Rumi, because the latter felt that the mark of true manhood was the ability to rise above sensuality **(Barks 1997:61)**. In another description of perverted sexual activities involving a sensual woman, Rumi's advice was *"Don't sacrifice your life to your animal-soul"* (or mind) **(Barks 1997:182)**.

Reincarnation is strongly implied when Rumi asserts that we have no idea where our pain is from and we do not know all that we have done. He adds that it is probably good that we do not remember, although we still have to suffer for it **(Barks 1997:60)**. Rumi concludes that God's silence is necessary because men are weak and could not stand the power and authority of His Voice. Men are also weak because of the enemy that resides within them, that is, the mind. All of our sins and failures are the result of listening to this mind instead of to the higher conscience or spirit. Rumi states that if he described the enemy within, even the most courageous would be paralyzed with fear **(Barks 1997:203)**. And yet each of us must overcome and vanquish this inner power. We do this by one-pointed or internally focused meditation. As Rumi put it, *"A good gauge of spiritual health is to write down the three things you want most. If they in any way differ, you are in trouble"* **(Ladinsky 2002:72)**. In other words, your desire should be for one thing: God. If you want several things, you do not have a proper objective.

Although Rumi apparently taught the same truths that all Master Teachers gave out to the world, he did so in his own unique manner. Just as ice cream comes in many flavors, yet all of it is ice cream, each spiritual teacher who has visited earth has described the distinctive *"flavor"* of the divinity he or she has tasted via inner experience.

Many mystics have incarnated in the Middle East, especially in the Sufi tradition. We have already mentioned Shams of Tabriz, the teacher of Maulana Rumi. There was also Khwaja Hafiz (1325-1390), a great poet and Persian saint of Shiraz (now in Iran). Other saints from areas dominated by Islam include Sheik Farid (1173-1265). a disciple of Khwaja Qutab Bakhtiyar Kaki and Rajjab (1567-1693), a Moslem seeker who became a disciple of Saint Dadu at the age of 19. He wrote many spiritual poems and collected the works of many saints in a large volume known as *Sarbangi*. There was also Sheikh Sadi (1184-1291) a Sufi saint of Persia and author of *Gulistan* and *Bostan*. And of course the great female mystic Rabia of Basra who died in A.D. 801. It is difficult to find authoritative descriptions of the lives and teachings of many of these great souls, and there would not be room in this volume to include all of them even if adequate reference works were available. We will now consider the great Saint Kabir who bridged the gap between the various faiths existing in the Middle East and the Far East.

Kabir

Kabir (1398-1518)

Religion devoid of love is heresy.

Where there is love there is no law.
Love knows neither ritual nor reason.

Kabir

The Medieval Saint Kabir is one of the best-known and venerated of India's great spiritual teachers. The legend of his life has been passed down through oral traditions for over 400 years, and his teachings and hymns are included in the scriptures of several religious sects. Although many orthodox Moslems and Hindu believers reject Kabir's spiritual precepts, millions of humble villagers throughout India and adjacent nations embrace his spiritual teachings and consider them to be part of their own beliefs. Therefore it is difficult to distinguish the original Kabir and his message from the accretions added by enthusiastic devotees who have amended his life and teachings to harmonize with their personal beliefs. However, most of these additions probably relate more to Kabir's life and social situation than to the teachings expressed in the poetry attributed to the great saint.

There is much disagreement among biographers regarding details of Kabir's early life, partly because the earliest accounts of his activities and teachings did not divulge much about his parents, birth, youth, caste or even about his teacher. These works do not indicate whether Kabir was married or single, whether he had children or not, or even suggest where and when he died. The earliest existing mention of Kabir is by Nabhadas, a devotee who wrote a poetic account of various saintly men in his ***Bhaktamal***, a volume that was completed in 1585 A.D. Nabhadas simply tells us that Kabir did not accept caste distinctions, the orthodox religious doctrines taught by six schools of Indian philosophy, rites and rituals of the various sects, popular yogic practices and such ascetic disciplines as fasting and pilgrimages to holy places. *"Religion devoid of love is heresy,"* he said, and added *"fasting and alms-giving are, without meditation, empty"* **(Sethi 1984:4)**. The short account of Kabir given by Nabhadas is probably an accurate but abbreviated depiction of his personality and teachings.

Over the next several centuries the followers of Kabir, known as Kabir-panthis, added such popular accretions as an Immaculate Conception, or they presented the notion that Kabir descended from heaven on a shaft of light and assumed the form of a child on the lotus leaves of a pond. Various legendary stories of such miracles as raising the dead, healing the sick and creating an abundance of food from a few loaves of bread apparently were expounded at this time. Some of these concepts may have been adopted from accounts of the miracles of Jesus **(Ezekiel 1979: xiii)**. Some commentators even tried to imply that Kabir was of Hindu lineage or the son of high caste parents. The motives behind such inventions apparently were to avoid admitting that a great saint was born in a family of low caste and also to assimilate the great Kabir into the Hindu religious fold.

The most reliable information available suggests that Kabir was born in North India about 1398 as the son of a poor Muslim weaver named Niru and his wife Nima. Religious custom dictated that Niru go to a local Muslim priest who would select a name for his son from the Koran. This qazi opened the holy book at random and found the name Kabir, an Arabic word that means *"The Most High."* Unwilling to confer such an exalted name upon a poor weaver's son, the priest again opened the Koran and once more came upon the epithet for God, and so the name was given. While some scholars doubt this account's reliability, this was a common naming procedure at the time of Kabir's birth and it is difficult to imagine that any parents at this time would have conferred such a name on their own child.

Although Kabir probably did not have a formal education because he was of a low caste, he obviously had a discerning intellect and a strong spiritual inclination as a youth. In his childhood he learned weaving techniques and made weaving his profession in life. Apparently he did not write on paper the many poems attributed to him but composed them orally as songs that were memorized by his disciples and then committed to writing. As Kabir put it in one poem, *"Paper would turn to flame if I touched it in an ecstatic mood. And ink dries if it comes within a hundred feet of the radiance of one who will not let God leave (his) arms."* **(Ladinsky: 2002:209)**.

His introspective nature and tendency to spend much time in spiritual contemplation as an adolescent annoyed his parents, but a loving disposition and mild manners endeared him to them anyhow. His compassion as a youth is reflected in the account by **Sethi (1984:8)** of how a young Kabir begged his father not to sacrifice an animal at a religious festival, and how the father finally gave in to the tearful pleas of his son and released the animal.

No contemporary accounts tell us whether Kabir was married or single. However, Priyadas in 1645 stated that Kabir was married and the ***Parichai of Anantdas*** (A.D. 1595) implies that Kabir had a family. Oral traditions state that his wife was named Loi, that a son was called Kamal, and a daughter was named Kamali **(Sethi 1984:13). Ezekiel (1979:14)** says that the Sikh scriptures indicate that Kabir was married twice. After his first wife died, he married Loi, a girl that he met in a forest hermitage. She gave birth to his two children. In order to support the acetic life style that some Brahmin yogis endorse, various legends regarding the miraculous arrival of his children evolved. Since many great saints had sons and daughters, none of these stories need be taken seriously.

Ladinsky (2002:211) said that Kabir lived in a crude shack in a very poor section of town where several butchers had their shops. This challenged the attitudes of his Hindu disciples who were strict vegetarians. Since all Masters of recent times have been vegetarians, Kabir probably was too; he simply chose to live in such an environment to attract only those disciples who could sincerely see beyond mundane circumstances. A true seeker will look only at the inner spiritual nature of a teacher and discard the opinions of those who are concerned with outer appearances.

Both **Ezekiel (1979:16)** and **Sethi (1984:15)** relate an incident in the life of Kabir that may well have happened. When several sadhus visited Kabir's home one evening, the saint asked his wife to prepare food for them. Loi told him that she had neither food nor money to purchase it. So Kabir asked her to go to a nearby grocer and procure the food on credit. The grocer was infatuated by Loi's beauty and told her that he would give her the requested food if she would come back that night and indulge with him. She went home and told Kabir and he suggested that she accept the conditions. So Loi brought home the provisions and the sadhus were fed very well. After the sadhus left, it began raining, so Kabir carried Loi to the grocer's home on his shoulders. When the grocer opened the door, he noticed that neither Kabir nor Loi were wet. The expression of purity on her face and the presence of Kabir made the grocer ashamed of his immoral mind and he begged for forgiveness. Legend has it that he later became a disciple of Kabir. This incident, whether actual or a later fabrication, certainly is indicative of the methods that a saint might use to convert a sinner to spiritual living.

The honesty of Kabir is depicted in various accounts. One of the most memorable events happened while he was yet a youth. He was sent to the market to sell cloth, but no one purchased his product at the low price that was asked. A salesman decided to help him so he yelled out: *"Excellent cloth, going very cheap, only twelve takas!"* A crowd gathered around and someone bought the cloth for eleven takas. But Kabir would only take five takas since that is what he thought was a fair price **(Sethi 1984:16)**.

One of the great stories about Kabir, told by many later saints, was the account of a proud Brahmin scholar who had defeated many of his most learned contemporaries in theological debates. He then changed his name to *"Sarvajit,"* which means *"the conqueror of all."* His mother, an initiate of Kabir, told him that she would consider him a conqueror only if he defeated Kabir in a debate. So her proud son loaded up a bullock cart with books and went to the home of Kabir. The latter told him that he was honored by the visit of so great a scholar and added that he had never seen so many books before. When Sarvajit offered to debate him, Kabir acknowledged that he could not debate one so learned, so he admitted defeat. Sarvajit then asked him to write a note saying that he had defeated Kabir in debate. However, Kabir suggested that Sarvajit write the note and he would sign it. So he wrote, *"Sarvajit has defeated Kabir"* on a piece of paper and Kabir added his name. When he got home, he proudly showed his mother the paper, only now it read, *"Kabir has defeated Sarvajit."* He returned and obtained a second note, but it read the same when he returned home. Sarvajit then accused Kabir of being a magician, but his mother told him that Kabir was truly humble and that arrogance could never defeat humility **(1984 Sethi:21)**. Later it is said that Sarvajit realized the greatness of Kabir and became his disciple.

Once in his travels Kabir met a devotee who claimed that whenever he sat in meditation and remembered Lord Krishna, he saw his teacher dancing before him. Kabir asked him to meditate in his presence, so the holy man closed his eyes and as he was watching Krishna dance, Kabir told him to catch hold of his hand when he came near. The form of Krishna tried to release himself from the grip of his devotee and in the struggle the holy man opened his eyes to see that he had firmly grasped one of his own hands with the other. Kabir then told him that what he had been seeing was a projection of his own mind, an illusion. He added that if the entity he had seen was real, he would have spoken to him, answered questions and would have taken him into higher spiritual regions. Kabir told the holy man that he could not visualize someone he had never actually seen and that forms created by his mind could not give him competent guidance **(Sethi 1984:25)**.

There are dozens of interesting stories about the alleged activities of Kabir. Some of these are probably based upon fact but enhanced by centuries of relating the event. Enthusiastic devotees probably created others long after the lifetime of Kabir. It is difficult today to distinguish between the actual happenings and the fabricated ones. **Sethi (1984)** relates many of these alleged incidents.

During his lifetime, Kabir had many followers including two famous disciples. One of these was Dharamdas, a wealthy worshipper of several idols. After a series of frustrating experiences involving manifestations of Kabir, Dharamdas finally realized that his rituals and devotion to idols were useless and he became a disciple of Kabir. The second famous disciple was Ibrahim Ibn Adham, the king of Balkh Bokhara. He is the subject of Leigh Hunt's much-admired poem *"Abou Ben Adhem."* After several perplexing experiences, the king abdicated his throne, went to India and, after he imbibed genuine humility, became a disciple of Kabir.

The subject of Kabir's guru has been debated for several hundred years. Some people say that he had no guru but was born as a perfect saint. Kabir did say that he had served as a master in earlier ages, so the idea that he had no need of spiritual guidance may be correct. Masters who have allegedly been born perfect include Jesus, Kabir, Guru Nanak, Guru Gobind Singh and Soami Ji in the east and Meister Eckhart in the west. However, most of these great masters did adopt a guru either from motives of humility or to show others that a guru is necessary for most people. Many authorities accept the concept that Ramanand was an early guru of Kabir. Ramanand, a Vaishnavite or devotee of Vishnu at Banaras, had a large following. He accepted Kabir after the latter convinced him that he had given him the mantra of *"Ram Bolo,"* or *"repeat the name of Ram"* accidentally en route to his morning bath **(Ezekiel 1979:20)**. According to later Sikh and recent teachers, Kabir ultimately became the master of Ramanand.

Some scholars in recent years have suggested that Kabir was a disciple of Sheikh Taqi (or Taqqi). Sethi (1984:9) said that these scholars have based their opinions upon Khazi-nat-ul-Asifia of Ghulam Sarvar (1868), a book that describes Sheikh Taqi as the guru of Kabir. Regardless of whom Kabir may have seemed to follow, especially early in his career, almost all commentators agree that Kabir was the greatest and most influential Saint of his time and that he exerted a powerful influence upon more recent Saints.

Modern scholars debate the year when Kabir left the physical world. Most of them accept the date of 1518 as the time of his death at the age of 120, but a few writers have advocated other dates that place his age at death between 70 and 80 years. Anyhow, when Kabir died, his disciples were shocked at the departure of their guru. Legend has it that his Muslim disciples wanted to bury the body according to their customs, while the Hindu disciples desired to cremate the body, as was their custom. A strong argument ensued until someone suggested they look at the physical form of the saint. When the cover was removed, all of them saw a heap of fragrant flowers where the body had been. These were divided into two clumps. The Hindus cremated their portion while the Muslims buried their share. Both classes of disciples had forgotten that Kabir often declared that he was neither Hindu nor Muslim, and he placed no significance upon material objects including abandoned physical bodies **(Sethi 1984:41)**.

Many passages in the writings of Kabir extol the qualities and importance of a Saint. His poem *"The Propitious Moment"* indicates that the man of God graced his home and the veil fell from his eyes as he heard the divine melody within. Says Kabir: *"I love, I adore the Saint; through his grace I found the Supreme One"* within my own body (Sethi 1984:195). In his poem, **"Bliss of Sahaj,"** Kabir says that he attained the supreme knowledge when the compassionate Master took mercy upon him. The darkness vanished before the dazzling Inner Light and *"I live in eternal repose."* The negative power, or Kal, has fled and the Peerless One is now visible **(Sethi 1984:492)**. In the poem, *"The Master's Gift,"* Kabir asserts that the Master in his mercy has given him a gift that enables him to know the Unknowable (Sethi 1984:516). In a passage translated by **Ezekiel (1979:306)** Kabir says that the Lord and the Perfect Master are one. All of the outer creation is an illusion. With the guidance of a perfect Saint he merged in the Eternal Sound (or Word) and met the Lord. Many similar passages could be quoted from the writings of Kabir, but these mentioned examples are typical of Kabir's praise of the Perfect Saint.

Of course Kabir was aware of the fact that many so-called gurus, swamis, masters, murshids, yogis and priests bear titles they have not earned by disciplined meditation. In one neat poem he suggests that one hold each teacher over the edge of a steep cliff for a few hours. If he doesn't wet his pants, you may have found a genuine spiritual adept **(Ladinsky 2002:217)**. This is because events in the objective world neither frighten nor gratify a teacher who is in harmony with the divine source of all.

During the time of Kabir much emphasis was placed upon the visiting of holy places such as sacred shrines and bathing in holy rivers. Kabir disagreed with such lower forms of devotion, saying that if one made ten trips around every holy shrine in the world, it would not get you to God as quickly as controlling your anger **(Ladinsky 2002:220)**. Kabir recommended that devotees meditate upon the Lord's Name, via repetition of this thought, and contact the Divine Word, a music that resounds within every individual at the core of their being. *"Wake up! Be aware of your true self, says Kabir: Only they gain liberation who remain absorbed in the Lord's love."* **(Sethi 1984:222)**.

Kabir asserted that without love one could not merge into ultimate divinity. This love must be for all units of the creation as well as for divine teachers and for God. He said, *"The wine of love have I drunk with avid thirst and I am intoxicated with the experience."* He then added, *"Love, love, say all, but few realize what love is. Whose heart is absorbed in love all day and night, he alone can be called a true lover."* Then he continued, *"Where there is love, there is no law. Love knows neither ritual nor reason. When (one) stays absorbed in love, who will keep count of dates and days?"* **(Sethi 1984:579-580)**. In another poem **(Sethi 1984:583)** he said that one devoid of love was like a cemetery or place of death. Such a person was *"like the bellows of a blacksmith, which breathe but have no life."*

In addition to love and self-control, Kabir advocated humility. He told how proud pundits deceived many into believing that they were messengers of God when all they did was quote scriptures and practice useless rituals. He said that the humble could not tolerate such pride. *"Those who give up pride of status and lineage and search for the Pure One destroy the shoot and seed (of error) and while yet in the body, transcend its bounds."* **(Sethi 1984:295)**. He told how religious authorities teach about a heaven that they have not seen and base this instruction upon books that they do not understand. *"They are ignorant of the mystery of their own selves,"* said Kabir, yet they describe an imaginary paradise. *"So long as a man's mind longs for heaven, he will not find abode at the feet of God"* **(Sethi 1984:467)**. This is because the attitudes most people have about heaven constitute an ego trip on their parts. They see themselves being rewarded with eternal bliss because they believe correctly, while they imagine that others will descend into a place of punishment because they did not accept the one and only *"genuine faith"*.

Kabir also attacked selfish greed. He said that he did not think there was such a thing as an intelligent person with superfluous wealth. *"For who with a fine mind can look out upon this world and hoard what could nourish a thousand souls?"* **(Ladinsky 2002:221)**. Hoarding material things is a product of desire and attachment. It shows a lack of security and wisdom, since the wealthy individual believes that his or her money will provide safety in an unstable world. However, accumulators of property and money can take none of this wealth with him or her at the time of death, and such persons deceive themselves when they allow greed to dominate their behaviors. Said Kabir, *"Only when you abandon harboring desires will you enjoy* (higher) *bliss. All diseases are centered in desire."* So be detached, eliminate desires and obtain a release from this uncertain world. **(Ezekiel 1979:285)**.

The essence of Kabir's teachings was that God was within each individual and that the Almighty could be approached by purification of the inner nature under the guidance of a competent teacher. As he put it, "The one for whom you search in all corners of the world is within your own body, but the veil of illusion covers your (inner) eye. Wake up and realize Him. When I met the Master, I became cool within, alleviating desire. Night and day I float with joy in the ocean of bliss, and within my own body, O Kabir, God has revealed himself" (**Sethi 1984:540-541**). In the poem *"He Is What He Is"* Kabir wonders how he can describe God and who would believe if he made an effort to do so. He finally concludes that all one can do is *"Keep the Wonder that you have seen concealed within your heart, for it is beyond the reach of Vedas and Koran, and no one will believe you if you try to speak"* **(Sethi 1984:542).**

Many masters have tried to describe the Ultimate Goal or Divine State, and all of them have admitted being ashamed of their feeble descriptions. The great Shiv Dayal Singh or Soami Ji, considered later, could only utter that it was "all Love." But this is not the love spoken of by most poets and lovers. It is an indescribable state of intense divinity that is all embracing and pure. **Sethi (1984:492)** translated a portion of one of Kabir's poems called *"Bliss of Sahaj"* in these words:

Now I have attained, O friend,
I have attained supreme knowledge;
I am absorbed in the bliss of Sahaj.

When my compassionate Master took mercy on me...
The darkness of delusion vanished.

Kabir goes on to state that all fear has departed, night has fled and the Peerless One, the invisible and unknowable Source of All has manifested in the eternal bliss of sahaj. The raw nugget is now gold, the restless mind is pure and calm and he is like a drop that has merged into the ocean of love and peace.

Kabir stated that he once searched outside in the objective world, bathed in holy rivers and worshipped many deities, but all in vain. Only when he looked within did he realize his true self and then realized the Lord's identity. Now he knows the oneness that has always existed. Kabir once was lost in the wilderness of the world. Today he rejoices in the bliss of divine love.

Sethi (1984:494) concludes his translation of *Bliss of Sahaj* of Kabir with these words: He *"who contemplates within will know his own self; No longer, O Kabir, will he come and go."*

Sarmad

Sarmad (? – 1660)

If greatness as lofty as the sky is bestowed upon you,
be humble as the dust of a doormat.

Ever present in my mind's eyes is my beloved master;
this affects me every moment and cleansers my Soul.

Sarmad

The great saint Hazrat Saeed Sarmad was born of Jewish parents and in early life probably embraced the Jewish faith. Apparently he was born in Palestine where he received a good education and became a prosperous businessman. The exact year of his birth is not known. His interest in trade and enthusiasm for learning led him to India at an early age. He traded Persian and Armenian rugs for silk textiles and gold, silver and copper works in India and sold these items throughout the Middle East. **Ezekiel (1966:7)** states that Sarmad spoke and wrote Arabic, Persian, Sanskrit and Urdu in addition to his native tongue. While living in India he visited many places of pilgrimage and consulted various sadhus and holy men in a search for God. He read every religious text he could obtain and studied the religions that he encountered but to no avail. As he said: *"Men find their happiness in religion and the world; deliver me from both."* He also found no comfort in nature. As he put it, *"From the breeze my heart sought thy fragrance. From the blooming garden, this eye craved for thy vision."* Then he added, *"Grieve not in this world, nor* *seek relief in mountains and wildernesses. This world is but a mirage. Look carefully at it. It is the mere froth of a bubble"* **(Ezekiel 1966:3)**.

Sarmad had a large circle of friends and business contacts during his early years in India and achieved much financial prosperity at this time. He makes no mention in his many rubaiyats or poems what caused him to abandon his business and social interests in favor of a spiritual pilgrimage, but this apparently happened after he met a spiritual teacher named Bhikha, a saint of great stature. Then he gave up all of his material prosperity and lived in humble poverty. Sarmad stated that his master asked him to search for God within himself instead of in the outer world. As he put it, *"The light of truth I saw in my citadel; when I had renounced all, I was bathed in it"* **(Ezekiel 1966:4)**.

In modern India Sarmad is considered to have been a Muslim Saint of the highest order. This is possibly due to the fact that he quoted many Muslim mystics in his writings and because Islamic rulers dominated India during his lifetime. However, he did not embrace or teach traditional Islam but expounded a Sufistic spiritual doctrine. Because of his unorthodox life and teachings, the tyrannical emperor Aurangzeb cruelly executed him about the year A.D. 1660.

Since there are few English translations of the Rubaiyats of Sarmad, one cannot give a detailed summary of the teachings of the Jewish saint from several perspectives. **Ezekiel** (1966) has published translations of 321 of his rubaiyats. These are based upon an Urdu translation of the Persian text *Rubaiyat-e-Sarmad* as published by Munshi Sayyad Mohammed Kurban Ali Bismil. All quotations given here except one are derived from this source. However, these statements agree with the teachings of other saints from all parts of the world.

According to Sarmad God has abounding love for all units of his creation and is the source of all glory and beauty. He adds, *"Without thy grace no man can see thy hand at work"* **(Ezekiel 1966:296)**. Sarmad stressed the quality of divine forgiveness in these words: *"The almighty God, ever so compassionate, looks not at my sins and wrong doings, but maintains his reputation as the merciful one"* **(Ezekiel 1966:352)**. And yet Sarmad asserts that without the guidance and grace of his master, he could never have looked upon the light of God.

The role of the master teacher is extolled by Sarmad in beautiful poetic lines. In **Rubaiyat 111**, as translated by Ezekiel, he stresses, *"Oh Master! Thy contemplation cleans away all earthly dirt; thy virtue kills the hunting leopard pack (of passions). The master softens greed and ambition that make one stonehearted."* In **Rubaiyat 172** Sarmad declares, *"I passed my life in grief, misery and restlessness when I was ignorant of the real object of life. I could get no profit until my master made everything clear."* In **Rubaiyat 207** Sarmad exclaims, *"Oh Master, within thy power are grief and joy. But for Thee, who can relieve me of sorrow's burden. All failed me when I needed them most. Thee alone and thy gracious mercy stood by me when the world left me abandoned."* He emphasized in **Rubaiyat 242** that he had seen the foreheads of many emperors of the world, and they were furrowed with anxiety. His advice was to become a devotee of a perfect master and eliminate all fears. In fact the genuine devotee contemplates his master at all times. As Sarmad states it in Rubaiyat 285, *"Ever present in my mind's eye is my beloved master; this affects me every moment and cleanses my soul."* Although many of the Rubaiyats of Sarmad praise the master, these few quoted examples clearly express the devotion he had for the one who could introduce him to God.

Saint Sarmad spoke eloquently about love, although he admitted that most people did not understand its nature. In **Rubaiyat 147** he said: *"Seekest thou happiness in this world? Vain is thy search. Sincere love exists not here."* Only the Nam or Word can relieve your distress. Love is encountered and understood as a transcendent experience. Sarmad said **(Puri 1940:390)**, *"If you are asked 'what is love?' say thou that it is the relinquishing of one's rights (or ego)."* He stated in **Rubaiyat 157** that he had seen the light of love in his body from head to foot after discarding the ego. This reminds us of the statement of Jesus that if one's eye is single, the whole body shall be full of light **(Luke 11:34)**. But the eye can only be single if the attention rises above the lower nature. Sarmad said (in **Rubaiyat 9**) that the flag of love had been raised within him and that he only beheld radiating love. In **Rubaiyat 50** he explained that by God's love he gained everlasting truth. You are freed from all of the lower worlds when you are captured in the trap of God's love **(Rubaiyat 93)**.

Sarmad, as have all real masters, extolled humility. In **Rubaiyat 311** he stated that *"thou art ignorant of thy real self and are intoxicated with ridiculous pride. You seek earthly glory, but that is like a brief flame."* He further suggested **(Rubaiyat 279)**: *"If greatness as lofty as the sky is bestowed upon you, be humble as the dust of a doormat. Worthless as straw are all earthly things."* In **Rubaiyat 259**, he advised a spiritual seeker to abandon ego and fight the tyrant mind with an unyielding spiritual discipline in the context of humility. Spiritually lazy people believe that their schemes are more powerful or more important than such things as karmic law, but vanity is weak and cannot prevail when it comes time to reap what one has sown.

Sarmad taught that life on earth is short and that everyone must die sooner or later. In **Rubaiyat 305** he asserted that people in utter madness pursue treasures that never can be theirs. Life is an egotistical bubble drifting in the mind-stirred air. Unless one seeks for spiritual wealth, he or she is wasting time in intoxicating activities. His advice **(Rubaiyat 13)** is that one should not seek for joy among the anxieties of a transitory world. If you long for eternal happiness, abandon the world and seek for solitude. There you should meditate upon His Word and attain inner peace **(Rubaiyat 230)**. You will then reap spiritual treasures and realize the eternal love that is your genuine inheritance.

In one of his rubaiyats, not numbered by Ezekiel, Sarmad explained his mission on earth. It was, he said, to revive the message of Mansur, an earlier saint who was blinded and cruelly executed. Since Mansur's holy influence had become faint, he must restate it. In other words, when well-intentioned but misled followers corrupt one master's teachings, a new saint is sent to correct this misunderstanding. Sarmad obviously knew he would also die in a similar way as Mansur, at the hands of fanatical secular leaders, for he stated that executioners and death give a longer life to the sons of God **(Ezekiel 1966:380).** Certainly it is true that martyrdom makes a teacher and his message famous in spite of attempts to subdue both. But it is also true that this message will sooner or later become distorted and a new saint will be sent to restore the original teachings. The world is never without one or more genuine spiritual adepts.

Namdev

Namdev (1270 – 1350)

The thundering resonance of the Word has liberated me while living, and I have experienced the glory of freedom

For (The Lord) is present in each particle and every being. Know Him as perfect ... and realize Him in His totality.

Namdev

Although Namdev lived before the great Kabir, his life and teachings are being considered after Kabir because of the tremendous influence Kabir has had on many different faiths. In this way, one does not consider the Sufi Saints, several of whom have already been studied, with the lines of Indian saints. Being of Moslem ethnicity in an Indian cultural environment, Kabir bridged the gap between the Sufi saints and those who incarnated in India. While the teachings are the same among both schools of masters, it is probably best to de-scribe several of the many Indian saints in one sequence so no reader becomes confused regarding the ethnicity of the teacher being considered.

Namdev, according to one of his own poems, was born on October 26, 1270 in Maharashtra, India. It is very difficult today to separate biographical facts from later additions and alterations made by ardent devotees, so a discussion of the life of Namdev must be brief. Tradition states that his father's name was Dama Seth and his mother Gonai. Namdev inherited the profession of calico printer from his ancestors and became a tailor. He earned a meager living by making clothing for others. In fact, his wife, Rajai, complained that his earnings were inadequate **(Puri and Sethi 1978:2)**.

As a child, Namdev was very devout, extremely pure of heart and most sincere. According to tradition, his father, Dama Seth, was a devotee of Vitthal (another name for Lord Krishna). He regularly took an offering of milk to an idol of Vitthal. Of course, Dama drank the milk after offering it to the stone image. One day when he had to be away on business, he asked his son to make the offering for him. The simple and sincere child took the milk and offered it to the idol. When the idol did not drink the offering, Namdev felt deeply hurt and wondered why Lord Krishna would not accept his milk. He began crying and said that he would not leave until the milk was consumed. According to legend, the idol actually drank the milk (or at least the milk vanished).

According to **Puri and Sethi (1978:3)**, Namdev met his master, Visoba Khechar in the temple of Nagnath when he was a young adult. In this temple, he found an old man suffering from leprosy and lying with his feet resting upon an image of Shiva (an important member of the Hindu trinity). Namdev sternly ordered the man to remove his feet from the idol. The old man said that he was too weak to do so and asked Namdev to kindly place his feet where God was not. The profundity of this remark instantly struck Namdev with the understanding that God was everywhere and that the idol was not a genuine manifestation of God.

Upon realizing that the old man was really a spiritual adept, Namdev begged him for spiritual enlightenment. Visoba Khechar asked him to carry him out of the temple since he was unable to walk himself. Namdev forgot about the stigma of leprosy and immediately carried the old man to a clean place outside. When he put his diseased body down on the ground, the leprosy vanished and a gracious and magnetic Visoba Khechar initiated him into the path of God-realization.

After his initiation by Visoba Khechar, Namdev abandoned his former practices of devotion to images of Vitthal, going on pilgrimages, bathing in holy rivers, and the performance of austerities and rituals. He practiced meditation as taught by Visoba Khechar and achieved divine realization within himself. Namdev's teacher may have given his pupil the name *Namdev* because it has a deep spiritual meaning. Nam (or Name) refers to the primal creative current, while *dev* (from Deva or radiant being) refers to angelic entities. In other words, Namdev means radiant exponent of the Word or simply *Radiant Word.*

At age 27, Namdev traveled on foot to many parts of central and northern India. In fact he spent over 50 years in northern India, moving from town to town until he finally settled down in Gurdaspur district in the Punjab. Many of his disciples moved into the area to be with their great teacher and a small village (known as Ghuman) sprang up. Namdev spent his time in meditation and instructing his devout followers. He left the physical world in A.D. 1350 **(Puri and Sethi 1978:10)**.

Namdev taught that God is all pervading and is the one reality behind all apparent diversity. As he stated **(Puri and Sethi 1978:21)**, *"For (the Lord) is present in each* *particle and every being. Know Him as perfect…and realize Him in his totality."* He compared the divine reality with the thread that runs through a string of beads and suggested that God could be found within at the core of each living person. As he put it, *"the formless One has taken the form of Name (or Word) and within Namdev He has made his abode."* (Puri and Sethi 1978:18).

In **Shri Namdev Gatha**, (poem number **1988**), Namdev praises the Word or Nam as beauty incarnate. He advises us to meditate upon Nam and become fearless. He states that Nam is the true ritual, the true religion, the real purity and the perfection that sustains creation for all time. It dispels darkness and delusion. **(Puri and Sethi 1978:19)**. The Word or Nam guides the soul safely through all higher regions. As Namdev puts it **(Puri and Sethi 1978:61)**, *"The ambrosial melody resounds within me, and I am enlightened. I gain deliverance from the world when I cease to be entangled by Maya."* Saints define *Maya* as the phenomenal realms of illusion where things are not what they seem to be. It includes mind and all things contacted by the senses. Mind is the highest and subtlest form of matter with an affinity for more gross categories of matter or crystallized energy in Astral and physical dimensions. Thus mind orients the attention or spirit (the real entity) outward into objective realms of Maya. Proper meditation reverses the direction of attention and allows the consciousness to rise into realms beyond illusion and regain a vision or awareness of God.

In his poem *"The Mystic Experience"* **(Puri and Sethi 1978:57)**, Namdev said: *"Where the effulgent light is seen, there rings the boundless Shabd* (or Word). *I became fused in Divine Light through the grace of my master. The Unstruck Melody has the lucency of the sun… (and) Namdev has realized the truth and attained the blissful state of Sahaj."* The word *Sahaj* means a condition of oneness with God. In another poem **(Puri and Sethi 1978:30)**, Namdev says that *"the thundering resonance of the Word has liberated me while living…and I have experienced the glory of freedom. Even the (scriptures) have no conception of my state and… remain baffled."*

In his **Shri Namdev Gatha 841**, Namdev lists the characteristics of a genuine saint. He says that the true saint sees God in all of his creation and provides shelter for those seeking peace and protection. He drives out lust and anger from the minds of his devotees and liberates them from delusion. The saint is not concerned with material property or mundane realms. He is in constant communion with God or the Word and never forgets this Power for a moment **(Puri and Sethi 1978:23)**. But how does one meet a genuine saint? Namdev says that one must have intense longing to meet God, and then he adds, *"to get the company of a saint is a rare fortune"* **(Puri and Sethi 1978:44)**.

A few of Namdev's poems praise higher meditation. One recorded in the Adi Granth of the Sikhs (page 485, and quoted by **Puri and Sethi 1978:51**) states: *"During all of the eight watches (or all hours) of the day, I meditate on my beloved. I repeat the Name of God day and night."* This is the highest form of meditation. The saint stated very clearly that *"Namdev has attained realization through meditation. My soul is merged into him who is the life of the universe"* **(Puri and Sethi 1978:65)**. Every true saint teaches his disciples the proper way to meditate and turn the attention from the world to God.

Saint Namdev also discussed the subject of death. He stated that in physical death consciousness departs from the mortal frame and the elements within the body decompose. But he speaks of another death, that of rising above body consciousness while still in the human form. Namdev said that he had realized his true self through the Word of his Guru or teacher and thus had passed through death and had no fear of it. He was now beyond death and could not die. He added: "*Visoba Khechar says, 'death we transcend, oh Namdev, when we experience it while living.'*"

Frequently certain yogis and other meditators obtain seemingly miraculous powers through intense concentration. Using laws of the Astral and Causal planes, one can perform what seem to be miracles. And yet Namdev says that such powers prove to be a hindrance to the one who uses them. First of all, the performing of so-called miracles usually inflates the ego and draws attention to the meditator for the wrong reasons. Secondly, the practitioner becomes engrossed in doing miraculous things and forgets to conserve energy so higher consciousness may be gained during meditation **(Puri and Sethi 1978:34-35)**. It is especially serious if a meditator performs so called miracles in order to obtain money. Such a person will soon lose the ability to manipulate higher laws and will bankrupt himself or herself spiritually.

Healing is another poorly understood practice. The main problem is the fact that many yogis and well-meaning healers do not understand why a specific malady assaulted someone, and one may actually harm a person by healing that individual. Nothing happens by accident or chance. A genuine friend will point out reasons why a particular disease invaded the body and suggest means whereby the afflicted individual can heal himself or herself. In this way the sufferer can learn what laws were violated to cause the particular disorder and avoid such infractions in the future. When Jesus healed a man who had been disabled for 38 years, he told this person to *"sin no more lest a worse thing come unto thee"* **(John 5:14)**. When he healed someone, Jesus often said, *"thy sins be forgiven thee"* **(Matthew 9:2, Mark 2:5)**. These biblical passages indicate that many maladies are caused by violation of spiritual laws or sins. Most faith healers and poorly informed practitioners simply postpone the effects of an unwise cause or they spread the penalty over a whole audience. In the early 1950s, the writer saw a well-known faith healer have each person in the audience raise his or her right hand and place the left hand on the person in front of that individual. Then he prayed and demanded that an infirm individual be healed. And healing happened, but I felt energy being drawn out of me. In other words, everyone in the audience shared the karmic debt. It is certainly probable that the one healed repeated the infraction of natural law that caused the malady in the first place.

Namdev states that if one wishes to know God, he or she must transcend desires and keep the mind focused upon meditation as instructed by a perfect saint. One must leave the forest of passions and not be attracted by the lures of wealth and fame. The devotee must transcend traditional religious practices such as rituals, pilgrimages, muttering of prayers or fingering a rosary, singing hymns or bhajans, and the wearing of distinctive or symbolic garb. The seeker cannot be led by the blind but by one whose spiritual eyes are opened.

Guru Nanak

Guru Nanak (1469-1539

One cannot comprehend Him through reason, even if one reasoned for ages; one cannot achieve inner peace by outward silence, not though one sat dumb for ages;
one cannot buy contentment with all the riches of the world, nor reach Him with all mental ingenuity.
How may one know the truth and break through the cloud of falsehood? There is a way, oh Nanak, to make His will our own."

Guru Nanak

The great saint Nanak was the first in the Sikh line of gurus. He was born on April 15, 1469 in the village of Talwandi Rai Bhoe, about 40 miles from Lahore, Pakistan. His father was Kalian Das Bedi, a village accountant, and his mother was named Tripta. He had a sister named Nanaki **(Khushwant Singh 1963:29-30)**. A brilliant child, Nanak was asking questions about the purpose of life and about God by the age of five. When he was seven, he learned the alphabet and basic math from a pundit and later learned Persian and Arabic from a Muslim mullah **(Khushwant Singh 1963:30)**.

Sometime between his twelfth and sixteenth year Nanak's relatives arranged a marriage between him and Sulakhani, a girl from Batala in Gurdaspur District, Punjab. **(Dhillon 2006:48)**. In those days, a young man or woman had no choice in a marriage arrangement. Nanak's father, noting that his son had no worldly interests, tried to engage his mind in such activities as farming, herding buffalo, dealing in horses, and working in a store. But Nanak was more interested in talking to wandering mendicants or *"holy men"* and various religious teachers **(Puri 1982:10)**. He performed all work conscientiously but his heart was not in it. Much time was spent in meditation and singing of devotional hymns. Although he traveled and taught much of his later life, he did father two sons, Sri Chand and Lakshmi Das during his earlier years.

Nanak's first mystical experience took place early one morning while he was bathing in Kali Bein, a rivulet flowing near Sultanpur. According to the *Puratan Janamsakhi*, Nanak was led from the stream into a nearby forest where he encountered the presence of God. Apparently this divine communion continued for three days **(Puri 1982:11).** According to Khushwant Singh, the Lord told Nanak that He was with him. He added, *"Through you will my name be magnified, and whoever follows you will be saved. Go into the world to pray and teach mankind. Let your life be one of praise of the Word or Nam, charity, service and prayer* (or simran)." He was then told to let this be the mission of his life **(Kushwant Singh 1963:31)**.

The traditional Sikh view is that Nanak received the divine commission to serve as a guru from God during his spiritual experience in the forest. However, some teachers, **Kirpal Singh (1967:20)**, for example, considered Nanak to have been a Swateh Saint, in other words a saint who came into this world with a direct commission to serve as a guru or teacher. Such masters need no special training and begin giving instructions at an early age.

Often Swatah Saints do adopt a guru as an example to others in order to stress the need for the guidance of a qualified teacher. For example, the Swatah Saint Kabir became a disciple of Ramanand and later liberated this idol worshipper **(Sethi 1984:10-12)**. The great teacher Seth Shiv Dayal Singh, popularly known as Soami Ji, apparently was a Swatah Saint, but he adopted Tulsi Sahib (another local saint) as his mentor **(Kirpal Singh 1973:10)**.

Several scholars have stated that Nanak did have a guru. For example, Gulam Husain Khan asserted that Sayyed Hasan, a Muslim scholar and dervish, was the master of Nanak **(Puri 1982:13)**. **Puri (1982:14)** states that an inscription in Baghdad reads: *"Guru Murad died. Baba Nanak Fakir helped in constructing the building that is an act of grace from a virtuous follower. 927 A.H."* This inscription suggests that a Guru Murad was the teacher of Nanak. The Kabir panthis (modern followers of Kabir) assert that Kabir was the master of Nanak. So there are differences of opinion regarding the guru of Nanak. While the physical teacher of Nanak cannot be determined by modern scholarship, many statements by Nanak indicate that he had a guru. For example, *"This is how I tamed my mind. I attached myself to the Word given by my Master and, through his grace, the Lord united me with Himself."* **(Puri 1982:14-15)**. *Also, "I bow low at the feet of my Master, by whose grace I have seen the Lord."* **(Puri 1982:16)**. In many other places, Nanak praises his master, so it seems apparent that he did recognize someone as his guru.

Kushwant Singh (1963:33) suggests that Nanak traveled extensively throughout India and journeyed as far west as Baghdad. He spent much time in the Punjab and traveled southward through Tamilnad and Ceylon. His final journey was a visit to Mecca and Medina (cities sacred to Muslims). During all of these travels, his companion was a Muslim disciple named Mardana. Finally the great saint settled down at a village named Kartarpur on the banks of the Ravi River. It is said that his garb when he traveled was a mixture of styles worn by Hindu sadhus and Muslim fakirs. This was to emphasize his oft-repeated statement: *"There is no Hindu; there is no Musalman (Islamic adherent)."* Apparently he meant that saints were above secular and religious labels and that in the Divine State such distinctions were not made.

An interesting account of Nanak's attitude toward orthodox Islam is told by **Puri (1982:17)**. Nanak accompanied several Muslim believers to afternoon prayer at a local mosque. When the qazi conducted the prayer service, the guru kept standing instead of kneeling as was customary. The qazi complained that Nanak did not show proper respect during prayer. When he was asked why, Nanak stated that the qazi's heart was not in the prayer, so he did not kneel for an insincere utterance. According to Nanak, the qazi was thinking about a newborn foal that he had placed in his yard before going to the mosque. There was a well nearby, and he was afraid that the foal might fall into it. The qazi admitted that this was true and no longer complained about Nanak's lack of proper respect.

Guru Nanak beautifully praises God in the *Jap Ji*, a wonderful hymn that serves as a prologue to *Guru Granth Sahib*, the voluminous Sikh scripture. Many translations of the *Jap Ji* are available in English. **Puri (1982:111-139)** renders a simple and accurate translation, and portions of his version will be quoted below. The inspiring and poetic translation by **Kirpal Singh (1959: 123-181)** will also be cited. A comparison of the two translations indicates that the basic message of Nanak is conveyed by both renderings.

God, or the Supreme State of Being, is, according to Nanak **(Puri 1982:113)** a state of Oneness. *"He is the first. He is all that is. Eternal Truth is his Name. He is the creator of all. Not begotten, He is self-existent. Through the grace of the guru, He is made known to men."* **Kirpal Singh (1959:123)** renders this passage in these words: *"There is one Reality, the Unmanifest-Manifested. He is Naam (or Word), the Creator, pervading all. (He is) timeless, unborn and self-existent. Through the favor of the Guru...He may be realized."* Because God is formless, omnipotent, and resides in every individual, the seeker has to inquire within to realize or become one with the Divine One **(Dhillon 2006:149)**.

The next portion of the *Jap Ji* explains the difficulty of knowing God by mental and emotional means. **Kirpal Singh (1959:125)** translates it in these words: *"One cannot comprehend Him through reason, even if one reasoned for ages; one cannot achieve inner peace by outward silence, not though one sat dumb for ages; one cannot buy contentment with all the riches of the world, nor reach Him with all mental ingenuity. How may one know the Truth and break through the cloud of falsehood? There is a way, O Nanak, to make His will our own."* Merging into the will of God after eliminating the ego (or rising above the mind) is the method recommended by Nanak to overcome physical, emotional and mental limitations. This divine realization only takes place via the guidance of a saint or teacher who has risen to spiritual consciousness. As **Puri (1982:120)** translates Nanak: *"The pundits (scholars) know naught of the dawn of thy creation."* Then he states that each scholar speaks of God as if he or she is wiser than any other person is. This is basically an ego trip, because the few who know of God by personal experience are very humble. Puri's translation continues: *"If anyone says he knows Him, he is but a fool in the eyes of dwellers of higher regions... (one) cannot reach the end of His vastness."*

In countless passages Nanak praises the Word or Nam, that creative current that emanates from God. According to Nanak **(Puri 1982:125-126)**, Nam is responsible for all existence. It provides all creatures what they need, and yet no one possesses the bounty of creation, for it is all God's. What can we offer to win His delight? *"Meditate upon His Nam at morn, wet with the ambrosia of the daybreak!"* Then by the light of His glance we shall all become free. **Kirpal Singh (1959:128)** translates these words in this way: *"At the ambrosial hour of the early dawn, be you in communion with the Divine Word (or Nam) and meditate upon His Glory. (For) salvation comes only by His Grace."*

Extracting the basic ideas from a lengthy translation of **Puri (1982:127-136)** we learn that the Word changes people to spiritual adepts as they overcome all sins and death. Such a hearer of the Word becomes wise, content, and full of peace and bliss. One gains cosmic consciousness, traverses all realms, and redeems not only himself but countless others. In conclusion, Nanak says: *"How can I conceive of thy creative power? Too poor am I to sacrifice myself for Thee. Whatever pleases Thee is good; thou art forevermore, O formless One."* **Engle 1980**: translates part of **Nanak's Rag Ramkali M.1** in these words: *"Through the Divine Word is God revealed to us, and in the company of the saints is the fire of ego destroyed."*

Nanak taught that the Word (or Nam) is the real guru and that the physical form of a saint is but an expression of the Word. The objective teacher attaches the consciousness of the disciple to the ever-present Word and helps the disciple to contact it consciously. Thereafter, the Word will guide the disciple back to the divine presence. As **Kirpal Singh (1959:130)** translates part of **Stanza 5 of the Jap Ji**, *"The Master is the Song Eternal or Word personified... The greatness of the Master, even if known, cannot be described with mortal eloquence."*

Nanak, as have all saints, spoke eloquently of love. As he put it **(Puri 1982:415)**: *"Come beloved friend and let us speak of love! (Let us) talk of the perfect, powerful Lord... the repository of goodness."* Nanak made it clear that God is not realized through intellectual cleverness. He said, *"He is attained through love"* **(Puri 1982:432)**. In another passage **(Puri 1982:428-429)** Nanak indicates that love is reciprocal: *"Night and day let me remain lost in my Lord's love. Love of the Word keeps one fresh forever."* In a passage reminiscent of Rumi, Nanak said: *"(Those) who obtain not the elixir of love know not the taste of God. They are like guests in an empty house."* **(Puri 1982:446)**.

Guru Nanak often referred to the subject of death. He said that the angel of death catches men like a fisherman catches fish. He added: *"The entire world is within death's compass. Without the guru there is no means to conquer it"* **(Puri 1982:368-369)**. He continued: *"Union with the beloved will give you peace, (and) the demon of death will poison himself and die."* This reminds one of **John Donne's** famous **Sonnet (10)**, *"Death be not Proud"* in which he concludes that *"one short sleep past, we wake eternally, and death shall be no more: death thou shalt die"* **(Spencer 1963:430)**. Nanak's recipe for realization of truth is contact with the Word. He concludes: *"Where the immortal Word of the guru abides, there death shall have no access."* **(Puri 1982:369)**.

All higher teachers have advised their disciples to overcome each negative tendency of the mind. Usually they attribute to mind five qualities that are often compared to thieves since they rob the person of noble character. These five traits are lust, anger, greed, attachment and ego. Nanak says that when lust fills men's hearts they are prey to dissipation where they lose much energy. Then, he says frustration and anger prove their undoing; they lose both poise and honor. The wealth of others lures their minds, and greed then puts halters about their necks **(Puri 1982:378)**. They thus become attached to impermanent material goods. Ego provides the false assumptions that these things are really theirs and that death awaits others, not them. Ego even attacks virtuous individuals who have overcome lust, anger and greed, patting them on the back and suggesting that they are virtuous souls. Ego is the last and most difficult characteristic to overcome because it is so subtle. That is why the humility of saints is truly outstanding: ego no longer bothers them.

Of course mind is essential if one is a denizen of the Causal, Astral or physical worlds. Minds can be trained to think and react in many ways, good or bad. Mind should be a servant of the higher spirit in each person, not the boss. It draws its energy from the higher spirit in each individual. Mind has its job, and that is to prevent people from concentrating upon things higher than the Causal plane, the source of mind. Nanak said that *"the mind is like a rogue elephant, wild and intoxicated with its own power. It wanders about in the jungle of delusion and* (desires). *Without the guru's Word, the mind will not be stilled"* **(Puri 1982:384)**.

Nanak was the first of the ten Sikh gurus. He was followed by Guru Angad (1504 – 1552), Guru Amardas

(1479 – 1574), Guru Ramdas (1534 – 1581), Guru Arjan (1563 – 1606), Guru Har Gobind (1595 – 1644), Guru Hari Rai (1630 – 1661), Guru Hari Krishan (1656 – 1664), Guru Teg Bahadur (1621 – 1675) and Guru Gobind Singh (1666 – 1708). Most of the *Granth Sahib* (Sacred Book of the Sikhs) was assembled by Guru Arjan. The later gurus made additions to the holy book. A few things should be explained for the benefit of those unfamiliar with Sikh history. Guru Hari Krishan began his mission at the age of five and served as master for three years until Guru Teg Bahadur was ready to assume the leadership of the Sikhs. **Engle (1980:118-119)** gave an example of the wisdom of this youthful leader. When he was called to the court of Aurangzeb, he told the assembled members of the royal household: *"Guru Nanak extends happiness to those of unwavering faith. He is ever with them, giving His protection; and those who live by his will, will be loved by God. But one who has not tasted the fruits of true discipleship, must, like a high peak, ultimately meet his fall. Devotion is like rain which does not gather on lofty peaks."* From the time of Guru Har Gobind through the days of Guru Gobind Singh, the Sikhs were persecuted severely by such Muslim rulers as Aurangzeb and by certain Rajput leaders such as Raja Bhim Chand of Bilaspur **(Kushwant Singh 1963:78)**. Although the later Sikh gurus were pacifists at first and tried to live in peace, they were finally forced to defend themselves on the battlefield. Self-defense is acceptable to God because the injunction *"Thou shall not kill"* applies to oneself as much as to others. If one allows a tyrant to kill him or her without protest, he or she condones murder. Self-defense devoid of hatred for the aggressor is ethical, while murder of innocent people carries a heavy penalty.

Several scholars have translated the writings of Guru Nanak into English, so it is relatively easy to study his teachings. One of the more accessible studies of the life of Guru Nanak as well as translations of many of his poems is the book *Guru Nanak* (1981) by J.R. Puri published by the Radha Soami Satsang of Beas, India. This work streses the spiritual or mystical nature of his teachings instead of functioning as a study of his works from either a literary or sociological perspective. Professor Puri was head of the Department of Philosophy of Punjabi University from 1969 to 1976 when he retired. After retirement, he concentrated upon practice of spirituality.

There is much repetition of ideas in the verses of Nanak, but this repetition has value in that it tends to drive home important points. The great master stressed the same spiritual teachings that all masters have taught in his own inimitable way. He spoke of God as the Absolute and self-existent eternal being or source of all. This source is above time, space and causation. Human minds cannot conceive of Him because this power or focus of love exists above the mind and lower creation. In the Jap Ji Nanak emphasized that one cannot realize God even if this person meditated for ages because mind gets in the way. One cannot employ thought to rise above causal mentality. And yet there is a way to make the divine will our own and thus realize the Ultimate Power. But we need the assistance or guidance of someone who has risen above the mind in realms beyond time, space and causation. We must contact a teacher who can link us consciously with the Word (or Naam, Shabd, or Voice of the Silence), because, as Nanak has said, it is hearing of the Word that enables one to triumph over death and cross the vast cosmic, celestial and spiritual realms to reach the feet of Divinity. The Word purifies the soul, separates it from mind and all material influences and draws it to self awareness and then to the blissful state of God realization.

In conclusion, Nanak tells us that human life is a precious jewel, but we exchange it for trivia. He adds **(Puri 1982:375)**: *"You have lost your nights in sleeping; you have lost your days in eating"* and you spend much time in unnecessary labor. Certainly one must earn an honest living while residing in this imperfect world, but earning a livelihood does not require spending over eight or ten hours in daily labor. And even while working one can remember God or the Master. If this is not possible because a job requires much concentration, one can dedicate the work to the Divine One and work in His name. In this way work becomes worship.

But worship with love is not what we do. Most people continually try to keep the mind amused or entertained and thus valuable time is lost forever. Lovers of God fix their attention upon the Divine One and lovingly serve the human beings they meet in daily life.

Mirabai

Mirabai (1498 –1547?)

Mira's beloved is almighty; the drop is now one with love's great ocean.

In my life I met two saviors: the saint and the Lord's Name. The saint adorns my forehead and the Name is embedded in my heart.

Mirabai

Those who make a cursory study of the history of spirituality may assume that all saints of the highest order have been men. This is certainly not true. While the Catholic Church has canonized many female "*saints,*" and all of these were noble souls, few of these "*saints*" seem to have ascended to the highest levels of being. But several female disciples of great saints did achieve sainthood themselves. One of the earliest examples was the famous Rabia of Basra. This woman was sold to a house of prostitution when she was a very young girl. Being extremely devout, she asked each man who came into her room for sex to pray with her. Her sincere and humble prayers made all of them ashamed of themselves and each of them left without touching her. Owners of the brothel noticed that no man ever returned when he went in to see Rabia. Upon inquiry the brothel owners discovered why, and they set Rabia free since she was bad for *"business."* After she was dismissed from the brothel, Rabia met a saint named Khwaja Hasan, also of Basra, and was initiated by him **(Maheshwari 1971:182)**. Saint Khwaja Hasan would deliver a discourse when Rabia was present at spiritual meetings, but he would not speak when she was absent. Some of his disciples wondered why he would not talk unless she, a woman, was present, and he replied: *"When I have been given nectar for elephants, how can I distribute it to lesser creatures?"* The Moslem attitude toward women made this statement especially disconcerting, but Saint Hasan was trying to make an important point.

Another famous female saint was Mirabai, a princess of Rajasthan, India and a disciple of the great saint Ravidas or Raidas (1414? – 1527). She was born in A.D. 1498 in the village of Kudki, Rajasthan, India (some authorities say her birth took place in Bajoli, another village in Rajasthan). Her father was Ratan Singh, a chief of twelve villages near Merta. Her mother died when she was two years of age, and her grandfather, Rao Duda, a man who often entertained holy men at his palace, reared Mira. Thus she was in contact with saintly persons at an early age and developed a deep interest in spiritual matters while she was yet a child **(Sethi 1996:4)**.

Mira's education included a study of available scriptures, music, spinning and sewing. As a princess, she was also expected to learn fencing, archery, the riding of horses, and driving of chariots. Being endowed with determination, courage and intelligence, she excelled in all aspects of her training. She was quiet and soft-spoken, mild mannered and affectionate. According to legend, she was one of the great beauties of her time **(Sethi 1996:4-5)**.

Rana Sangram Singh, the King of Mewar, asked Mira's grandfather for her hand in marriage for his eldest son and heir, Prince Bhojraj. Although Mira objected to a conventional marriage, neither she nor the prince had a choice in the matter and an engagement ceremony was performed. In 1516, when Mira was eighteen, an elaborate marriage took place. Mira was given numerous gifts of clothing, jewelry and the revenue from many villages (alleged to be 300,000 rupees per year). The kind-hearted Mira spent most of this money feeding spiritual devotees and holy men and helping the poor **(Sethi 1996:5)**.

Mira faced many traumatic events early in her life. Her beloved grandfather Rao Duda, who had essentially reared her, died just before her wedding, and her husband was killed in battle about 1525. Her father, Ratan Singh, died in 1527, also in battle, and Rana Sanga, a close adviser, was poisoned soon thereafter. This series of events caused the deeply spiritual Mira to reflect upon the transient nature of the world and seek for higher truth. As she wrote in one poem: *"Life in this world is short; why involve yourself in it? The body is false and all material objects are false. False is the entire creation"* **(Sethi 1996:6)**.

Throughout childhood and early youth, Mira was a devotee of Lord Krishna, and she believed him to be the Supreme Being. At an unknown time in her life, she met Saint Ravidas (or Raidas), believed to have been a disciple of Kabir. This low-caste cobbler lived from about 1414 to about 1532, a span of about 118 years. Mira confirms that Raidas was her teacher in several of her poems. In one of them she says: *"I kept searching for the secret of that realm. When Saint Raidas, my Master, I met, he gave my soul the clue to that Eternal Abode"* **(Sethi 1996:8)**. In another poem, she wrote, *"When Raidas, the perfect Master, I met, the severed twig rejoined the tree"* **(Sethi 1996:9)**.

After Ravidas initiated her, Mira took to the path of devotion with fervent zeal, and her meditations bore fruit. However, her unorthodox spiritual practices and her reverence for a lowly cobbler disturbed the royal family and the orthodox Brahmin priests in her area. At this time most people fervently believed in the caste system, especially those who were members of the upper castes, and a princess simply did not go to a cobbler for spiritual guidance. Rana Ratan Singh, now the king of Mewar, looked upon Mira as a royal disgrace and had her maligned and tormented by her sister-in-law Udabai and others. Udabai was unrelenting in her scorn until she encountered Mira in meditation one day. A brilliant light flooded the room, and Udabai, overwhelmed by the radiance, repented of the fact that she had persecuted Mira, and became a devotee of the saintly queen **(Sethi 1996:10-11)**. The harsh actions of Rana Ratan Singh did not deter Mira from her path of devotion. Whenever she could, she visited her master daily, although the Rana forbade her to do so. Finally he placed a guard in her section of the palace to keep her from visiting Ravidas, but she would climb down the palace walls using a rope **(Sethi 1996:13)**.

When Rana Ratan Singh died in 1531, his successor, Rana Vikram, continued to persecute Mira. He tried to have her poisoned, but the virulent poison had no effect upon her. Then he arranged to have a deadly viper sent to her in a jewel box. Mira was told that the box contained a precious necklace, and she opened it to discover a strand of rare pearls. **(Sethi 1996:17)**.

Mira regularly entertained holy men and devotees at the palace, and many members of the local public began to admire her and attend the meetings where she spoke and sang songs of devotion. Mira was a vigorous champion of human rights, including women's rights, and with wit and penetrating insight would expose the corruption and superstition present in politics, orthodox religion and in the caste system **(Ladinsky 2002:241)**. Finally, the treatment she received at Chittor became unbearable, so Mira left the palace and journeyed to Merta, her paternal home. From Merta she traveled to various places, but these travels are not well documented. **Ladinsky (2002:241)** states that Mira spent the last few years of her life helping the sick and impoverished people near the Ranchhorji temple and writing ecstatic poems. The exact date of her death is controversial.

Although there are many books on the life of Mirabai (or Mira) in the Gujarati and Hindi languages, there are very few biographies of Mirabai in English and few translations of her poems in English. The book ***Mira, the Divine Lover by*** **V. K. Sethi (1996)** was used extensively while writing this section on the life and teachings of Mirabai. Various other publications quote Mirabai in a limited way along with other saints, and some of these translations were considered.

Mira rarely describes the nature of God, although she often expresses a longing to meet the Divine Source of all. In one of her poems, she compares God to an ocean of love and considers herself to be a drop from that ocean. She says, *"Mira's beloved is almighty; the drop is now one with love's great ocean"* **(Sethi 1996:193)**. Mira also refers to God as the Immortal One, and she stood in awe of that Divine Power. As she put it, *"If one unveiled word from God touched this earth, it would ignite like a rag soaked in oil"* **(Ladinsky 2002:265)**.

Many of Mira's poems praise the Word, Nam (or Name) or Shabd, the Divine Creative Current. As she said, *"The Lord's Name is all that I own. Nothing else belongs to me"* **(Sethi 1996:118)**. In another poem she states, *"The jewel of Nam have I found, a precious wealth have I obtained. My original treasure I have regained. It can never be stolen or squandered, (but) keeps on increasing from day to day"* **(Sethi 1996:133)**. Mira makes it clear that the Word is something that one hears within. She says, *"The master joined me with Shabd (Word), my source, and I am absorbed in its sweet melody. The bliss of this union has stilled (my) mind* **(Sethi 1996:105)**. She explains to seekers that *"within your body resounds sweet strains of eternal song."* And then she adds, *"Within your body burns a flame in resounding waves of brilliant light.* **(Sethi 1996:170).**

Perhaps more of Mira's poems praise the perfect saint than any other topic. She said, *"In my life I met two saviors: the saint and the Lord's Name. The saint adorns my forehead, (and) the Name is embedded in my heart"* **(Sethi 1996:** In another poem she states, *"The boat of Truth I occupied, with the Master at the helm. With (Him) I was ferried across the deadly ocean of the world"* **(Sethi 1996:133)**. Again, she stated, *"At her master's feet (Mira will) forever stay. Now she is truly a queen"* **(Sethi 1996:188)**. In another poem she asserted, *"Mira is one with her master as a thread (is part of) the cloth. People say Mira has gone astray (but) they are a prey to their own delusion. What can a crow ever know about the flight of a swan? Mira lay asleep in the vale of darkness until her master shook her from the sleep of eons."* **(Sethi 1996:175).**

All saints have praised the blessing of love, but Mira is especially eloquent regarding this primal characteristic. She said, *"I am intoxicated by the Lord's love. (It is like a soft rain around me (saturating) my every pore with bliss"* **(Sethi 1996:115)**. In another poem she wrote, *"Love* (is) *so strong a force (that) it broke the cage and (Mira) disap-*

peared from everything. I write of that journey of becoming as free as God. Don't forget love; it will bring all the madness you need to (hurl) yourself across the universe" **Ladinsky 2002:251)**. And finally she said, *"I am absorbed in his love. My misery of wandering in the world has ended. The lily bursts into bloom… (and) my heart blossoms in joy. Peace permeates this body of mine (and the) very Lord has become my own. The pain of duality has vanished"* **(Sethi 1996:72)**.

Mira frequently mentioned meditation as an essential practice for realizing the Divine Nature via the help of a saint. She said, *"Engage in the Lord's devotion. Persist in your meditation (and) be steadfast, (for) far is the abode of the Lord. (The one) who climbs and reaches the top tastes the sweet fruit of love"* **(Sethi 1996:73)**. In one of her poems she says, *"In the calm of the night I will arise and go to Him, and return at dawn. Night and day I'll remain engrossed in communion with my Lord. My love for Him is ages old"* **(Sethi 1996:95)**. Those who are capable of rising above physical consciousness can meditate all night while the body sleeps and is refreshed with energy. Of course beginners cannot do this, but anyone who meditates under the direction of a realized soul can reduce the amount of sleep required to maintain good health and, at the same time, will transmute the procreative energies to centers in the brain. This can help one both physically and spiritually.

In conclusion, Mira asserted that the world is a dark place where pain and misery reign. She suffered a lot in physical clothing. But then she found Ravidas (or Raidas) and her roving and troubles ended as she was carried across the *"terrible sea"* of the world. Great was her joy in the saint's company when finally she found peace **(Sethi 1996:100)**.

Dadu

Dadu (1554 – 1603)

Like ice dissolved in water, in God is merged the lover of God.

Where God is, there I am not; where I am, there God Is not.

Dadu

The sixteenth century saint Dadu is not as well known as Kabir, Nanak or even Mirabai in the western world. But he taught the same truths as other saints of the highest order, and his teachings give the seeker a refreshing look at these basic concepts. He was a contemporary of the great Moghul emperor Akbar, one of the most brilliant and open-minded rulers in history. It is difficult to obtain books in English that give many details of Dadu's life and teachings. An especially recommended volume is ***A Sixteenth Century Indian Mystic, Dadu and His Followers*** **by W. G. Orr.** Mr. Orr was a missionary who went to India to preach Christian doctrines. However, he noticed that the teachings of Dadu were extremely similar to those of Christ, and he studied the history of the Dadu Panth (pronounced "*punt*") with much open-minded insight and documented his study unusually well for the 1940s.

Dadu was born in 1554 at Ahmedabad, India. Local tradition asserts that his father, Lodi Ram, desired to have a son. One day a religious mendicant told him to go the next morning to the banks of the Saraswati River where his prayer would be granted. He did so, and noticed a basket floating in the stream. In it lay a beautiful child. He carried it home to his wife who was immediately able to nurse the infant. In all probability, this legend is apocryphal, and Dadu was born in the same way as other saints. As **Orr (1947:26)** wisely observed, *"The story (of Dadu) has undergone many transformations in the course of its passage from lip to lip and from pen to pen."*

The scholarship of Orr suggests that the parents of Dadu were Muslim, although his ancestors were probably Hindus who were converted to Islam during the reign of the Lodi dynasty. **Orr (1947:50)** points out the fact that some Hindu adherents are in the process of trying to claim that Dadu was of Hindu descent and are gradually rewriting the history of this saint. The vocation of Dadu was that of a *naddaf* or cotton carder. There was no Hindu caste for this vocation. The study by Orr of Dadu's life is especially valuable because it shows how a religious or mystic tradition can change through time.

Tradition states that when Dadu was eleven years old, the child was playing with some companions when a stern-looking mendicant arrived and asked for alms. All of the children fled except Dadu who gave the old man a small coin and *pan* (a preparation of the areca nut). The old man placed some of the pan in the boy's mouth, put one hand upon the boy's head and instructed him in higher truth **(Orr 1947:27)**. According to some scholars, Dadu's guru was Sheikh Buddhan, a Sufi Saint of the Kadiri line **(Upadhyaya 1980:7)**. Although Dadu may not have understood all of this direction at the age of eleven, it lodged deep within him and, seven years later, Dadu was given a sublime vision. He was told to abandon the world and give himself up to a life of meditation. He left home and for six years led the life of an ascetic before he settled down at Sambhar, a town in the province of Ajmer. Here he would meditate for hours on end. Much to the dismay of local Hindu and Muslim religious leaders, he began to attract a large following of local seekers. In fact, these seekers interrupted his private devotions so much that Dadu spent more and more time carding cotton. As **Orr (1947:27-29)** points out, Dadu's attempt to play the part of a poor cotton carder was as unconvincing as Kabir's appearing in public with a noted harlot. The true character of both Dadu and Kabir could not be obscured, and the character of each saint stood out even more clearly.

One legendary event in the life of Dadu is reminiscent of an incident in the life of Kabir (where wording of a note was miraculously changed). The local authorities at Sambhar, in order to stop the flood of people going to Dadu, passed out an order stating that anyone who went to Dadu would have to pay a fine of 500 rupees. Two devoted followers were arrested for violating this decree. In court, the government order was read aloud, only now it said *"Whosoever does not go to Dadu shall pay a fine of 500 rupees."* Needless to say, the devotees were released and the order rescinded by the perplexed authorities **(Upadhyaya 1980:9-10)**.

Dadu became the father of four children, two sons (Garib and Miskin) and two daughters (Hawwa and Shabbo). Legends of their miraculous virgin births are probably inaccurate attempts by later ascetic followers of Dadu who could not reconcile his family life with their concepts of renunciation **(Upadhyaya 1980:8)**.

At the age of 35, he left Sambhar and traveled to Amber where he was given a warm welcome and many valuable gifts. He kept none of these but immediately distributed them to the needy. He would not accept money (a characteristic of all true saints). In Mandota, a self-appointed sadhu pretended to be a disciple of Dadu and was loaded with gifts and money. But his conscience began to trouble him. What kind of man was Dadu, whose name stirred such generosity? He then hurried to Amber and became a true disciple of Dadu **(Orr 1947:31)**.

While Dadu was at Amber, he was brought to the attention of Akbar, a ruler who welcomed all holy men. The emperor sent a retainer, Suja Khinchi, to invite the saint to Faatehpur Sikri for a meeting with Akbar. The saint refused, saying, *"What have I to do with kings and emperors?"* Suja refused to eat, drink or leave until Dadu made the visit. The saint finally relented, and Akbar was delighted, asking to see him as soon as possible. Two courtiers received Dadu first. One of them greeted him with the words *"homage to the Divine Akbar*." Dadu replied, *"Homage to him, whom all the saints adore, whom gods and men and choirs of angels praise: homage to Him, the pure indwelling* (One)." Then he added, "He is the one with whom we have to do. What profit is there in falsehood?" The courtiers were shamed into silence **(Orr 1947:31-33)**.

Dadu met with Akbar on two occasions. At the first meeting the saint answered all of Akbar's questions. The emperor finally stated, *"You have arrived at the root of the matter, but how is this inward state to be obtained?"* Dadu replied that the seeker needed to express a passionate yearning for God. Such a person needed to cease from indulgences of the body and abandon all attachment for the three worlds (the physical, Astral and Causal realms).

The emperor was deeply moved and asked for Dadu to visit him daily. At a second meeting, the emperor asked Dadu to speak of divine things, but the saint remarked sadly, *"When the body is not pure, what can one understand of divine things?"* Akbar then asserted that something was being held back and stated that he would not have sent for Dadu unless he believed that he could impart truth. He then asked him how one so immersed in worldly affairs could find God. Then the emperor added, *"I am ready to love him with every power of my being and to school my heart in truth if I may learn His secret."* "Well spoken," said Dadu. *"That is the sum of all I have to say. May God keep you ever in this mind."* Akbar bowed his head and Dadu gave him a blessing before he departed **(Orr 1947:34-35)**.

For over ten years, Dadu traveled from place to place teaching higher truths. Finally, he settled in Naraina where he resided beneath a tree in a garden. Many sadhus and disciples visited him there. In 1603, he left the physical body in the presence of his two sons and a few noted disciples. According to legend, the body of Dadu was carried in a bier to a hill some twelve miles distant where both the bier and body of the saint disappeared from view (Orr 1947:43). Although Dadu had said *"the open plain befits the sadhu, where (there) is neither burying place nor burning ground,"* a higher power chose not to allow the body of Dadu to decompose on the hill of Baraina **(Orr 1947:37, 43)**.

Dadu used many words to denote the Supreme Being. Often he called this Power Rama or Hari, both Hindu terms for God. However, it is clear that the Divine One he is in reference to is well above the Rama of Hindu lore. Saints often use the name of a lower manifestation of deity to attract believers in that deity. The holy book attributed to Dadu is called the *Bani,* which is another term for the Word or Divine Music. **Orr (1947)** has translated many passages from the *Bani* into English, Upadhyaya (1980) has translated numerous poems of Dadu into English, and various other writers have translated a few hymns of Dadu into this language. The books by Orr and Upadhyaya served as sources for most of the quotations from the *Bani* used in this study.

Dadu stated that the invisible God dwells within each person. He refers to God as the true and bounteous Creator of everything, and asserts that Truth abides deathless from age to age, but only one in many finds this Transcendent One **(Orr 1947: 92-93)**. In another passage he said that *"There is but one spirit: the Lord is in all. Let your union be with the Lord, not with a sect or mode of dress"* **(Orr 1947:103)**. Dadu speaks eloquently about the delusion of Maya (the Negative Power and outer nature or illusion). He said, *"Maya has destroyed our* (awareness of reality). *Neither God nor the Negative Power is visible"* **(Upadhyaya 1980:42)**. He implies that only the saints and their true disciples see beyond the show of creation and realms of delusion. The Supreme Power is truly awake, while the souls encased in matter sleep and dream in the realms of Maya.

The *Bani* of Dadu eloquently praises the Divine Word. He clearly equates the Word with the objective expression of the master. He said, *"Uttering the Word, the Satguru awakens the soul at will; at will he speaks within."* In a personal vein he added, *"He snatched me from the jaws of death, speaking the Word in my ears."* Then again he suggested ways that the Word affects others. Dadu said, *"Arrow-like the Word of the saintly guru flies in all directions; it arouses the sleeper, and he whom it smites finds salvation."* He concluded, *"The disciple* (hears) *with his ears, and is stirred to remembrance of God"* **(Orr 1947: 84-85)**. In another part of the *Bani*, Dadu says, *"Within the Word is divine wealth. Whoever takes it with discrimination knows not defeat."* *He adds, "The one who applies himself deeply to the Word is united with the Lord"* **(Upadhyaya 1980:117)**. Upadhyaya also translated the expression Bani or Word as Name. He rendered one utterance of Dadu in this way, *"Grant me the true Name, O Lord, so that the trammels of the Negative Power may be destroyed. Fearless then does one become, and the Negative Power consumes him no more"* **(Upadhyaya 1980:119)**.

Dadu contrasted saintly teachers with those who preach before they have learned the higher truth. He said, *"On the one hand, there are lovers of the Lord who annihilate their egos and transcend the body. On the other* (hand), (there are) *nominal holy men of the world (who are) engaged in maintaining their bodies, (and who) resort merely to empty talk"* **(Upadhyaya 1980:134)**. Genuine saints are not concerned with mundane pleasures, choice foods and drinks, or accumulating material goods. They come to rescue those souls who cry out for guidance from the depths of their being. Saints do more than merely talk about a God they have not seen. They lead sincere disciples to a Divine Power that they have realized by hard work and love. As Dadu stated it, *"Lo, the Guru has shown the way to the Merciful One; key in hand, he has opened every door"* **(Orr 1947:84)**.

Dadu advocated meditation where the chattering mind is controlled. He said, *"As long as the attention is not withdrawn and the mind is not made motionless, the Beloved touches me not"* **(Upadhyaya 1980:143)**. Control of the mind is made possible by constant remembrance of God and the saint who is leading you to the Divine Presence. Most saints recommend keeping a series of charged words (or names of stages of being) firmly in mind instead of thinking about the world and mundane or emotional things all of the time. As you think, so you become. This is a basic law.

When Emperor Akbar asked Dadu about the caste, color and nature of God, the saint replied, *"God belongs to the caste of love. Love is dear to Him. Love is His body, and love alone is His color"* **(Upadhyaya 1980:132-133)**. He continued, *"Like ice dissolved in water, in God is merged the lover of God."* Dadu considered love to be the only true worship of the Divine One. He put it this way, *"Where the ardor of love is lacking, worship is* (like) *water where there is no thirst"* **(Orr 1947:168)**. Dadu told Akabar that he, the emperor, wished to play the game of love, but that he was too immersed in the world and sense pleasures to imbibe the divine fragrance of love. Sensuality and spirituality do not occupy the same house. Ego and selfish desires permeate sensuality, whereas spirituality leads the soul above all temporal feelings, desires and things. As Dadu concluded, *"Where God is, there I am not; where I am, there God is not. The* (Divine) *Palace has no place for two"* **(Upadhyaya 1980:132)**.

Dadu associated humility with death of the ego in several memorable passages. He said, *"Let one reduce oneself to dust while living, then will the Lord reveal Himself. Let one die before death, O Dadu; all die sooner or later"* **(Upadhyaya 1980:138)**. He taught that only the dead could tread the trail to God. On this path, he said, *"No coward can stand,* (for) *it is the battlefield of a warrior who offers body, mind and* (ego) *to God"* **(Upadhyaya 1980:137)**. As Dadu put it, *"When a man has abandoned false pride, arrogance and vainglory, when he has become humble and meek, then does he find true bliss"* **(Orr 1947:105)**. The *"death"* referred to by Dadu was not an annihilation of the soul or spirit, but rather the awareness of one's true nature that is accompanied by self-realization. Speaking in a personal way, Dadu said, *"My enemy I is dead; now none can slay me. 'Tis I who slay myself: I have died, and* (yet I) *live"* **(Orr 1947:162)**.

Saint Dadu taught that men and women must reorient their lives properly while they are in physical forms on earth. He strongly disagreed with the widely held belief that one can repent at the moment of death, have all sins washed away, and be ushered into some wonderful paradise. He stated, *"Where you fix the mind while living, there shall* (you) *go at death"* **(Orr 1947:96)**. It is impossible to become angelic by the simple act of repentance. Instant changes in character cannot be made. One who has lived a life of wickedness could not withstand the awesome light and power found in a Causal Plane heaven, for example. A sensual and dishonest entity could not maintain consciousness in such a refined setting. His or her personal negativity would gravitate the soul to a lower realm such as one of the dismal Astral hells. In the words of Dadu, *"He whose life is spent in worship, self-discipline, and good works will travel heavenwards; he who follows the lusts of* (the body) *will fall into hell and* (then) *return to earth"* **(Orr 1947:96)**.

Saint Dadu did not agree with those mendicants and ascetics who performed such harsh austerities as trying to meditate in the midst of four fires on a very hot day, melting blocks of ice with their bodies, wearing uncomfortable garb that irritated the skin and sitting on sharp objects in an attempt to control the mind. He said (Orr 1947:107), *"Pay reasonable heed to the claims of the body,* (but avoid) *all that would separate you from Hari* (or God)." The practice of austerities keeps one from divine awareness just as successfully as indulging in sensual pleasures, because such attempts to overcome physical drives relate to ego as strongly as actually engaging in lustful physical activities. Dadu taught that one should happily accept what God has provided, regardless of whether this is pleasant or some form of adversity. If the disciple is faithful and sincere, all will be sweet to the taste because it comes from God and is intended for improvement of the disciple. As Dadu concluded, "For others' good He created all, and not for selfish ends. Heedful for others is the Supreme Being…few there are that understand. He takes not pleasure in receiving: His pleasure is to bestow" **(Orr 1947:142-143)**.

It is unfortunate that the life and teachings of Saint Dadu are not better known in the western world. Many here have heard of the great Kabir and even Guru Nanak, but few are familiar with the spiritual contributions of Dadu. This master stressed such important qualities as love, humility and truthfulness. His praise for the master guide and the importance of devotion to a saintly teacher was exceptional. And of course Dadu stressed the value of concentration upon the divine Word as one returned to the real home of God. He contrasted the realized saint with the preacher or lecturer who only spoke from the theoretical learning about a given subject.

Dadu emphasized that the truth and the divine source lies within each soul incarnated today. As Jesus said, the kingdom of heaven is within. It is not an objective manifestation. Dadu certainly taught this essential truth in his own day and he lovingly guided hundreds of true seekers through subjective realms to the real home of peace and divine love.

Upadhyaya (1980:141) summarizes the teachings of Dadu beautifully in his translation of one hymn. Dadu says, *"Recognize the path to the beloved, and take the route of the anguished lover in separation. One who treads as the living dead crosses the impassable* (gulf). *Keep the Master's grace and reflect on his pure teachings. Develop love and devotion and keep the thought of the Creator always before thee."* He then advises the seeker to fix the mind in the Sound Current (Word or Nam) and merge into God like a drop of water into the Divine Ocean.

Seth Shiv Dayal Singh

Seth Shiv Dayal Singh

(Soami Ji)

(1818 – 1878)

So long as the Soul does not reach its real home, it will not rest in peace.

To control the mind, look to the Guru. If you follow his dictates, you will control the mind; but if you follow the mind, you will go astray.

Seth Shiv Dayal Singh

Many saints lived, taught and departed from the physical world between the time of Dadu and the emergence of Soami Ji. Bulleh Shah (1680 – 1758) has already been mentioned. Paltu Sahib (1710 – 1780) taught the same spiritual truths, but not much is known about his life. Some of his poems have been translated into English. They strongly condemn fanatical orthodoxy and expose hypocrisy and religious fraud while extolling the value of the Word of God and the message of saints. Then of course there were the later Sikh gurus. Most students of Sikh traditions believe that the line of Sikh gurus ended with Gobind Singh. **But Kirpal Singh (1973:9)** suggests that Ratnagar Rao of the Peshwa family was authorized to carry on the work by Guru Gobind Singh. This saint initiated Sham Rao Peshwa, known later as Tulsi Sahib (1763 – 1843), the famous author of *Ghat Ramayana*. Tulsi

Sahib was the teacher of Soami Ji. Even if one considers Soami Ji to have been born a saint, he still was closely associated with Tulsi Sahib and obviously admired him.

Seth Shiv Dayal Singh (later known as Soami Ji) was born in Agra, United Provinces, India on August 25, 1818. His father's name was Seth Dilwali Singh and his mother's name was Maha Maya. Both of Soami Ji's parents were followers of the Hathras saint, Tulsi Sahib, who apparently initiated him at a very tender age **(Maheshwari 1971:28)**. From early childhood Soami Ji began teaching deep spiritual precepts to a few people around him, although he did not lecture openly to the public until he was much older **(Seva Singh N.D.:2)**. On the last day of his life, Soami Ji told his disciples that he had practiced the inner Word from the age of six (**Kirpal Singh 1973:11)**.

In all probability, Soami Ji was a Swateh Saint (one born with Divine knowledge). All it took was brief guidance from Tulsi Sahib for him to become firmly entrenched in divinity. Clearly, Soami Ji loved and respected his mentor because he visited him often and even helped carry him about when he was unable to walk. **Puri and Sethi (1981:7-8)** tell how Soami Ji, when he received word that Tulsi Sahib was about to leave the body, ran 20 miles with bare feet to get a final glimpse of his beloved master. Tulsi Sahib gave him a deep penetrating final look and departed from the world. Soami Ji was 25 years of age at the death of Tulsi Sahib. He did not start teaching openly until he was 43 and after he had spent 17 years in meditation in a dark room **(Seva Singh N.D.:2)**.

Soami Ji married a lady who, he said, had come to earth with him from a higher state and was destined to be his life partner. In later life, she was called Radhaji. She cooked food for sadhus and for others and took care of the three sons of Soami Ji's youngest brother. She survived Soami Ji for over 16 years, passing from this life on November 1, 1894 in Agra, India **(Maheshwari 1971: 144-146)**. The one photograph of Radhaji seen by this writer suggests that she was an extremely radiant and spiritual soul.

In January of 1861, Soami Ji started publicly teaching at his home in Punni Gali, a street in Agra. He expounded the doctrine of the Word or Nam in lucid terms and initiated over 4,000 disciples during his lifetime. Soami Ji was one of the first saints to give a complete initiation at one time. Earlier saints often gave a partial introduction to the higher path initially and then, after the disciple had purified himself or herself to some degree, the saint would give the rest of the initiation. The first part of the initiation was usually a mantra (or simran) of charged names that represented levels of divinity, and the second part was an inner connection with the Word or Nam. However, sometimes the teacher left the body before the disciple had made much progress and thus a complete initiation was not obtained. Soami Ji and subsequent saints corrected this problem by giving both portions of the initiation simultaneously.

Soami Ji left the body on June 15, 1878. He authorized four advanced initiates to carry on the spiritual work. These disciples were Baba Jaimal Singh, Rai Saligram Sahib Bahadur (also known as Hazur Maharaj), Partap Singh (younger brother of Soami Ji who was also known as Chacha Ji), and San Mukh Das. Another disciple of Tulsi Sahib, Gharib Das, also expounded the spiritual truth at the same time. This means that there were five spiritual teachers active in a limited part of India immediately after the passing of Soami Ji. Baba

Jaimal Singh, Rai Saligram and Partap Singh all established lines of teachers. Some of these lines still exist, although certain authors do not recognize the validity of these lines.

The august personality of Soami Ji and the clarity with which he explained the higher spiritual teachings endeared him to many disciples and others. He taught the same concepts expounded by Kabir, Guru Nanak and Tulsi Sahib, but he openly explained to everyone many esoteric spiritual truths that previously had been taught clearly to a limited few close disciples. Many saints had mentioned these aspects of divinity in the form of symbolic allegories only. This is the reason why some people today consider Soami Ji to be the founder of the Radha Soami Faith and look upon it as a recently introduced religion. Actually his disciple Rai Saligram popularized the phrase *Radha Soami*, which means *Lord of My Soul* when he realized that Soami Ji was exactly that. Kabir had hinted at the term *Lord of the Soul* earlier, but the term did not become commonly uttered until the time of Rai Saligram. Because he was a man of inner realization, the spiritual path enunciated by Rai Saligram was just as valid as the slightly different format taught by Baba Jaimal Singh **(Sawan Singh 1984: xiv)**.

Soami Ji taught that the ultimate and nameless Being could not be described in the words of any mortal language. This first and eternal region is a place of power and love that circumscribes all. This is the stage from which the Word emanated to create all lower dimensions. According to Soami Ji, this is the realm of grace where love, mercy and bliss reign eternally and spiritual consciousness is absolute. Death, karma, sin, evil and pain are not present in this Primal State. It has been called Anami (Nameless), Akah (Untold), and Radha Soami

(Lord of the Soul). This is the region of Supreme Saints **(Seva Singh N.D.:48-49)**.

Three stages below the Anami condition is Sach Khand (true home) or Sat Loka (true realm), a region of pure spirit or consciousness. A subtle form of duality exists here in that entities maintain individual identities, but no negativity is present in this exalted state. Souls or spirits descended from the true home into inferior realms and finally entered dimensions of mind and gross matter where they forgot their blissful origin and became lost in the vast expanses of the lower creation. When Baba Sawan Singh, a perfect saint in later life, complained to his teacher, Baba Jaimal Singh, that his mind gave him a lot of trouble, Baba Jaimal replied, *"This is the mind's job, my son, because it is the creator of all gross and subtle evil tendencies"* **(Jaimal Singh 1998:128)**. Soami Ji taught that saints reveal methods by which the mind can be controlled and used as an asset. He made it clear that austerities, such as maintaining silence, torturing the body in various ways, fasting for lengthy periods and residing naked in jungles, did not promote control of the mind. Many persons praise these ascetics because they believe they have achieved great spiritual stature. But Soami Ji said that it is easy for a careful investigator to tell whether such ascetics are sincere but unenlightened practitioners of austerities or pretenders, who seek fame, honor or even wealth **(Seva Singh N.D.: 98-99)**.

Soami Ji praised the true Master, calling him an embodiment of Sat Purush, the manifestation of deity at Sach Khand. His Word-Form guides the soul of the true seeker through all gross and subtle realms. A real guru, said Soami Ji, will only discuss the true way back to God via the Word, encourage correct meditation where the mind is controlled, and encourage love. The true teacher will explain the nature of the inner path and give personal guidance to each of his students **(Seva Singh Ji N.D.:96-97)**. The society of a living teacher is essential, for no scripture can change a person into a saint. In fact it is impossible to traverse all of the inner subtle planes without guidance. One's own mind will trip him or her if nothing else is successful in causing this person to fall. As Soami Ji **(Seva Singh N.D.:125)** said, *"To control the mind, look to the Guru. If you follow* (his) *dictates, you* (will) *control the mind; but if you follow the mind, you will go astray."* In fact Soami Ji considered the master to be the most important entity of all. After praising all of the manifestations of deity in the several dimensions, he said that it was only by the grace of his teacher that he could meet and know them. And it was only by the guidance of his guru that he could return to the Primal Home. This is why he believed that the master teacher was of prime importance **(Puri 1940:437)**.

Throughout the Sar Bachan (teachings of Soami Ji), one finds praise of the Word. He said **(Seva Singh N.D.:184)**, *"Without the Nam, or Word, inner or outer purification is not possible. There must first be a purification of the gross being, and then of the subtle"*. Soami Ji **(Seva Singh N.D.:245)** says in Bachan (or statement) 218 that the Word revealed by a perfect saint will uproot all evils and give one perfect control of the mind and senses. No other method will do this. In another passage, Soami Ji said, *"Of Shabd* (or Word) *in its various forms have I made the ladder. Step by step do you ascend and reach the True Home"* **(Puri 1982:11)**.

Love is mentioned many times as essential in spiritual liberation. First of all, one should love the perfect saint who has awesome love for you. Love will carry you to the Word or Holy Name and to the subtle or radiant form of the master within **(Seva Singh N.D.:256)**. In another paragraph Soami Ji **(Seva Singh N.D.:172)** says that love for a living saint should be like the love of a child for its mother. This reminds us of the statement of Christ that one must become as a little child in order to enter the Divine Kingdom. But few people love with the simplicity of a child. Love for a saint will translate as love for all, and such love will help liberate the seeker.

Soami Ji spoke eloquently about humility. He stated that the Lord loves humility, so it is important to do whatever induces it. Then he adds that the society of saints is the best place to obtain this quality since saints are embodiments of humility **(Seva Singh N.D.:166)**. In another passage he said that the dirt of vanity must be cleared away by service to the master and others and by constant hearing of the Word. As he put it, *"The root of all bonds of the world is egotism"* **(Seva Singh N.D.:156-157)**.

A true seeker is one who has become disillusioned with the world and its conditions. Such a seeker for God may obtain worldly luxury and great fame but he or she considers these things of no value because all mundane things have a price tag on them and cause people to become slaves to so-called necessities. All of these things and conditions are impermanent. As Soami Ji stated **(Seva Singh N.D.:160)**, "So long as the soul does not reach its real home, it will not rest in peace."

Baba Sawan Singh

Baba Sawan Singh (1858 – 1948)

He out of His mercy has bestowed upon you such a noble gift that all of the treasures of this world stand in no comparison with it. But it will not improve your condition unless you use it.

If mind could throw away all worldly desires this moment. The Soul would go up like a shot..

Baba Sawan Singh

Those authorized to perform spiritual work by Soami Ji included Baba Jaimal Singh, Rai Saligram, Seth Partap Singh and San Mukh Das. All of these disciples started lines of successors except San Mukh Das, who initiated mostly sadhus. Successors of Rai Saligram included Shiv Brat Lal, Brahm Shankar Misra and Ajodhia Prasad. Many other teachers followed these individuals in branching lines of gurus. Shyam Lal succeeded Seth Partap Singh, and Baba Jaimal Singh authorized two successors to carry on spiritual work, Baba Sawan Singh of Beas, India and Bagga Singh of Taran Taran, India. We will now consider the life and teachings of Baba Sawan Singh as a conclusion to this brief treatment of eastern mystics. Various other teachers have appeared since the time of Baba Sawan Singh, but these enlightened souls will not be considered at this time. The teachers from the west and from the east, and from various time periods, which have been discussed earlier in this book, have all taught the same basic truths. Although there are some modern followers of these saints who may disagree with this statement, a thorough study of the basic teachings of these noble souls will convince the open-minded seeker that this is true.

The radiant Baba Sawan Singh was born on July 27, 1858 in Ludhiana District of the Punjab, India. His father was Sardar Kabul Singh and his mother was Shrimati Jiwani. Sawan was the only son born to this couple. Kabul Singh often kept the company of holy men, serving them lovingly, and he passed this trait on to his son. As a young man, Sawan spent much time with a renunciate and yogi named Bhoop Singh and became impressed with his sincerity and lack of worldly attachment. He also met other holy men and learned what he could from them **(Kirpal Singh 1978:4)**.

When Sawan was 25 years of age, his father suggested that he enter the military service and arranged for a commission. He taught briefly at an army training school before he entered Thompson College of Engineering at Roorkee, India. After graduation, Sawan was offered an army commission as well as a job in civil engineering. He chose the latter and accepted a job as an overseer in Nowshera. Here he met Baba Karam Singh of Mardan and listened to his discourses. Then he went to Peshawar and became acquainted with Baba Kahan, a man with substantial inner enlightenment. Sawan asked him for guidance but was told that another person would give him the direction that he sought **(Kirpal Singh 1978:6)**.

In August of 1894, while Sawan was inspecting work on the Koh-marie road, he met his teacher, Baba Jaimal Singh. After four days of attending Baba Jaimal's discourses and asking a volley of questions, Sawan received initiation from his mentor. From this time on, as long as Baba Jaimal lived in the physical world, Sawan spent as much time as possible with him **(Kirpal Singh 1978:8)**. Many letters were exchanged between the master and his disciple when the two were physically separated. The Radha Soami Satsang at Beas has published the letters of Baba Jaimal Singh to Sawan Singh in a book called ***Spiritual Letters***.

Before he passed from his physical body on December 29, 1903, Baba Jaimal Singh authorized Sawan Singh to continue the spiritual work. He also authorized Bagga Singh of Taran Taran, India to initiate seekers for Truth, but not as many people knew about this commission as knew about the authorization given to Sawan Singh. In fact, Baba Jaimal announced publicly at Beas that Sawan would succeed him.

For over a year after the passing of Baba Jaimal Singh, Sawan Singh did not initiate seekers, although his teacher had authorized him to do so. He visited the Satsang (spiritual meeting) of Seth Partap Singh (Chacha Ji) at Agra who asked him why he was not doing the spiritual work. Sawan stated that he was not strong enough and suggested that someone else do it instead. Finally, after many days of refusal, Chacha Ji asked Sawan what he took him to be. Sawan replied that he was the brother of Soami Ji and the spiritual form of that great master. Chacha Ji said that if Sawan believed that, then the issue was settled and Sawan would have to obey his instructions. So Sawan took up the duty, serving as an agent of his beloved teacher. However, he asserted that this was not a burden that any sensible person would wish to carry **(Munshi Ram 1979:200; 1984:226)**.

Saint Sawan tirelessly performed the spiritual work for many years, giving guidance and loving encouragement to over 150,000 souls until April 2, 1948, when he left the physical form at age 90. On October 12, 1947, Saint Sawan authorized Saint Kirpal Singh to carry on the spiritual work **(Kirpal Singh 1978:27)**, and on March 20, 1948, he authorized Saint Sardar Bahadur Jagat Singh to continue the work at Beas **(Munshi Ram 1984:266)**. It is not unusual for a master soul to leave two or more successors. Soami Ji left four and Baba Jaimal left two. It is tragic, however, when disciples who do not know the full story quit behaving like loving disciples should and create disharmony and dissension. We should have love for all and let a more competent judge decide who is right and who is wrong.

Most of this discussion of Saint Sawan Singh's teachings will be extracted from a series of letters that were originally distributed in manuscript form, but recently were published by an anonymous group **(Sawan Singh 2010)**. These letters, written in English between January of 1911 and November of 1934 to a few disciples in America, are unusually long and explicit because, at that time, almost nothing had been written in English regarding the teachings of Saint Sawan or his immediate predecessors. The writer received this collection of typewritten letters many years ago from a disciple of Saint Sawan. Excerpts from some of these letters have been published in the book *Spiritual Gems* **(Radha Soami Satsang, Beas, Punjab, India 1980)**. However, the volume *Spiritual Gems* consists of randomly chosen excerpts, and the dates of writing are not given. In this book, documentation will consist of the date for the letter being considered. Unfortunately, a publisher for the 2010 edition cannot be referenced because the publication does not state the name of the publisher. The personal quality, clear presentation, and the fact that they were composed in English early in the 20th Century make them especially desirable as a source of Master Sawan's teachings. It is very important to point out that some letters were specifically directed to the personal problems of specific individuals and the suggestions may not apply equally to everyone. However, many paragraphs are valid for any seeker. It is some of these that are quoted.

Saint Sawan spoke lovingly about God. In a letter dated November 12, 1911, he wrote, "*Father* (God) *is always with you. You live, move and have your being in Him. The nearer you get to Him, the more fully will you feel His presence and His help. As the love for Him increases in you, you will get deeper and deeper realization of His Radiant Form* (inwardly)." In a letter of August 1, 1912, Sawan writes, "*Our Father is love, and we are small drops from that ocean of love. So try to bring yourself in harmony with this principle of love.*" Saint Sawan reaffirmed that God is within at the core of each entity in a letter dated March 23, 1914. He said, "*Never think of going into the wilderness to find* (Him)." He added that one could go about life as a man or woman engaged in business or as a householder and still remember God (via simran) and spend time in meditation and reach the goal one-day. In a letter dated August 29, 1929, Sawan wrote, "*Union with God is not attained through any particular religion, caste or creed. This union is attained by going within and by rising on the Sound Current* (or Word)."

In a letter dated July 27, 1919, Sawan says that saints are always present in this world. Their job is to take the souls back to the true home (Sach Khand) by connecting them to the Word within. This audible arm of God removes all impurities of mind and leads the cleansed souls back to God. On May 23, 1915, Sawan wrote that external music captivated the mind but caused a downward flow of spirit because its source was external. He added, *"The internal music is a thousand times sweeter and more melodious than that heard in this world."* It augments the powers of the spirit by focusing the widely scattered attention into one focal point. Since the source of this music is God, it attracts the spirit like a magnet. Sawan added (October 27, 1927 letter), *"if the spirit were not covered by the rust of mind and matter, it would go up like a shot."*

In a letter written on October 10, 1923, Saint Sawan responded to the lament of a husband and wife that they lived so far away from him. Sawan said, *"Never think for a moment that you are such a long distance from me. The master in the form of Shabd* (Word) *is within you and is watching you and looking after you in every way. If you rise a bit more, you can talk with him when you like."* In a letter of August 29, 1929 Sawan quotes Guru Nanak who said that the Word was ringing in every atom. Nanak said that we do not hear it because we are not in touch with it within, but this Word is there for us and to help us. It is the mission of the Saints to connect us with the Divine Word and lead us back to our true home.

Saint Sawan often refers to the Word or Nam as the Sound Current. In a letter of May 10, 1928, he said, *"the Sound Current is at the bottom of all faiths. Mohammed called it* Kalma, *Christ called it the* Word, *Nanak called it* Shabd, *and the Vedas called it Nad. They all mean the same; the difference is in the language only and in the extent to which the lift was made within."* He goes on to explain that many ancient seers and teachers used the Word as a means of rising into higher dimensions. Some stopped at the top of the Astral Plane, others journeyed on to the Causal Plane, while others followed the Word up to purely spiritual realms. Saint Sawan considered the Word to be the greatest treasure. In a letter dated August 29, 1929, he wrote, *"Is it not strange that* (many people in) *this world* (are) *poor when everyone is carrying the treasure* (within)?" He then added that the treasure of Nam or Word belongs to each person, but people only encounter it through the assistance of a saint.

As we have already indicated, all saints have praised the guru or teacher as an objective manifestation of the Word. Saint Sawan defined the duty of saints in a letter of July 6, 1926. He said, *"The object* (of saints) *is solely to assist true seekers and lovers of God."* In a letter dated May 17, 1923, Sawan said, *"The master never fails to do his part toward those whom he has taken into his fold."* He then added that those who do their duty will see how the master helps them from within. Even those who fail to meditate properly and disobey his injunctions will find that he comes to their rescue when everyone else has forsaken them. In a letter of October 10, 1923, Sawan indicated that the inner connection with the Word was permanent. He said, *"My connection with you is not limited to this life but is for all times."* In other words, the Guru as Word stays with the disciple until the True Home is reached. In a letter of December 17, 1925, Saint Sawan explained that death of the physical master was not a reason for dismay. In answer to the question of whom to see for guidance when the guru who initiated you dies, Sawan said, *"The master leaves the physical frame like other people, but he remains with his disciples in the astral form."* He then stated that the teacher would continue to give internal guidance and would discharge his duties as before. Outer guidance could be given by a successor, but it may be difficult for a beginning disciple to recognize the successor.

Love for God and for all of his disciples permeates the beautiful letters of Sawan Singh. In a correspondence of December 17, 1925 Sawan said that the way of the saints is *"not a platform for debates, it is the glory of love."* In a letter dated July 3, 1924, Sawan asserted that the path to God was based upon pure and simple love for the guru, God and for all incarnated souls. In a letter of June 9, 1932, Sawan writes, *"Mind and intellect keep the fires of hopes and desires kindled. In these fires the soul suffers. Therefore pass on both the mind and intellect to the master, and take from him in exchange the wealth of love and devotion."* As he put it in a letter of March 24, 1933, *"Our path homeward is lit with the brightest of suns and moons, and our home is peace personified and our father love and grace."*

All saints have indicated that the mind is the most obdurate enemy any disciple could face. It is the mind that conceives the most sensuous thoughts, indulges in anger and greed, and daydreams constantly to satiate the ego. In a lengthy letter of July 3, 1924, Sawan wrote, *"The Sound Current* (Word) *and the master do not appear* (within) *as long as there is low karmic dirt in the mind. The process of cleansing is going on. The time* (required to clean the mind) *depends on mental attitude, and cases are known in which development has been phenomenal."* In a letter of December 17, 1925 Sawan states that most evil resides in the mind, but such is curable. Saints look at the disciple's soul and not at his or her mind or body. They feed the soul and help it become strong so that it can overcome all tendencies that are less than divine. A purified and disciplined mind makes a good servant of the soul, but an untamed mind is a poor master. In a letter of May

10, 1928, Sawan stated that the mind and soul are so intricately intertwined that unless the mind is trained to go within, the soul cannot do so either. If the mind and higher attention are in the Word, the karmic bonds are loosened. But, he affirmed, *"It is an uphill task."*

All saints and spiritual teachers have recommended the discipline of meditation. As Sawan said in a letter of August 1, 1912, *"He out of his mercy has bestowed upon you such a noble gift that all of the treasures of this world stand in no comparison with it. But it will not improve your condition unless you use it. A hungry man is never satisfied simply by* (stating) *the names of various dishes that lie before him. Though the teachings you have* (been given) *are invaluable, yet they cannot be of any good* (to you) *unless you act* (upon) *them and daily engage in* (meditation) *for as long a time as you can spare from your worldly engagements."* Saint Sawan admitted, in a letter of March 20, 1916 that meditation is a difficult task at first, but after one becomes proficient in it, it is most joyful. As he put it, *"most practitioners become despondent in the beginning, but still they cannot give it up because they can find no other and easier path. Therefore, they resume their journey and succeed in the end."* Sawan often gave clear and detailed descriptions of what happened in successful meditation. In a lengthy letter dated April, 1927 (no day given), Sawan wrote, *"When the attention has been withdrawn from the body below the eyes, and has become fixed in the eye-focus, we become unconscious of the body below the eyes, but we are superconscious within."* He then added that one is now oblivious to the physical world and passes through an aperture into the Astral dimension. After experiencing the Astral Plane, the attention can return to the physical world and remember the Astral experience clearly. In a letter of October 14, 1931, Sawan took the meditation experience much further. He said, *"Inside the phy-*

sical is the Astral and inside the Astral is the Causal." He then explained that when we reach the Astral plane we travel to the top of it and pass through a tunnel into the Causal Plane. Then at the top of the Causal Plane we are able to enter the state above mind or the *"Empty Realm"* of some faiths. Sawan compared this process to the removal of a series of coats.

Saint Sawan taught that one was drawn to the spiritual path because of noble past karmas and because they inwardly cried out to God for guidance. It was God, therefore, who decided to bring them home. In a letter of February 6, 1914, Sawan wrote, *"You should not be anxious to scatter these teachings far and wide. If anyone comes to you with love and is a real and honest* (seeker for Truth), *you may (help) him understand all about this* (spiritual path)." In another letter (November 22, 1922) Sawan emphasized that *"it is not our object to increase our followers* (through proselytizing); *the object is to help the sincere and truly loving seekers."* In another letter (dated only April, 1931) Sawan emphasized that saints were not interested in attracting large numbers of adherents, making money or gaining fame, for such things are forms of poison on the path of truth. Sawan wrote, *"If you come across a real seeker, give him* (or her) *a hint. There is no necessity to go out of your way to influence others. Things happen when the time is ripe."*

In a letter dated simply September, 1918, Sawan makes it clear that all of those who have received initiation from a genuine saint are protected throughout life and met at the time of death by the Astral form of the master. Those who meditate much and purify their minds go within where they can converse with the inner form of the saint throughout their lives. If the mind has not been cleansed of deficiencies, and concentration has not been developed via meditation, the master will still appear before the gaze of the disciple at death and take the soul up to whatever level it can maintain consciousness. It can then progress from this point to higher spiritual levels. Sawan concluded, *"If mind could throw away all worldly desires this moment, the soul would go up like a shot."*

Hopefully, this brief consideration of partial teachings of selected saints from Western, Middle Eastern and Far Eastern spiritual traditions has adequately demonstrated the fact that all genuine saints have taught essentially the same thing. Teachers have been sent to the world from many different levels of being such as purely spiritual, Causal, and Astral realms. But all of those from higher spiritual levels taught about the Word (often referred to as Logos, Shabd, Nam and various other names). Adepts from Astral or Causal levels often used pranayam breathing procedures and certain asanas (or exercises), along with a satvic diet (foods conductive to Hatha Yoga and Raja Yoga discipline) and a mantra of sacred words, to steady the mind and harness the vital pranas. Prana is the sum total of natural energy in the universe. Pranayam exercises enhance sense perceptions, grant mental powers, and awaken the Kundalini energy stored at the base of the spine. The attention then ascends from chakra to chakra (centers where nerves and/or energy channels converge) to centers in the brain and to consciousness upon Astral and Causal Plane levels. The object of Raja and Ashtang yoga practices is to achieve conscious or superconscious samadhi (states of heightened consciousness and freedom). The difficulty of negotiating this intricate path and the scarcity of genuine adepts in these practices mean that few adherents are successful in rising to elevated spiritual levels. In defense of these methods, it can be said that those without backgrounds of purity and discipline usually see light quicker in one of the yoga systems that use pranayam because the exercises begin at lower chakras. Most saints start their disciples at the third eye center and go up from there, so it may take quite a bit of time before progress becomes apparent to the devotee who has limited spiritual background. Both Astral and Causal Plane teachers may employ methods other than the Word, but the Word can be used to carry one to any of these levels as well as to purely spiritual realms. Saintly teachers from all religious traditions have practiced and taught the way of the Divine Word. Spirituality is a prayer mat upon which all religions may sit or kneel.

Chapter 7

SPIRITUALITY ON A NATIONAL LEVEL

Righteousness exalteth a nation:
but sin is a reproach to any people
(Proverbs 14: 34)

Factors of cause and effect operate on national levels the same as they do in individual life experiences. Unfortunately, most nations do not consider the probable or potential effects of corrupt or wicked living and thus fail to steer a course of righteousness. Whether the citizens of a nation believe in laws of cause and effect or not, they are affected by them and have no choice but to accept the consequences of their life styles. Look at the Roman Empire, for example. Amid a few talented and skillful administrators such as Augustus (63BC – AD 14), Hadrian (AD 76 – 138), Antoninus Pius (AD 86 – 161) and Marcus Aurelius (AD 121 – 180) were a number of dissolute tyrants. Examples of the latter include Nero (AD 37 – 68), Commodus (AD 161 – 192), and Elagabalus (AD 204 – 222). Incessant wars and political corruption decimated the national treasury, so increasingly heavy taxation was practiced. Gladiatorial games in which combatants fought to the death before cheering crowds, public torture of Christians and political opponents (including exposing them to starving beasts in an arena and burning them alive) were common forms of "entertainment" in Rome. Public displays of sexual perversion and private practices of gross sensuality on the part of political leaders and common citizens took place throughout the Roman Empire. All of these activities yielded karmic results, and the Roman Empire collapsed. Other great political systems have also fallen for similar reasons. Each nation today must face the results of oppressive governmental leaders, political corruption, and selfish commercialism in the course of time. Although modern politicians may not be quite as degraded as the worst Roman emperors, current American political leaders have created their own arenas of despair. There will be no escaping the consequences of their dissolute actions.

All nations need sound governments that help and protect each citizen under their jurisdictions. This means that leadership must be honorable, just and virtuous. In fact an ideal leader serves as an ethical and moral example to all young people in that nation. Fairness to everyone, honesty, thoughtfulness and a genuine concern for the welfare of each citizen characterizes a true statesman and leader. Such a person rises above partisan political levels to the status of a servant of the people. As Christ put it **(Mark 10:43-44)**, *"He who would be the greatest among you shall be the servant of all."* Unfortunately, instead of electing capable and totally honest social servants to positions of authority, we support politicians whose connections with political parties and special interest groups render them incapable of being just and unbiased. So many political leaders with commitments to certain commercial agendas and powerful lobbyists legislate on behalf of these entities and fail to consider what is best for the nation now and in the future. Unless we change our ways of government to promote justice for all in the context of maximum freedom, we too must ultimately travel the road to defeat and collapse. And like the Egyptian dynasties, Roman Empire and Nazi dictatorship in

Germany, we too will reap what we have sown and are sowing.

War has been a human plague throughout history. Millions of young men and women have been sacrificed in religious wars and in conflicts started by egotistical or thoughtless political leaders. Only Satan, or whatever one calls the negative power or ego-driven mental tempter, leads armies to wars of aggression. Only he can inspire the hatred and selfishness that makes people fight like beasts in the night. Certainly the defense of one's nation is moral if your country is attacked by another country, but aggression or preemptive striking of what may possibly be a potential threat is never a sound moral decision. Also, it is not right to push another nation to desperation by economic sanctions, naval blockades or other strategies so that they have no alternative other than to attack you. A righteous nation will always take the moral high ground and will not sanction or encourage a despot or dictator simply to obtain oil or some other commodity at special prices. A truly democratic government will stand up for the freedoms of others irrespective of the cost in terms of temporary financial advantages. Such a nation will only respond militarily when forced to do so by aggression. A righteous country tries to live in peace and is fair to all other nations.

In the event that an aggressor forces war upon a nation, the spiritual society will practice moral and humane treatment of all prisoners captured regardless of how the opposing forces treat their captives. Even if they use inhumane tortures and starve captives to coerce them into revealing what they know, the truly democratic and just nation will not sink to that level. Such a nation will emulate the giants of spirituality who have advocated love and justice and not join ranks with tyrants and terrorists. Righteous nations will allow the negative karma of wicked countries to fructify, which it will, and payment will be made in due course. Remember that Revelation 13:10 says, *"He that leadeth into captivity shall go into captivity: he that killeth with the sword must be killed with the sword. Here is the patience and faith of the saints."* This is a very clear statement of karmic law or cause and effect. Any nation that engages in cruel and inhumane practices is really sowing the seeds of its own demise.

Public servants in each nation are responsible for the welfare of the citizens that they are supposed to serve. They must allocate resources wisely and make efforts to promote future world peace. If most of the money spent upon expensive weapons of war were used to enhance the welfare of the citizens of a democratic nation, that society would become so strong that no forces of tyranny could subdue it. This is real national security. No nation really needs huge stockpiles of weapons of mass destruction. It actually needs only the minimum forces required to defend itself adequately regardless of what another government may possess. While military strength may dissuade an aggressor sometimes, an enhanced moral strength and a free society are far greater protections. Directly or indirectly, poverty, ignorance and social injustices fuel the fires of rebellion and civil strife. The main culprits here are bad governments. Our political leaders in the twenty-first century must wake up and expound spiritual values or be responsible for our downfall.

Any genuine democratic society maintains freedoms of speech, press, protest and worship even when threatened by terrorists or those who oppose democratic processes. The strength of a genuine democracy resides in the freedoms enjoyed by all. To paraphrase Ben Franklin, *"Any nation that sacrifices individual liberty to gain security deserves neither and loses both."* A nation under surveillance by *"Big Brother"* is doomed to failure by its own oppressive methods because those who have once tasted freedom cannot tolerate the bitter flavor of oppression. A truly compassionate political leadership concerns itself with maintaining a strong social security system so elderly people can live decently, promotes an exemplary health care system that stresses prevention via healthy living and attends to the needs of each citizen, and has a well conceived emergency preparedness plan. Such measures reflect a wise use of wealth. Above all, good leaders are totally honest. If an answer to a reporter's question might compromise national security, a true lover of freedom will state as much; but all other answers should be truthful and clear. A free society can never be based upon lies.

A spiritual nation considers the fact that life on earth is a continuum and plans for tomorrow as well as today. We live in the context of a fragile and vulnerable environment. If we think only of modern economic factors and then pollute or destroy the natural landscape so a few millionaires can become even wealthier, we do a disservice to the present population and prepare a tragedy for future generations. Unfortunately, our children and grandchildren must reap the chaos being sown by shortsighted political leaders of today. There is an old Cree Indian saying that may be paraphrased in this manner: *"Only when the last tree has died, and the last river has been poisoned, and the last fish and animals have expired will we realize that we cannot eat money."* Americans today would do well to consider the example of Andrew Carnegie (1835 – 1919) who gave away his millions before he died. Two of his statements are worth repeating. 1. *"He who dies rich dies disgraced."* 2. *"Beyond this ($50,000.00 per year) never earn, but spend the surplus for benevolent purposes."* During his lifetime Carnegie gave away over 350 million dollars to promote education, culture and peace. The millionaire who tries to amass more money when millions are in poverty or starving cannot be looked upon as a compassionate member of the human race.

Every species of plant in the world has significant importance in the overall scheme of life. Many plants and trees have medicinal value, others are useful for food, and still others exemplify beauty in a desirable landscape. Wise people will maintain the genetic diversity they have inherited. Unfortunately, many species have been allowed to become extinct simply because they were not of immediate economic value. Take the apple for example. Thousands of varieties have been developed over the last two centuries, but many of these have been lost to cultivation simply because they did not possess bright colors, such as red or gold hues, or have favorable shipping qualities. Many of these antique varieties have fantastic flavor and are wonderful for a home orchard, but commercially minded nurseries promote only a few popular varieties. Every nation needs to have a botanical institution that keeps a few examples of all known species so a wide genetic diversity will be maintained. This would not be an expensive project. We spend millions on wars and destruction; why not allocate a moderate amount of money for preservation of all botanical resources, especially our supply of medicinal and food plants?

Many mammals, birds and fish have either become extinct or are on the verge of extinction. Since modern humans did not create any of these life forms, what makes us think we have the right to exterminate any biological species so some large corporation or wealthy entity can make more money? Most of our streams, rivers and oceans are now contaminated with heavy metals, pesticides, chemical residues and agricultural wastes. Oil companies are allowed to drill in all environmental contexts in order to extract the last drops of a rapidly vanishing resource. We need to use our remaining petroleum reserves as a source of raw materials for lubricants, plastics and other products and develop the hydrogen fuel cell and renewable energy sources. But instead of planning for tomorrow in a thoughtful manner, the political leadership and many major corporations of today think only of immediate profits at the expense of environmental concerns. While it is true that the health of major corporations must be appraised in a modern democratic society, we must also consider impacts upon total populations and our collective futures in devising sound economic strategies. Theoretically, our government is supposed to be of the people, by the people and for everyone in the nation. And yet, most governmental procedures are devised and implemented by huge political organizations or parties in affiliation with the giant corporations that fund these political systems. Small businesses, including family farms, are unable to compete with corporate giants and are forced into liquidation. People are losing the right to choose between natural and inexpensive health therapies with long track records and heavily promoted but untested medications because giant pharmaceutical companies mislead doctors into prescribing expensive and poorly evaluated drugs in order to make huge profits. Take the recent Vioxx scandal, for example. This widely advertised drug for pain turned out to be deadly for many individuals. Natural remedies exist for most maladies, but pharmaceutical giants discourage their use because such remedies cannot be patented and sold at tremendous profits.

Corporate titans and governmental agencies supported by them are not being honest with the American people. The same is true with other nations in the world. We run a serious risk of developing what might be called a corporate federalism where a very few gigantic corporations own almost all real property and people are forced to work for them under their conditions. Any spiritual approach to government considers each citizen to be as important as any other individual, and it recognizes the God-given right of each species to exist on a thoughtfully managed earth.

While it may be wise for spiritual precepts to infuse our educational structures, indoctrination in specific religious viewpoints must be avoided. America's founding fathers advocated a separation of church and state because the history of most nations in Europe and elsewhere indicated that rulers had all too often selected the state religion. And people were forced to participate in religious systems that were not in harmony with personal consciences. In a nation like America it would be wrong to try to establish a fundamentalist Christian State, a Catholic State or an Islamic State. Spirituality can permeate every religion, but one size does not fit all when it comes to personal creeds. Take the issue of prayer in public schools. If everyone in a community agreed on religious doctrine, one prayer might be suitable in a specific educational institution. Problems arise in a community where many individuals are members of numerous Protestant denominations, a large percentage belong to the Catholic Church, several families are of the Jewish Faith, a few practice Buddhist devotional methods, some families are of Islamic persuasion, a limited number belong to the Bahai faith and a few people are atheists. In a community with such varied religious views, there is no way that everyone can agree on a format for public prayer. Protestant denominations usually pray aloud, Catholic adherents cross themselves as they pray, Islamic believers are required to face Mecca and prostate themselves as they pray five times a day, and Buddhist adherents prefer meditation to prayer. A possible solution to this dilemma would be to have ten minutes before classes begin during which each religious group could meet in private to engage in personal devotions or, in the case of atheists, could engage in whatever activity inspires them. But no one should be forced to perform a religious ritual or pray in a way that does not agree with personal conscience. After all, we are supposed to have freedom of religion or freedom to embrace no religion in America.

Most people of faith endorse devotion in some form. Places of worship, such as churches, synagogues, temples, and mosques should be available for religious services and personal devotions, and members of all faiths should engage in favored methods of prayer or meditation in the privacy of their own homes. It is doubtful that those who do not practice spirituality at home do so at religious services either. And, of course, atheists should not be coerced into following any religious procedure. Each person should respect the views of every other human being. Those who believe it is their job to "*save*" those whom they see as mistaken in the world should save themselves, and allow God, Allah, Brahm or whatever one might call an Ultimate Power to decide who is right or wrong. It is an ego trip of titanic proportions for one to assume that his or her faith is the only one that is theologically correct.

A sound educational system teaches students how to think and not what to think. It is good for each pupil to be familiar with the scientific method, but the limitations of science should also be stressed. Some things are beyond examination by modern scientific procedures. Initial causation is one example. While some cosmologists and astrophysicists have claimed that they can explain the development of life and consciousness without recourse to a divine concept, the postulations that they suggest cannot be proven by observation or by mathematical means. Unfortunately the scientists who develop such things as nuclear energy and superior technology are not the ones who employ such awesome powers. Unenlightened and economically oriented political leaders often decide how these developments will be used in the world. What should be a sound answer to dwindling natural resources becomes captive to blind ideology and to proponents of greed. Andre Malraux expressed both concern and insight when he wrote, *"Science in the twenty-first century will be spiritual, or it will not be"* **(Thuan 1995:274)**. The public needs to be educated regarding both the nature of and the limitations of science as well as sound political management of the fruits of science.

It would be of great benefit to teach comparative religions without bias or judgments upon the validity of the many faiths. In a closely-knit world, people need to know what others believe so they will not inadvertently offend them in word or deed. Open-minded discussions are important ingredients in education. In a discussion everyone learns something (at least the views of others), whereas in an argument hard heads collide as emotions erupt, and learning exits the premise.

Every great nation contributes inspired visual art and music to world culture. Such creative genius uplifts and strengthens society as it prepares the inner nature of each person to contact the Divine Wisdom within. While the artistic efforts of modern human beings are imperfect, each step toward the goal of spiritual awareness must be praised. **Cyril Scott (1933)**, in his perceptive book ***Music, Its Secret Influence throughout the Ages***, explained how the works of great classical composers as well as various other categories of music affected world societies. **Scott (1933:124-125)** suggested that music influences the physical consciousness as sound vibrations play upon the emotional and mental natures of each individual. Due to differences in emotional and mental development among individuals, music that inspires and delights one person may not appeal to another. But certain works of genius will impress a large number of individuals and thus uplift a substantial segment of society. Because of this, a responsible government will encourage all reasonable types of artistic expression.

Categories of popular entertainment are prone to constant change as one type of art or music gains popularity while a recently favored category gradually vanishes from public demand. Tastes are constantly changing. Television, movies and printed media try to maintain audiences or readership by introducing more daring and explicit entertainment. This can either be degrading or a positive factor in the development of taste. If a scene in a television program or in a movie introduces sexual promiscuity strictly for the sake of erotic titillation, it is objectionable. If there is a positive artistic reason for nudity, for example, then it may be acceptable. Some of the scenes in Shakespeare's *Romeo and Juliet* are quite explicit, but they contribute toward a positive impact. The great bard was *"holding the mirror up to man,"* as he put it, and he honestly portrayed both the sensual and sublime aspects of human behavior. A prudish Victorian attitude is just as bad as a lewd or vulgar tendency. The natural aspects of human nature, such as eating, sleeping and sex, are not bad or indecent in themselves. It is when such things are perverted that they have negative social impacts. For example, the marvelous film *The Miracle of Life* depicts both conception and birth openly. Only a seriously distorted mind could possibly find anything objectionable about this superb video. Since children have an innate curiosity about adult sexual matters, parents and religious leaders should properly teach such things in an accurate but non-sensational manner at suitable ages. No young person should learn the facts of life from his or her peers because such sources are often unreliable and there is a tendency to sensationalize sexual matters.

What is acceptable in one society is often frowned upon in another. Yet religious and political leaders in each nation can encourage certain standards of decency in entertainment. Inspirational and scientific productions as well as thoughtfully presented sports programming are always popular and should be promoted. A sense of sportsmanship and courtesy need to be instilled in all athletic personalities. The use of performance enhancing substances simply to set new records sends a bad message to youthful athletes and such *"records"* are not genuine since we are not using a level playing field. The argument that everyone else is taking steroids or performance enhancing substances indicates a lack of both clear thinking and genuine sportsmanship.

The media must realize that it is their responsibility to provide uplifting and wholesome entertainment and not allow the *"bottom line"* of immediate profits to dictate what is made available to listeners and viewers. On the other hand, the *"Big Brother"* approach of privacy invasion is altogether undesirable. The media should monitor themselves so legislative controls will not be needed. Media censorship in private homes and clubs is impractical and probably unconstitutional in the United States at least. But if religious, educational and governmental institutions do their part to encourage reasonable entertainment, social pressures will have tremendous effects.

Entertainment that encourages or unnecessarily depicts violence or racial hatred must be frowned upon by all sincere and sensitive souls. The constant depiction of violence on television, video games and in movies tends to make viewers insensitive to the sufferings of others. Keeping the mind constantly inundated by violent or aggressive actions reduces the ability to appreciate harmonious and thoughtful things. If we are to end up having a peaceful world, people must create serene conditions through collective mental and emotional contemplation of tranquility. As we think, so we become and our physical actions reflect what we are inwardly. Since habits are formed by repetition of attitudes and by processes of thinking, we can establish either a violent society or a harmonious and loving social structure. The choice is ours as a nation.

Chapter 8

SPIRITUALITY AS A PERSONAL WAY OF LIFE

Nothing from outside can give you peace,
because peace is within you always.

(Swami Satchidananda)

Everyone in the world is seeking for love and peace, but few people look in the right place to find it. Peace cannot be discovered in the outer world because everything in it is constantly changing and fraught with turmoil. Millions of battles are ceaselessly being fought, from the levels of microbes to human encounters, and even galactic changes can be observed. Certainly a tranquil landscape in our objective world can seem peaceful, but this is only because we fail to see the total picture. Behind a rock one could find an ant attacking an insect or, in a tree, an observer could discover a bird swallowing a worm. There is no real peace anywhere in nature unless a human observer who has found it within projects it outwardly and thus affects his or her immediate surroundings.

A great eastern sage, Bikha Sahib, once observed that every person has diamonds and rubies in his or her bundle, but how to untie the knot they do not know, so they remain paupers. Yes, love and wonderful peace both exist within each entity, but these jewels are kept behind locked doors to protect them from unworthy thieves. To those who believe they can personally obtain these gems unaided, one can only say: *"good luck!"* An extremely pure and highly evolved soul might gain part of this wealth, and a few have done so. But most of us are so mentally soiled and selfish that we cannot enter the inner realms where love and peace may be found. Also, there is as much deception and turmoil in the Astral dimension as in the physical realm, and the mind is a creative factor in the Causal Plane. The wisest thing for you to do is to find a teacher who holds the key to the door of your inner safety deposit box. Certainly you must do the seeking and finding, but you need guidance in order to avoid making many errors. You must adopt a way of life that leads you beyond the rituals of religions and the intellectual gymnastics of philosophy. This way of life is called spirituality.

All living things are rooted in God much like a tree is rooted in earth. Only our attention has dropped from the Divine State to lower realms where we learn by terse experience. It can return to God by passing through all lower dimensions if we engage in proper spiritual disciplines under the guidance of someone who knows the way home. This is what Jesus meant when he asserted that the kingdom of God is at hand **(Mark 1:15)**. **In Luke 17:20-21**, Jesus clarified this when he exclaimed that the kingdom of God comes not with (outer) observation: for the Kingdom of God is within you. He referred to spiritual guidance when he told his disciples: *"I am the way the truth and the life"* **(John 14:6)**. In other words, his followers could only approach God with his help. When our drop of attention rejoins the ocean of Divine Consciousness, we realize the awesome fact that we never really left God, for an essential part of us was always anchored in divinity. This was the only way that we could maintain our existence and the reason we could return to The Source by expanding our consciousness from self knowledge to an awareness of God. The re-focusing of our attention or spiritual essence is accomplished through the practice of meditation and spiritual living.

One of the major challenges one faces in each social context is that of making a living. The nature of one's livelihood has a tremendous impact upon his or her spiritual growth. First of all, the means of earning a living must be honest and contribute to the general welfare. A vocation should be morally and ethically sound in every way. Emphasis should be placed upon the importance of service to others and not strictly upon the bottom line of monetary income. An activity may be legal but ethically and morally questionable. We grow spiritually when we serve lovingly and unselfishly, and whenever we put others before ourselves, we will be blessed with such basic material necessities as shelter, food and clothing as well as other useful things, but most important of all, we will be blessed with spiritual insight and love.

Wealth can be a tremendous test of personal integrity and compassion. A billionaire who revels in luxury, having many times more wealth than he or she can use, cannot take this material opulence with him or her when death calls. But they do take with them the karmic load caused by selfishness and they have to answer for that greed before the karmic judge. They could have done so much good in the world with their millions, but they chose to hoard it and neglect the needs of others. Andrew Carnegie uttered a wise precept when he said: *"he who dies rich dies disgraced."* He also allegedly said, *"Money is like manure. Spread it around and it does a lot of good, but pile it up in one place and it stinks like shit."* There is nothing wrong with being rich if one uses the money wisely. If you have wealth, you can help others in so many ways.

But if your assets have you, and your god is the bottom line, your immaturity makes wealth a noose about your neck and chains about your feet as it exposes your inner selfishness. The dictum of Thoreau that *"one is rich in proportion to the number of things he can afford to leave alone"* represents another side of the wealth issue. Many wise people have chosen to eliminate attachments to material objects and property and live lives of simplicity. But this is not spiritually preferable to controlling wealth to help many others. These represent two forms of non-attachment. Each one of us must choose the route where he or she can be of greatest service to others, because selfless service reflects true spiritual stature.

Those who *"sell"* religion have much in common with those who sell questionable securities. Many ministers, priests and religious exponents are sincerely interested in serving others unselfishly, and such individuals are to be admired. They earn meager livings by teaching and inspiring those whom they guide. But so many dealers in religion serve themselves particularly and choose this profession because it is an easier way to make a living than engaging in manual labor or even serious intellectual activities. So many religionists on ego trips pretend to be agents of God and sure guides to paradise. They presume to lead and save others when they have not liberated themselves. Jesus and other genuine teachers have strongly denounced such hypocrisy. Humility, love and unselfish service toward others mark the genuine spiritual teacher. He or she is not busy laying up treasures on earth, nor are they striving for glory in heaven. They serve because they love others and see service as the right thing to do.

Another questionable vocation is that of the faith healer who pretends to be an agent of the divine. A certain acquaintance of mine once wrote to a well-known *"faith healer"* asking him to pray that she would recover from cancer. This *"minister"* responded by writing that if she would send him $50.00 as an offering, he would pray for her. A prayer from such a social leach would be worthless. On no occasion did Jesus demand money to heal the infirm, and in no instance did he advocate taking money for prayers or healing. Neither Jesus nor any other genuine agent of God ever said, *"Come unto me ye that are loaded with money and I will heal you for so much."* True healing, like all gifts of God, such as spiritual truth, is free. Those who try to make a living by *"acting"* as healing agents of God have yet to learn some basic things about living and true service.

Most psychics and charismatic fortunetellers, who advise the gullible on such matters as health, methods of obtaining wealth and securing true love, are of questionable veracity because they do this for money. Certainly there are genuine psychics and prophetic individuals, but these never charge for advice or guidance. As one loving and sincere psychic once told me, *"my abilities are gifts of God. If I charge for them or even take money for them, I lose them."* I once received a letter from a well-known *"psychic"* who stated that God had given her the gifts of psychic insight and healing ability and that for $30.00 per month she would act as my spiritual advisor and guide me to health, fortune and true love. I responded with a letter in which I stated that I was delighted to learn that God had blessed her with such a psychic gift. Then I added, *"by the way, what did He charge you for it?"* Needless to say, that was my last letter from Madame So and So. A few psychics as well as certain so called spiritual *"teachers"* or *"guides"* use hypnosis (focused or controlled imagination) or suggestion to make others see what they want them to see or experience. Since imagination seems *"real"* or tangible to some portions of the mind, this can be misleading. One test for authenticity in such matters is this: if the so-called guides are charging money for guidance or clearly seek fame because this brings wealth, they are acting from selfish motives. Avoid them!

A poll taken several years ago revealed that the public distrusted used car dealers, insurance salespersons and politicians more than any other vocational groups. The reason for this lack of trust was because most people felt that these individuals told each person what he or she wanted to hear not necessarily the truth. Now we have had a few honorable politicians and many generally good ones, but we have been deceived and lied to by hundreds of them. So many use patriotic motives to gain adherents while others promise improvements in a certain local infrastructure to obtain votes. The broad general good is seldom considered. It is indeed suspicious when a candidate spends several million dollars to obtain a job that only pays $60,000.00 to $150,000.00 per year. Few are willing to lose that much money personally just to serve others, and those who are funded by special interest groups have so many commitments to these entities that they cannot behave fairly and in the public's best interests. Influence peddling and under-the-table kickbacks are sources of income for many dubious political leaders. Very few of them retire from *"public service"* with limited wealth and incomes. The example of President Harry S. Truman is an unusual exception for one who obtained high office. He returned to Independence, Missouri and lived in a modest frame home after he left the nation's capitol. Some will complain that Tom Pendergast, head of the Pendergast machine of Kansas City, sponsored Harry Truman in his early political career as County Judge and initially as a U.S. senator. Certainly this is true, but Truman had no choice.

One either went along with Pendergast or you did not survive very long. But when Boss Pendergast died and Truman was his own man, he formed the Truman Committee and investigated waste in World War II defense spending. Although he made mistakes later in his career, they were honest misjudgments and he always did his best. Even in the decision to use the nuclear bomb to end the Japanese segment of World War II, Harry carefully considered the odds. It is estimated that it would have taken almost one million American lives and possibly as many Japanese lives to conquer Japan by going from island to island. As it was, about 120,000 Japanese citizens lost their lives. This was an awful decision for Truman to make. Perhaps only Lincoln had to consider such a difficult situation since early colonial times.

The American sage Henry David Thoreau had much to say about misguided patriotism in his great essay on **"Civil Disobedience."** Those who serve the state with their consciences must disagree with corrupt and arbitrary governments that enslave citizens and tax them for more than their money. Thoreau concluded, "*No man with a genius for legislation has appeared in America. They are rare in the history of the world. There are orators, politicians, and eloquent men, by the thousand...We love eloquence for its own sake, and not for any truth which it may utter.*" Thoreau felt that if we rely completely upon the *"wordy wit"* of legislators for guidance we would surely fail as a nation. Today we need statesmen and men of spiritual stature as well as intellectual depth to usher us along the path of real democracy.

Another career choice is a military one. A hasty thinking idealist will assert that since war is hell indeed, then serving in the armed forces either reflects a bestial quality on the part of the enlistee or strong governmental coercion on those drafted to fight. All of the higher teachers have frowned upon taking of human life, but all of them have said that defense is moral if one is attacked by others. The injunction that *"thou shall not kill"* is equally true for oneself as for others. In other words, to allow your own life to be taken when such could be prevented is wrong. The attitude postulated in the Bhagavaggita that one should fight without anger or hatred for others while realizing that death does not end existence for anyone is almost impossible to practice. But to say that spirituality is incompatible with a military career is refuted by the life of the great Saint Baba Jaimal Singh (1838-1903) who chose a military career because other options were unavailable. The caste system of his day stipulated career choices for each caste segment. Today most people can choose their own careers and this choice often reflects the state of personal spiritual development.

Popular entertainers and sports heroes should be moral and ethical examples for young people today; however few of them are. So many use their vast wealth to engage in personal dissipation via alcohol, drugs and constant sexual involvement. The abuse of performance enhancing drugs in endeavors to achieve new records is not fair to those of yesterday who did not use such substances to boost performances. To compare the records of Babe Ruth or Roger Maris to those who are today breaking those records is not fair to the sport of baseball (in this instance) or to devoted fans because one standard is not being applied to all participants throughout time. This same objection applies to football, basketball, cycling and many other competitive sports.

A spiritually oriented person should avoid those vocations that distort or abuse natural functions, especially sex. Certainly there are instances in history where a person believed to be a prostitute has made a complete reversal to become a spiritual entity. Mary Magdaline is an alleged example of such an individual. Frequently, a loving woman mistakenly associates physical involvement with men with genuine love only to discover later that she was mistaken. Spiritual leaders often recognize the potential for deep and pure love in a person who is temporarily engaging in immoral behavior. Saints are here to redeem errant persons, not to condemn them, and they feed the positive side of each soul. And a capacity for love is definitely a spiritual asset. Many people have yet to learn the difference between *"making love"* and being a real lover in a spiritual sense.

Those activities that sensationally distort the sexual function, such as graphic pornography, must be avoided if one is to live a spiritual life. People who engage in and those who view sexual abuse of children in life or on videos and those who engage in sex with animals have yet to be assaulted by vestiges of conscience. God did not design sex for such abuse. In some impoverished nations children or teenagers are sold to barbaric tourists so serve as sex objects. They are forced to perform every imaginable type of indignity for the amusement of their dissolute captors. Reaping the karmic penalties for such thoughtless behaviors will be intense and extremely unpleasant experiences. Yet, the karmic law will be satisfied in the course of time.

Another vocation that stifles spirituality is gambling where one person's financial gain comes at the expense of someone else. The winning of money in a state lottery, for example, is not the same as winning heavily in a poker game because in the latter instance others at the table lost what the winner gained. In both instances one must ask the question, *"did I really earn this money by a useful activity?"* Of course if one uses lottery money to perform charitable activities and not for a personal ego splurge, he or she may benefit many others. An infusion of money seriously tests the mettle of an individual far more than does abject poverty.

Finally, we will consider the workaholic who spends every possible second in life trying to amass material wealth and takes no time for self-improvement. When work becomes a *"god,"* it stifles spiritual development and this worker leaves the world impoverished because none of his or her wealth accompanies the individual.

One should not pretend to be something that he or she is not. Hypocrisy is detrimental to spiritual progress because it is a type of lie. One can tell outright falsehoods or one can lie by distorting the truth or by omitting something that is relevant to a situation. The most serious lie one can express is to pretend to be a spiritual teacher when he or she is not. This is the ultimate ego trip and carries the heaviest penalty. A spiritual person is totally honest at all times. He or she is not interested in impressing the world with personal learning or spiritual attainments. Fame, like material wealth, cannot be taken into the beyond at death. In fact, both of these temporary conditions are often maladies that infect and mislead the mind. When the instrument of thought is blind or deluded, it is never a suitable spiritual guide.

Spiritual people take a disciplined yet loving approach to life. They use the mind but are not led or misled by it. Mind relishes diversity and constant change, and it leads a soul like the proverbial sheep down a path of shallow diversions. Only when it is too late does the soul realize that it is on the edge of a precipice where it lacks the ability to change directions or reverse a forward momentum. Death is unexpected but inevitable in such a circumstance.

Something might be said about avocations or hobbies. These can be of value if they help one to relax and think more positively. Swimming, hiking, camping, golf and other similar recreational activities can be beneficial. Reading great books that make us think and watching inspirational videos can motivate us toward living spiritual lives. It is certainly all right to collect something that interests one, whether this is coins, stamps, old china or sports paraphernalia, but one should consider others when doing so and be fair about making acquisitions.

Spiritual people respect the environment and never contribute to pollution or environmental destruction for immediate or future financial gains. Also, spiritual people respect all life forms and do not promote the extinction of any species. They treat mother earth as they respect or should respect any mother.

Since the human body is a divine temple, a wise person treats it well, not indulging in tobacco, alcohol, junk food and excess sweets. If one has any addiction, it is best to overcome this habit now. It will be much harder to do so after you leave the physical body. Addictive substances have an effect upon the astral body and to some degree upon certain levels of mind, so break all binding habits at this time and become free of such chains.

Keep spiritual goals in mind and engage in activities that are compatible with them. A social life consisting of parties, frequent entertainment at movies, nightclubs, casinos, etc., is shallow and a waste of precious time. To that person who rationalizes *"I'm in the world, so I may as well participate in worldly activities,"* the wisest reply is, *"yes, you are in the world, but do you want to stay in it?"* We gravitate to that stage or condition where we keep our attention focused. If we concentrate upon mundane activities, including shallow entertainment, we stay in and return to this chaotic earth. If we think of God, love and higher truth, we gravitate toward such a state, for as we think so we become. Certainly we have to make a living and interact with those with whom we have karmic connections. And these essentials require some careful thought. It is great to maintain a sense of humor and engage in beneficial physical exercise to keep the body healthy. Such activities as walking, swimming and Hatha yoga are useful indeed. But we should perform our objective duties as a dedication to God and have love for all people because God is at the spiritual core of all living things. To paraphrase the poet Robert Frost, we dance round the margins of life and suppose, *"but the Secret sits in the middle and knows."* Our job is to move from the circumference to the core of existence.

When loneliness guides the chariot of a person's life, it rarely leads that soul in the direction of love, the state that everyone really seeks. Social friendship should never be confused with real loving concern. Let your fortunes or your appearance change, and your so-called friends desert you for more popular people. Often our loneliness leads us to all of the wrong places and we become enamored by seemingly charming and successful personalities. But glimpse beneath the social masks worn by these forlorn actors and you will see uncertainty, quiet desperation, misery, doubts about the present life and deep fear of an unknown future. One cannot depend upon someone who himself or herself is being tossed about upon the mental and emotional waves of uncertainty. Such individuals do not even make good friends let alone real lovers. Certainly a social life may seem to be fun at times, but the results of such experiences often are sexual relationships, dissipation, disease and death. But we should not despair, for true lovers do exist, but we have to BE one in order to find one. And regarding loneliness, remember that one who loves God is never alone and thus can never be lonely. Unfortunately most of us are too blind to see this, so we continue to assume that we are forever on our own.

Religious orders play important roles in the awakening process because they often inspire people to seek for higher truth. But they are not goals in themselves. At best they serve as lower steps on the stairway that leads to God. Illumination cannot be conferred by a ritual or by the study of scriptures. We can join churches, social clubs, learned societies and a host of other interesting organizations only to become part of various blind movements or groups that do not really know where they stand or where they are going. The typical social life is like trying to walk on thin ice. When it breaks, as it always does, we realize too late that the seemingly solid footing could never have supported us and that the water beneath the ice is deep indeed. And in this water hungry sharks are waiting to feed. These are the social parasites that prey upon those vulnerable and weaker souls who are lost and who misplace their trust and attention. Never forget your real goals: self-knowledge and divine consciousness. The spiritual life is more joyous and happy than a social one because it improves you, inspires you and takes you home.

Of course, everyone needs guidance on the spiritual return to God, and one's first priority should be to find someone who knows the way back to the Supreme

State by personal experience. Spiritual authority is never based upon apostolic succession, the votes of a College of Cardinals, family connections or political opinions. It is only sustained by inner experience. Anyone who cries out to God for God has made a good start, because the Divine One will send someone to assist that seeking individual. The Biblical injunction, *"Seek and ye shall find"* **(Matthew 7:7)** is very relevant to a spiritual life, but equally important is what you seek. In **Matthew 6:33** it says *"seek ye first the kingdom of God"* and the other things you need will be added to you. So petition God for God, and purify your life so you can maintain consciousness at that exalted level of being. Only pure souls can see the Ultimate Source of all that exists. Today each of us is floating rapidly down the tumultuous river of life, a stream that flows away from God. Those who continue to float this great stream will end up far from the Divine Source at the ocean of death. But if one wishes to return to God, he or she must be a strong swimmer and battle the current bravely. Returning to God takes effort. Spirituality, not religion or orthodox faith, is the genuine but arduous way back to the Divine Being.

Glossary of Terms

Aeon. – A spiritual being or Master sent by God to teach truth and help souls return to the Divine presence.

Allah. – An Arabic name for God.

Anami. – The ultimate state of divinity (Nameless One).

Arianism. – Teaching of Arius a fourth century Alexandrian who said that Jesus was not of the same substance as God, but was the best of created beings.

Ashram. – A Sanskrit term for a retreat or center of spiritual study and meditation.

Astral. – A subtle dimension penetrating and extending beyond the physical bounds of this world. Literally "star realm." Just as several radio or TV frequencies can pass through the same space, Astral matter is distinguished from physical matter by differences in speed of vibration of energy. Sahans-dal-Kanwal is the capital of the astral. The term may also refer to the body associated with this dimension.

Atman. – Supreme spirit or oversoul of all.

Aurangzeb. Shrewd but intolerant Mughal ruler in India (1658 – 1707) who executed the ninth Sikh Guru, Teg Bahadur.

Avatar. – An authority sent from the Astral or Causal levels to correct evil conditions in the world and to punish offenders.

Aum. -- The sacred sound associated with Brahm,, Lord of the Causal Plane.

Bani. – Literally "music" or "song." Often used as a synonym for Word or Shabd.

Bhagavad-Gita. – Famous section of the Mahabharata where Krishna instructs Arjuna in matters of attitude and duty.

Bhajan. – Devotional song, or the practice of listening to divine spiritual sounds.

Bhakti. – Devotion or intense love.

Brahm. – Lord of the Causal or mental dimension and accepted by many as the Supreme Being.

Buddha. – The enlightened Prince Siddhartha, inspirer of Buddhism.

Causal. – The subtle mental dimension above the Astral Plane. Home of Brahm. Also the energy form or the creation associated with this realm.

Celestial. – Literally "heavenly." Usually means the same as Causal.

Chakra. – Literally means "wheel" because of its shape. One of seven energy centers in the human body.

Darshan. – Literally "seeing." Viewing a saint or spiritual teacher with loving attention.

Deva. – An angel or nature spirit.

Elohim. – The word translated "God" in the first verses of Genesis. Actually, "El" is a name for God and "him" is a Hebrew plural suffix. The correct translation of Elohim is "the Gods or Authorities.

Essenes. – An ascetic Jewish brotherhood existing before and during the time of Christ.

Faquir. – A Moslem saint or holy man.

Gnostics. – An early Christian sect that believed the world was created by emanations from the Divine and that Aeons were sent from this source to instruct men.

Guru. – A teacher, especially a spiritual instructor.

Jihad. – A holy war. Originally the battle one fought with the mind to eliminate all negative tendencies.

Karma. – Literally cause and effect. As you sow, so shall you reap of Christianity.

Kharizites. – A division of Islam that believes Allah controls everything.

Krishna. – Famous teacher in the Bhagavad-Gita.

Kundalini. – A spiral of energy said to exist at the base of the spine in the areas of the sacrum or coccyx. When transmuted and elevated to higher energy centers this energy may induce enlightenment.

Macrocosm. – The larger greater cosmos or universe or higher inner cosmology.

Maha. – Literally "great."

Maha Sunna. – A vast region of darkness between Par-Brahm and the fourth division of creation (in the terminology of eastern saints).

Mahayana. -- A division of Buddhism that believes all people have the potential for enlightenment and emphasizes faith in the eternal Buddha and love for all.

Microcosm. – Man as a smaller copy of the greater macrocosm.

Mutazilites. – A division of Islam that stresses freedom of the human will.

Mystic. – A spiritual teacher who has practiced disciplined meditation.

Nam (or Naam). – Another name for the Word or Shabd.

Negative Power. – In the terminology of higher spiritual teachers, the Negative Power is the Universal Mind. The Positive Power is above the mind in purely spiritual regions.

Nero. – Roman emperor A.D. 54 – 68. Infamous for blaming Christians for the great fire of A.D. 64 and for elaborate and expensive building projects.

OM. – Sound or symbol of Brahm, the ruler of the Causal realm.

Pantheism. – The doctrine that God is the transcendent reality permeating a universe that is an expression of this power.

Par-Brahm. – The next spiritual region above Brahm or the Causal Plane.

Parshad. – Food blessed by the energy of a Master.

Prana. – Life force or vital energy, a subtle material force used by some yogis and healers to elevate consciousness or promote healing.

Pranayam. – Part of the Patanjali yoga system involving breath control.

Purush. – The supreme creative power.

Radha Soami (or Swami). – A term coined by Guru Rai Saligram for the Supreme Being. It literally means "Lord of the Soul."

Ram. – A name commonly applied to God in the East.

Rishi. – Literally "enlightened one.

Sach Khand. – Literally "True Home." The fifth region above this physical dimension.

Sadh. – One who has reached Par-Brahm or higher. A Sadh Guru has been authorized to engage in Spiritual work.

Sant. – Or Saint is one who has reached the fifth region above this world.

Sat. – Literally means "true."

Satguru. – A saint or teacher who has been authorized to act as a master or guru.

Satnam. – Literally "True Name." Term applied to the lord of the fifth region above the physical dimension.

Satsang. – Association with a spiritual teacher in person or via remembrance of this great soul by considering his teachings.

Shabd. – Word or Logos. The creative spiritual current emanating from God. Can also Refer to a hymn or verse written by a master.

Shiite. – A member of the Moslem Shiah belief system.

Sikh. – Technically, one who has attained the Astral level. Also, a follower of a Sikh Guru or a member of the Sikh faith.

Simran. – The mental repetition of a mantra or charged words to assist in concentration or to test the authenticity of something or someone in higher plaanes.

Soami (or Swami). – Lord, or spiritual teacher.

Sufi. – A mystical branch of the Moslem faith that is not accepted by Shiite or Sunni believers. Maulana Rumi is one example of a Sufi Master.

Sunna. – Traditional portion of Moslem law believed to be based on the words and acts of the prophet Mohammed as directed by Allah.

Sunnite. – A Moslem who accepts the Sunna as authoritative.

Tantric. – A school of Buddhism.

Theravada. – Division of Buddhism that believes most monks and nuns may gain Salvation or enlightenment and that Buddha is a human teacher.

Tisra Til. – Third eye or point in the subtle body between the two eye brows that opens with pure concentration and allows the devotee to see higher dimensions..

Upanishads. – Ancient Hindu scriptures.

Vedas. – A collection of ancient hymns or Hindu scriptures.

Word. – the Logos or creative aspect of God (defined in John 1 of the Bible).

Yoga. – Literally "union." Any system or discipline designed to unite one with a higher stage of consciousness. Hatha yoga consists mostly of physical Exercises or Asanas originally designed to prepare one for mental or spiritual Forms of yoga but now often used to enhance physical health.

Young, Brigham. – Mormon prophet following the death of Joseph Smith.

Yuga. – A cycle of time. According to Hindu adherents, there are four yugas. First is the Sat Yuga or golden age, next is the Treta Yuga or silver age, next is the Dwapar Yuga or copper or bronze age, and finally there is the Kala Yuga or iron age.

Zen. – A sect of Buddhism that developed in China and Japan. It has almost no theology and cannot be conceptualized by intellectual logic. Enlightenment is a sudden awakening to the nature of one's own being and to the oneness of all. Often a Koan or illogical statement is used to induce cessation of rational thinking and an awakening of higher consciousness.

References Cited

Arberry, A. J. (translator)

1949 The Rubaiyat of Jalal al-din Rumi: Select Translations into English Verse. London, Emery Walker.

1968 Mystical Poems of Rumi. Translated by A. J. Arberry. Persian Heritage Series, No. 3. University of Chicago Press, Chicago.

1979 Mystical Poems of Rumi. Translated by A. J. Arberry. Persian Heritage Series, No. 23. Westview Press, Boulder, Colorado.

Barks, Coleman

2001 The Soul of Rumi. Harper, San Francisco.

Barks, Coleman and John Moyne (translators)

1997 The Essential Rumi. Castle Books, Edison, New Jersey.

Blake, William

1969 Blake, Complete Writings. Oxford University Press. New York.

Bloom, Harold

2005 Jesus and Yahweh, The Names Divine. Riverhead Books, New York, New York.

Boehme, Jacob
1969 The Signature of All Things. The Attic Press, Greenwood, S. C.

Chand, Faqir (translated by B. R. Kamal)
N.D. Jeevan Mukti. Faqir Library Charitable Trust, Manavta Mandir, Hoshiarpur, Punjab, India.

Darling, David
1996 Zen Physics. Harper Collins Plublishers, New York, New York.

Day, Martin S.
1963 History of English Literature 1660-1837. Doubleday & Company, Inc., Garden City, New York.

Dhillon, Harish
2006 The First Sikh Spiritual Master. Skylight Paths Publishing, Woodstock, VT.

Ehrman, Bart D.
2005 Misquoting Jesus. Harper One, New York.

Eisenman, Robert
1998 James the Brother of Jesus. Penguin Books, New York.

Engle, Jon
1980 Servants of God: Lives of the Ten Sikh Gurus. Sant Bani Press, Tilton, NH.

Eusebius
1995 The History of the Church from Christ to Constantine. Barnes & Noble, New York,

Ezekiel, Isaac A.
1966 Sarmad. Radha Soami Satsang, Beas, Punjab, India.

1978 Kabir the Great Mystic. Radha Soami Satsang, Beas, Punjab, India.

1979 Saint Paltu. Radha Soami Satsang, Beas, Punjab, India.

Fox, Matthew
1980 Breakthrough: Meister Eckhart's Creation Spirituality in New Translation. Image Books, New York.

Funk and Wagnalls
1986 Funk and Wagnalls New Encyclopedia, Volume 20. Funk and Wagnalls, Inc.

Head, Joseph and S. L. Cranston (editors)
1999 Reincarnation, an East-West Anthology. AEON Publishing Company, New York.

Johnson, Paul
1996 The Quest for God. Harper Collins Publishers, New York.

Khan, Inayat Hazrat
1988 The Music of Life. Omega Publications, New Lebanon, NY.

Krishnamurti, Jiddu
1989 With a Silent Mind (Video). Mystic Fire Video, Inc., New York.

Law, William
1938 Selected Mystical Writings, Stephen Hobhouse, editor. C. W. Daniel Co., Ltd, London

Law, William (trans.)
1764-82 The Works of Jacob Behmen (Four Vol.), London.

Johnson, Paul
1997 The Quest for God. Harper Collins Publishers, New York.

Ladinsky, Daniel (Translator)
2002 Love Poems From God. Penguin Compass, New York.

Maccoby, Hyam
1986 The Mythmaker: Paul & the Invention of Christianity. Barnes & Noble, New York

Maheshwari, S. D.
1971 Biography of Huzur Maharaj. Universal Art Press, Belanganj, Agra, India.

Meyer, Marvin W.
1986 The Secret Teachings of Jesus: Four Gnostic Gospels. Vintage Books, New York.

Newton, Michael, Ph.D.
2002 Journey of Souls. Llewellyn Publications, St. Paul, Minnesota.

Nicholson, Reynold (translator)
1925-1940 The Mathnawi of Jalaluddin Rumi. 8 vols. Luzac, London.

Nikhilananda, Swami
1949 The Upanishads, Volume 1. Bonanza Books, New York.

Orr, W. G.
1947 A Sixteenth Century Indian Mystic. Lutterworth Press, London.

Peers, E. Allison
1950 Studies of the Spanish Mystics, Volume 1, Macmillan Co., New York.

Puri, Lekh Raj
1940 Mysticism, the Spiritual Path. The Sant Bani Book Depot, Beas, Punjab, India.

1982 Radha Soami Teachings. Radha Soami Satsang, Beas, Punjab, India.

Puri, Lekh Raj and V. K. Sethi
1978 Saint Namdev, His Life and Teachings. Radha Soami Satsang, Beas, Punjab, India.

Puri, J. R.
1981 Guru Nanak. Radha Soami Satsang, Beas, Punjab, India.

Puri, J. R. and V. K. Sethi.
1981 Tulsi Sahib, Saint of Hathras. Radha Soami Satsang, Beas, Punjab, India.

Puri, J. R. and T. R. Shangari
1986 Bulleh Shah. Radha Soami Satsang, Beas, Punjab, India.

Ram, Rai Sahib Munshi
1979 With the Three Masters (Vol. I), Radha Soami Satsang, Beas, Punjab, India.

1884 With the Three Master (Vol. II), Radha Soami Satsang, Beas, Punjab, India.

Scott, Cyril
1933 Music, Its Secret Influence Throughout the Ages. London: Rider & Co.

Sethi, V. K.
1984 Kabir. Radha Soami Satsang, Beas, Punjab, India.

1996 Mira, The Divine Lover. Radha Soami Satsang, Beas, Punjab, India.

Singh, Bahadur Jagat
1982 The Science of the Soul. Radha Soami Satsang, Beas, Punjab, India.

Singh, Baba Jaimal
1998 Spiritual Letters. Radha Soami Satsang, Beas, Punjab, India.

Singh, Khushwant
1963 A History of the Sikhs. Princeton University Press, Princeton, NJ

Singh, Kirpal
1959 The Jap Ji, the Message of Guru Nanak. Ruhani Satsang, Delhi, India.

Godman. Ruhani Satsang, Delhi, India
1973 Baba Jaimal Singh, His Life and Teachings. Sat Sandesh Books, Franklin, NH

1978 The Way of the Saints. Sant Bani Ashram, Sanbornton, New Hampshire.

Singh, Sawan
1980 Spiritual Gems. Radha Soami Satsang, Beas, Punjab, India.

1984 Discourses on Sant Mat. Radha Soami Satsang, Beas, Punjab, India.

N.D. Collection of letters of various dates written to American disciples between 1911 and 1934. Typed manuscript.

2010 Foreign Correspondence of Hazur Sawan Singh 1911 – 1934. Privately published.

Singh, Seva (translator)
N.D. The Sar Bachan. Beas Satsang, Beas, India.

Smith, William and F. N. and M. A. Peloubet
1984 A Dictionary of the Bible. J. C. Winston Co., Philadelphia.

Spaulding, Baird T.
1972 Life and Teaching of the Masters of the Far East. (four volumes) DeVorss & Co., Marina del Rey, CA.

Spencer, Hazelton (editor)
1963 British Literature from Beowulf to Sheridan. D. C. Heath and Company, Boston.

St. John of the Cross
1909 A Spiritual Canticle of the Soul. (David Lewis, translator). Thomas Baker, London.

1912 The Living Flame of Love. (David Lewis, translator). Thomas Baker, London.

Suzuki, D. T.
1956 Zen Buddhism. Doubleday Anchor Books, Garden City, New York.

Thoreau, Henry David
1969 The Best of Walden and Civil Disobedience. Scholastic Book Services, New York.

Thuan, Trinh Xuan
1995 The Secret Melody. Oxford University Press, New York.

Tolstoy, Leo
1984 The Kingdom of God is Within You. The University of Nebraska Press, Lincoln.

Upadhyaya, K. N.
1980 Dadu, The Compassionate Mystic. Radha Soami Satsang, Beas, Punjab, India.

Vagi, David L.
1999 Coinage and History of the Roman Empire, Volume One. Amos Press, Sidney, Ohio

Walshe, Maurice O'Connell
2000 Meister Eckhart (Volume 1). Element, Boston.

Weiss, Brian L, M.D.
1997 Only Love is Real. Warner Books, New York.

Williamson, G. A. (translator)
1965 The History of the Church: Eusebius. Barnes & Noble, New York.

Yogananda, Paramahansa
1975 Autobiography of a Yogi. Self Realization Fellowship, Los Angeles.